THE NIPUTI
...the Nephew

Life under the shadow of a Mafia killer

By

Joseph Bonpensiero
"The Niputi"

Samantha Bonpensiero
Photographer
Uplifting the Bonpensiero legacy
2014
www.Samanthabonpensiero.com
Niputi Cover Photo and design by: Samantha Bonpensiero,
Photo by Samantha Bonpensiero Copyright©2013

Published by Joseph S. Bonpensiero Copyright©2014
All rights reserved. No part of this book may be used or reproduced in any manner whatsoever without written permission except in the case of brief quotations embodied in reviews or critical articles. For information or use permission requests, contact the author at joebonpensiero@gmail.com

Published by: Joseph Bonpensiero, Henderson, NV 89002
Printed in the USA by Create Space an Amazon.com company, Charleston, SC 2014
Available from Amazon.com and other retail book stores.
Available on Kindle and other devices
ISBN: 0989795004
ISBN-13: 9780989795005
ISBN 978-0-9897950-0-5 (Paperback)
ISBN 978-0-9897950-1-2 (Kindle)
Library of Congress Control Number: 2014915639
CreateSpace Independent Publishing Platform
North Charleston, South Carolina

FRANK BOMPENSIERO

A Failed Legacy

"Like crushing life from almost everything he touched, Mafia killer Frank Bompensiero stained our Sicilian name and dishonored our family."

KIRKUS REVIEWS

"In the '70s, while serving in the Air Force, Bonpensiero was hit with the news of his uncle's murder through a high-profile article in *Time* magazine. Uncle Frank was a mobster, a black sheep from whom the author had been trying to distance himself.

"As *niputi* (nephew), the author was witness to his uncle's bullying tactics, his 'You ask, I give, you owe!' methods of extortion and forced allegiance.

"Bonpensiero delivers a detailed account of family history with a focus on his notorious relative [mobster/killer Frank Bompensiero]. Bonpensiero succeeds in painting a picture of a closely knit immigrant community and a wayward son who ... regularly tried everyone's nerves. Readers see the unfolding of an American life ... colored by the Sicilian immigrant experience."

Niputi sheds "... light on family ties ... Frank's disreputable activities ... and a distinctive cultural identity ... growing up in San Diego's Little Italy in the 1940s."

Sicilian Proverb

"Lassa di manciari, nunlassari di travagghiari."

"Forego eating but never forego working."

TABLE OF CONTENTS

Dedication xi
Author's Notes xiii
Trinacria xv
Preface xvii

    Part I FAMILY SECRETS 1
1 Time Magazine Obituary 3
2 Tell Me A Story 12
3 Wop Town—Little Italy 17
4 Call Me Niputi 26
5 One Dish Too Many 34
6 Sicilian Family Shame 42
7 Death Before Dinner 49
8 Baptisima ...and The Evil Begins 57
9 Killer on The Run 67
10 A Thief and More 77

    Part II LOYALTIES & LIES 93
10 Manhattan Misstep 95
11 Learning the Business ...non-delivered promise 105
12 Along Came the Man 113
13 Corsair Imbroglio 125
14 Travels with Leo 136
15 House Above the Bay 152

    Part III TEEN YEARS 165
16 Goons, Guys & Girls 167
17 Frank's Joints ...just ask him 179
18 West Coast Boyz 186
19 Hollywood Wishes 196
20 Vegas Dreams 203
21 Rowdy Day at Del Mar 213
22 NIPUTI PHOTO ALBUM 223

	Part IV IN THE MIX	251
23	Frank Blows It ....Big Time	253
24	Thriftco ...And The Top Dog	264
25	Date Night ...Scent Of A Woman	278
26	Retribution Raiders	291
27	Cockfight At Puccio's	300
28	The Camera Lies	310
29	England Getaway	327

	Part V COMING OF AGE	343
30	Bars, Banking & Business	345
31	The Star & Garter	354
32	The Rosenberg Connection	369
33	Dreaded Encounter	382
34	The Last Hurrah	398
35	A Father's Passing	408
36	Off We Go ...Into The Wild Blue Yonder	422
37	My Mafia Perspective	427

Epilogue	437
Special Remembrance To Nathan "Nate" Rosenberg	441
Bibliography	443
Acknowledgements	445
About The Author	447

DEDICATION

I dedicate this story to Patrick J. Montgomery, Colonel, U.S. Army, my pal, and lifelong friend who recently passed away. Pat witnessed many events written about in this memoir while having his own cross to bear. For over 55 years, he and I shared many good and bad times together. We met in San Diego while working at Rohr Aircraft Corp in the summer of 1957. We were teens trying to save a few bucks before entering San Diego State College and became steadfast friends. We were co-workers, college students, and commissioned officers. We finally arrived as brothers-in-arms serving our country and were always there for each other a phone call, or letter away. From our initial San Diego meeting to points east and west around the world, Arizona to Vietnam, Africa, and Western Europe, we stayed in contact and he was the brother I never had. He was there offering support during the tragic loss of my two children. A voice of reason and encouragement while I was under duress. He was a staunch sounding board through challenging times as a USAF Commander. All should be so lucky as I to call such a stalwart man my friend. I'll miss you, Patrick.

Your lifelong friend,
Joe

AUTHOR'S NOTES

1. *NIPUTI* (Ni-pu-ti) is a Sicilian word that means nephew. I heard it the first time as an eight-year-old when I was introduced to Frank Bompensiero, my father's brother. He said "Joey you are my *Niputi—as if he owned me.* As you will learn, Frank Bompensiero, a feared Mafia killer, and the story's main antagonist was my nemesis. What you will read happened after our introduction. It became the grist for writing this memoir.

2. BONPENSIERO is my surname and the name of the only father I ever knew, Salvatore (*Turi*) Bonpensiero. He was the younger brother of Frank BOMPENSIERO. The difference in surname spelling was a midwife's documentation error on my father's birth certificate. Ironically, the same midwife delivered Frank eight years before with the same physician certifying both names and birth certificates.

3. To the best of my knowledge and research, what you read in this memoir is true. However, with chapters one and two the names of officers and enlisted personnel in the USAF involving my military career are fictitious. There was no need to address individuals by real names when their role in the Niputi story was minimal. However, all incidents described and experienced by me in this memoir are true. They happened as I recall and I wrote what I saw and heard.

4. When I was a young boy around the family, the men and women spoke Sicilian and their form of English was dependent upon who understood what. Accordingly,

when I started to write this memoir, and recalled the past, I bounced around using common words as I recalled and addressed elders as *Ziu (Uncle)* or *Zia (Aunt)*. I referred to my father, Salvatore Bompensiero aka *"Turi,"* as Dad or Americanized to "Sam or Sammy." You will note that I called Francesco "Frank" Bompensiero, *"Ziu Chich,"* or *"Chichu"* (Uncle Frank). These were slight variations in Sicilian pronunciation which I used respectfully. I interchanged them in the story as often as I did in conversation when I spoke.

5. For clarity, I use the italicized term *Mafia* throughout the manuscript. It is a word of mystery and not found in my Sicilian dictionary, but referred to in an Italian dictionary as "swagger." The word Mafia to my knowledge has no definitive or specific criminal meaning in either language. But from an etymology standpoint, the Arabic word *Marfud* gives credence to the similiarity to the Italian as it means *swagger or boastful*. The Muslim Arabs do have a foothold in Mazzara, Sicily. I also use the terms "La Familia" interchangeably with the term "Mafia" the "La" is a feminine definitive article in the Sicilian language. According to the Sicilian Dictionary and phrase book, "Sicilian is the first Romance (Roman) language to have been formed from spoken Latin (Vulgar Latin) And, it is older than Italian, French, Spanish, Portuguese, or Romanian. Italian, which in truth is a dialect of Tuscan, is called a language, since there only can be one official language for a country.

6. The Trinacria, a Greek iconic gift to Sicily, was used as scepter on the rear cover to representative Sicily's people and their multi-cultural history, as they openly do not declare Italy their primary country. To them, it's all about Sicily.

TRINACRIA

Geographical anthropology tells us that Sicily had a triad of aboriginal tribes known as the Sicans, Elymians, and the Sicels who inhabited the island about 8,000 years BC. However, with the arrival of the dominant yet reasonable Greeks in 734 BC, the isle of Sicily-smaller than Cuba-entered history and for the next 600 years, the Greeks enriched the culture. Those were times of growth and learning, but things would change as feudal and warring nation states came, conquered, and replaced the previous regime. For over two thousand years, countless marauders including the Vandals, Ostrogoths, Byzantines, Romans, Arabs, Normans and Bourbons oppressed the Sicilians.

Over time, the indigenous people's bloodlines became an amalgam resulting from ravishes of war and rape. A deep and prideful people, the Sicilians made accommodations in culture, language, politics, and religion to survive. Today, the Sicilians are a mysterious people indeed. They hold to pagan rituals as much as they hold to Catholicism. Yet, they retain their folklore of the early Greek infusion. That brings us to Sicilian notoriety over the past one hundred fifty years: Their Greek Trinacria, the icon depicted on the back cover, depicts a feminine head, crowned with snakelike hair akin to sirens of Greek lore, and three human legs folded at the knee—as if running away. The Sicilians identified with the mysterious Greek symbolism and based their traditions upon them.

As my Uncle Frank boasted on numerous occasions, "I am Sicilian, not Italian! We Sicilians have our own flag." To this day, Sicilians post the Trinacria symbol proudly in lieu of the Italian flag. One day, some say in the mid-1860s, a small band of jailed Sicilian miscreants vowed to retaliate against civil oppression be it the papacy, Italian bureaucracy or rich landowners. They named their organization—Mafia. Of all the oppressors, The Mafia was the kindest of all to the peasantry . . . but only time would tell. Were the Mafia members pureblooded Sicilians, as Hollywood would like you to believe? We now know there were few if any purebloods left in Sicily.

PREFACE

By 1976, my troubled memories and my difficult times had come and gone. And I could reflect on the past with the ease of looking at old scars and feeling no pain . . . just memories. However, one year later while I was serving as an Air Force officer in Germany, the USAFE Inspector General made me painfully aware of an expose in *Time* magazine revealing that my uncle Frank Bompensiero had finally pissed off *Ah Familia* brotherhood. To no one's surprise, he became February's assassination target. With his departure, the river Styx felt no ripple as another hood crossed into hell and another chapter closed on American crime annals. However, with my position as a Command Inspector having Top Secret clearances and having been an associate of the deceased Mafiosa, my professional integrity came under scrutiny. I was now under a microscope.

Years later, in 1999, while I was living in Oregon, my cousin Tina telephoned. She sounded distraught. "Can you believe it, Joe? The bullshit never stops when it comes to Uncle Frank and the family. Here we go again . . . being dragged through the mud." I learned that the *San Diego Reader* led the show this time. Judith Moore, a senior editor apparently, had an association with Frank's daughter Mary Ann, and Moore created a melodramatic twisted series on the infamous San Diego bad man-Bompensiero. Later in 2009, after Judith Moore died, her estate and the *Reader* published "A Bad, Bad Boy." It sparkled like a Tom Sawyerish takeoff of fun times on the Mississippi. As I read, I thought this had to be a joke:

Frank the ruthless, evil and self-centered deviant would kill for his pagan Mafia principles or for a dollar. Make no matter. Along the way, he flaunted his lifestyle—while using his family as cover, collateral damage.

I found "A Bad, Bad Boy" to be a bleeding-heart tale about a man I didn't know. Portrayed as a misunderstood, loving man and father who provided financial support for his elderly mother, poor sisters and brother while making a good home for his wife and daughter. While badgered by the press, he still had time to become papa Frank, the teary-eyed TV audience of one watching "Lassie." Most of this tripe, no doubt, came from the mouth and imagery of Frank's fawning daughter, Mary Ann. Speculation over her motives, be they celebrity, money or whatever, only supported Mary Ann's actions. However, wrapping her father's escapades in a shroud of boylike peccadilloes, then flaunting her own slanted view with utter disregard for reality and the feelings of other Bompensiero offspring was unconscionable.

In a few years, the enigmatic word *Mafia* would be nothing more than an overused euphemism for any culture's criminal association that spanned the globe. Then, more importantly, on September 11, 2001, the USA experienced its worst tragedy as nearly 3,000 souls lost their lives at the World Trade Center. This event ushered in a new, more deadly fear as political and religious zealots committed acts of terrorism on U.S. soil.

I, for one, took umbrage after reading the *San Diego Reader's* series and the follow-on book, "A Bad, Bad Boy" and the faulty innuendo and idyllic perceptions about Frank, his reality, and my father. Had it not been for the inaccurate re-creation of events involving the family; I would have never written this memoir. Here then, with an in-depth family history stressing a family's evil seed gone awry, I detail my memoir. Though I had a solid relationship with both men, I sought validation and through added research and investigation, I could get it right. With my inside family knowledge, I could document the story from an enlightened perspective. Who could tell it better? I lived it. Here then is "Niputi the Nephew."

PART I
FAMILY SECRETS

CHAPTER 1

TIME MAGAZINE OBITUARY

For over seventy years, I carried the Bompensiero surname with its hundred-year-old origin straight from the pebble-stone roads of Sicily. It roughly translated to "Good Thoughts." I was proud of the name and those who came before. As children, my cousins and I heard the stories told by the elders. We honored our heritage. Years later, I became embarrassed as the press attacked our family name. They accused Frank, my father's brother, of having Lo Mafia affiliations. They painted him with a broad brush. People believed it. His exploits, real or made up, were news and sold papers. Epithets like "Wop," "Dago" and "Lo Familia" became commonplace. As I matured, those terms stuck in my throat. Like the word 'nigger' to a black man, the belittling words were like a slap in the face demeaning. My scar tissue grew. I became spring-loaded to any wiseass remark that denigrated my Sicilian heritage or associated me or mine with crime. Finally, after my years of living with the guilt through association, Time magazine laid bare Frank's gory death. It glaringly depicted an account of his sordid exploits and his gangland-style execution. It hit home for me in a world far away and across the sea.

✶ ✶ ✶

Mid-May 1977 caught me at my desk in deep thought, reading a classified operations war plan when something slammed into the side of my head. I almost passed out, but my military training kicked in.

"Incoming!" I shouted to my four teammates and dived for cover.

We hunkered down and braced ourselves for another round. My head pounded and I glanced around to determine my best course of action when I heard a blaring voice.

"Bomb Dispenser! Goddamn it, Bomb Dispenser!"

Like a cluster bomb tossing crap all over the place, Colonel Head's blustering of his pet name for me cut through the silence.

Colonel Richard Head, termed "Dick Head" (behind his back), was chief of the Maintenance Inspection Branch and our boss.

My eyes blinked as I noticed the bright and garish colors of a missile-like object lying on the floor next to me. It was a May 1977 issue of *Time* magazine, European edition. All became clear as I realized that it ricocheted off my head and struck my reference stack of "Secret "document files. It scattered them all over the floor like tenpins on a bowling lane.

With two pistols facing each other, the magazine's cover told all in two-inch garish mustard letters on a tomato-red background.

MAFIA
BIG, BAD AND BOOMING!

Realizing that we were not under attack by the "Baader-Meinhof Gang"—my initial guess—I crawled out from under my desk, magazine in hand, to face Colonel

Head, whose voice was still ratcheting upward toward the highest alto range.

"Why the hell is your name plastered all over *Time* magazine?"

I opened my mouth to speak, but Head continued his harangue.

"The general is up in arms over this trash! I want an explanation and I want it now! Why in hell—."

Head stopped mid-sentence. He noticed that the rest of the team members were still down under their desks.

"What are you all doing on the floor?"

Lt. Col. Richard Head, a hefty six-foot-six hulk, leaned forward with the finesse of a twelve-year-old bull elephant. I didn't like his manner. Moreover, he and I had the kind of history you do not need while working your way up the military ladder. I had been instrumental in our Inspector General chewing his ass out a couple of months earlier. This did not endear him to me.

Head closed the gap between us like a tiger on the hunt, ready to leap and chomp on my ass. I positioned myself behind my desk and stood at my full height, which seemed almost half of his.

"Regarding your question, sir, since 'Bomb Dispenser' is not my surname, I wasn't sure you were talking to me. Most people call me Joe, Joseph, or captain. Some even manage to get their tongues around 'Bonpensiero.' However, if calling me 'Bomb Dispenser' is easier for you— go right ahead. I just wouldn't want someone to misunderstand— like the lieutenant did in Aviano."

✹ ✹ ✹

The reference was to an incident months before when Head insulted me and Second Lieutenant Antonio Biasi in the presence of two other teammates.

"*Haya Goomba*—Bomb Dispenser," he yelled at us by way of greeting one day as Biasi and I were discussing Biasi's plans to improve the operation in his new job, since he had recently been assigned to the Aircraft Maintenance Division at Aviano. I chose to be his unofficial mentor, as I had been to many newly commissioned second lieutenants in the field. We had a kinship and I felt that Biasi could fit right into Aircraft Maintenance.

Colonel Head, however, put it differently as he addressed Biasi. "With a name like *Antonio Biasi*, you fit right into the Aviano fa-mil-ia WOP and Mafia community."

Biasi did not appreciate Colonel Head's inappropriate and insulting remarks. However, they were not new to me. He used them frequently, sprinkling his conversation with them to me and in front of others because he thought they were funny.

"Besides, Bomb Dispenser, I note from your partner's name tag that you've found another 'Dago Salami' to hang with. You 'spaghetti benders' are all alike."

Biasi, no doubt, thought Head's remarks were over the line. Later that day, he lodged a complaint against Lieutenant Colonel Head at the Aviano Air Base inspector general's office. By that afternoon, it arrived at the USAFE Command's IG desk.

Summoned later that day to testify at a formal military IG hearing, I hurried off to attend. It resulted in a verbal reprimand for Head, and the word spread rapidly that the colonel's ass and career were now blowing in the wind.

✷ ✷ ✷

"I asked you a question," Colonel Head repeated.

I came to the forefront and said, "Apparently, sir, my Sicilian name has too many syllables for some to pronounce. Actually, I understood from Captain Jobs that you came up with 'Bomb Dispenser.' I'm just not used to hearing it used officially, sir."

There was a ripple of laughter from my teammates in the office.

Colonel Head's voice raised an octave and his cheeks turned red. "God damn it! This is no joke, Captain Bonpensiero."

"I'm sure not, sir. And it wasn't a joke with the IG at Aviano either!"

"You no doubt misunderstand, captain," Head was nearly screaming now. "Why in hell is your last name in this friggin' story about the Mafia?"

I thought for a second and figured I would give him a bone to gnaw. The prick.

"Look, colonel, I 'm at a disadvantage. I haven't read the article, but if I had to guess, I would say it is about my uncle—Frank Bompensiero, an alleged Mafiosa. Hell, Colonel, the FBI knows our family had inroads into the Mafia! Are you saying the Air Force doesn't?"

My comments finally connected with Head. His expression was pure shock as his jowls sagged, his eyes glazed and you could see the gears in his brain start to turn. His expression was priceless. I thought a wisp of garlic breath could knock the SOB over.

"Captain, do you mean to tell me you actually know the dead guy and what the hell do you mean, alleged Mafia."

"Yeah, I know—knew—him well, sir. Ever since, I was about eight years old. It's no big deal. He's my uncle, my father's brother."

"Well, what about the . . . alleged Mafia?"

"Colonel, if you can prove my Uncle Frank or anyone else in the world is a member of the Mafia, you'd be the first one. All those who said they could prove it are dead.

Besides, how would you prove it? You don't know any Mafia criminals, do you? Hell, the FBI hasn't proven that it exists. Ask J. Edgar Hoover." I had to laugh at my own words.

"Why then is the name spelled differently?"

Head's insistence on grilling me on a personal matter in front of the team was really starting to piss me off.

I straightened my desk, mumbling something about an overzealous midwife transcribing my father's name incorrectly and using an "N" instead of an "M," hence the error on the birth certificate. When I finished, Head had not budged and he was still glowering.

"Listen, colonel," I began. "I have lived over thirty years trying to escape my association with Frank Bompensiero's sordid life, as well as all the slurs and bigoted comments about my heritage from a lot of people."

My stare did not waver. "But, for now, you'll have to wait until I've read the article."

"Article my ass!" he growled. "They even have pictures."

"So do I, colonel. So do I. As soon as I clean up the classified as required by our regulations, I'll give you my critique."

Unwilling to accept my explanation, Head wanted my ass and was determined to put me through the grinder. He started to speak again. "Ah . . ." is all he got out when I interrupted.

"Sir, if that is not good enough I'll be heading down to file an IG complaint as well."

I turned my back on him and continued to restack and verify an exact accounting of the secret files that the magazine missile had displaced.

Head turned on his heels and delivered his parting shot before he stomped out.

"You'd better have an explanation for the IG, Bonpensiero."

"Yes sir, colonel sir!" I picked up the magazine and started to scan the article. The artist's rendering of Uncle Frank lying face up on the ground was good. He captured Frank's shock as the assassin's gun blasted away. *It appeared to be creative drama. The artist wasn't there to capture the scene, so he created one.* "Notorious Mobster and Murderer," read the caption.

My first emotion was visceral. It was relief; and there was something else—satisfaction. *Finally, they nailed Frank.*

The reputed Mafioso, the San Diego crime family member and suspected killer had finally been put down like the mad dog the press always claimed him to be. His killer got to him three months earlier in February 1977. His body, found in a blood-smeared phone booth in Pacific Beach, California, was just blocks away from the small, unpretentious house where he lived with his second wife, Marie (Adamo) Bompensiero. There he lived quietly, conducting his business, lying low and hopefully unnoticed by all. The caption claimed that the police, FBI, and the media were aghast that something like this could occur in idyllic San Diego. *If only they knew what I knew.*

I stared at the *Time* cover and article as reality finally sunk in. *Frank was dead, no bullshit!*

My father used to say, "Never talk ill of the dead." However, the finality of the graphic caught me off guard. I began to smile as reality set in. *The maniacal prick was dead and I am free of his stain—finally.* Or, so I thought.

But, knowing Colonel Head as I did, I knew this was not going to go away. I assumed there would be a meeting with the general to explain myself. I was concerned. I knew

I had to stay calm and keep my act together. My career was on the line. With a nutcase like Colonel Head watching my bleeding carcass like a vulture, I could be in trouble.

With many years invested in the Air Force, I was older than my peer group entering the promotion board cycle. With a wife and two sons to support, I needed some long-term security. That meant a field grade promotion. However, published Air Force statistics indicated that fifty percent of my peer group would be tubed and sent packing home. It was now a numbers game. The fact that I filled all the squares to be competitive: assignments, degrees and military training and education, made no matter. They were prerequisite. The odds of promotion were not in my favor. With this new gangster bullshit hitting the fan I was desperate, yet I needed to remain calm. I had to plan my meeting strategy.

My history with Frank had always hung overhead like an ominous cloud beneath his shadow, paying Sicilian familial respect where none was due. It would have been nice to simply nod, cross myself, and walk away, keeping whatever emotion I had to myself. Nevertheless, I could not escape the reality of my name—Bonpensiero. Frank was no longer a threat to me. *Or, was he? Who in the hell knew what the Air Force would say? Maybe I should remain quiet and let the general ask the questions. Hell, would he even know what to ask?*

A Sicilian Niputi was expected to *Stai-Zitto* (stay quiet). *Hell, it worked for Frank and his boys when the cops and FBI pressed them.* That is why everything said about him was conjecture. No one could prove anything. Frank would do a job, bury the evidence, and keep his mouth shut. When arrested, his first words were, "I want my lawyer."

That's it. He kept his mouth shut. Frank knew the *Spiru*—(spies/cops)—would have to prove him guilty. He often joked that if they didn't have a corpse, he'd be released.

Maybe I should follow suit. However, that wasn't my way. Years away from home, a combat tour in Vietnam, and the loss of my baby daughter in England had hardened me. I guessed my teammates expected me to say something profound, maybe to deny and disprove the allegations. As their eyes focused on me, I thought maybe they were looking for some sign of remorse at the death of a family member. But they didn't know anything about my life or me. I grew up in the shadow of a braggadocio Mafia killer. They didn't know the man I knew—Frank Bompensiero—Mafia enforcer—my uncle.

CHAPTER 2
TELL ME A STORY

It was autumn of 1976 and the Bicentennial year was passing quickly as my family and I enjoyed the tulips in the Keukenhof gardens in Holland. In the USA, Jimmy Carter succeeded Gerald Ford as president and a movie named "Star Wars" created space junkie enthusiasts worldwide. An obscure computer company known as Apple became incorporated and Super Bowl XLI saw the Vikings take a beating from the Raiders. And, Elvis Presley died. In short order it was now the summer of 1977 and fate found a way of ruining my day. I had been on temporary duty working for the Inspector General in Germany. Now, months in the field proved the traveling life was finally getting to me. And our boss, the USAFE--Europe IG, learned from the March 1977 issue of Time magazine that a Bompensiero execution had taken place in the U.S. The victim, my infamous uncle, had been dealt a righteous blow—most likely from his second family—the Mafia. I never shared my family history or tales about my relative's connections with the Mafia among my military circles. Need to know, right? None of their business! Wrong! My military supervisor—a bigot-master—and I were summoned to the Inspector General's office to air my family's dirty laundry... and try to save my career. Oh what fun!

✷ ✷ ✷

I chugged down my second cup of coffee and glanced up just as Lieutenant Colonel Head walked through the door.

"I just had a call from Vivian, the IG's secretary. She said the general wants to see us in his office today at ten hundred hours."

"Why'd she call you?" He seemed miffed.

"No idea, sir."

"Well, move your ass, Bomb Dispenser, we've got a twenty-minute drive ahead and I'm not going to be late."

"I'll drive if you want, colonel."

"Like hell you will. The Dutch probably gave you a learner's permit to drive a bicycle or a car. Right?"

"Yeah, you're right as always, colonel. I have both."

"Make sure your shoes are clean when you get in my wife's car. She'll have a hissy fit if I get it dirty."

We drove off and, within a mile, pulled up behind a line of cars stopped at a traffic light. Colonel Head started to sweat as he became agitated over the delay and began slapping the steering wheel, a nervous gesture I'd come to recognize. I figured he was seething because the IG secretary didn't call him directly. Protocol dictated that as the maintenance boss, he should be the one to get the call.

My assessment was correct. Not five minutes into the drive, he turned and started to stammer, something he often did when he was upset. He leered at me and stammered, "You know Ba, Ba, Bomb Disss-pennn-sir," if it wasn't for that frig-gen Jobs, I wouldn't be involved in his mess!"

Despite his reprimand two months before for racially bigoted remarks to junior officers (me included), he insisted on calling me "Bomb-Dispenser" when we were together alone or, as only a few days before, when he got the ass-strafing call from the IG's office about the *Time* magazine article about my uncle's death.

Take responsibility, colonel. You had to sign off on me joining the team. What a petty prick!

As nervous as he was, I secretly hoped he'd stress out and crap in his drawers in front of the general. *That'd be a hoot!*

Traffic started to move and we finished the ride to the IG's office in silence. I leaned back and reflected on what I would say to the IG about my association with Frank Bompensiero.

We cooled our heels in the general's anteroom for a few minutes before being ushered into his office. The general continued to read as we walked in, apparently engrossed in the dog-eared copy of *Time*. When he hit the last page, he looked up, "Please, gentlemen, sit."

"Captain Bonpensiero, have you had an opportunity to read this article in *Time*?"

"Yes, sir. Colonel Head was kind enough to provide it." Colonel Head's cheeks flushed red. I didn't miss it and the general didn't either.

"Well, captain, what did you think of the story?"

"I'm sorry that the Bompensiero family's notoriety has caused the Air Force any concern, sir. But I guess we all have a skeleton or two in a closet."

He stared at me over the rims of his reading glasses with an almost imperceptible frown at the crease of his lips. He didn't say a word.

Oh, shit! I figured I'd stepped in it this time. Maybe other people didn't have skeletons in their closets.

I tried for firmer ground, and a subject that I knew well.

"If I may speak freely, General?"

"Please do."

"Honestly, the article reminded me of the same crap I've seen for years. Mostly, it was conjecture with very little substantive proof to back up the reporter's creative story."

"What, then, is the truth?" he asked.

I began a summary of Frank's childhood in Milwaukee, prior to his accompanying his family to Porticello, Sicily, where, at eight years old, his mother expected him to help support the family. I followed up with some of the facts about his early bouts with the law and his return to the States. The general was surprised when I mentioned that Frank spent little or no time in jail over the years. I explained that with no witnesses, no proof, and cops on the take, he continually got away with murder, literally.

"Then, in 1955, sir, he was indicted for endorsing a bribery check and got hosed with a forty-two-year sentence in San Quentin Penitentiary. After serving about five years and, because of Dad's financial overtures, favors promised and other considerations—the system paroled Frank. The bureaucrats and liberal press most likely thought him rehabilitated, but the hounds outside the law—his *Mafia* brotherhood—and his family knew better."

The general seemed to accept my synopsis.

As I sat across from him, I had no idea whether my career was toast. I felt as if I had done my best of painting a picture for the general. I could only hope that I saved my career as well.

I waited for him to make the next move as he either took me for a dutiful nephew, angry informant—spilling insider information—or just trying to save my career. He finally spoke.

"I've heard enough, Captain Bonpensiero. What a tale. You've had a strange and interesting life. You have a heck of a story there. You may consider writing it down one day. But, for now, why don't you bury the past and move on with your Air Force career."

I was relieved to the core.

"Yes, sir. Thank you. Maybe one day I will write the story, once the players are all dead. But for now my Air Force career is number one on my agenda."

He smiled and stood. It was time to leave and he offered me his hand. I shook it, saluted smartly, and wheeled in place. With Lieutenant Colonel Head in tow, I departed. As an interesting reflection, Colonel Head never opened his mouth one time during the entire session in the IG's office. On the drive back to Kapaun Barracks, Colonel Head mentioned that the meeting went well and said nothing more, leaving well enough alone. I concentrated on performing my mission.

A few months passed and Colonel Head received orders. He elatedly departed, knowing he was going to the Pentagon—the pinnacle of military acclaim.

A moderate and affable senior officer took over as team leader and we all were pleased. I knew I could focus on my career without looking over my shoulder for something about Uncle Frank in the wind. With the clouded years of Frank's life of crime behind me, I could put my life in order. Still, I never forgot the general's suggestion.

It took over three decades before I thought about my journey along that crooked road. When I began reliving the past, an angry residue of guilt through association surfaced. I found it easy to tell my story, starting with the day I learned of Frank Bompensiero's death, which almost affected my career. But, to be truthful, it really started when I was a boy of eight and Frank Bompensiero walked into my life.

CHAPTER 3

WOP TOWN—LITTLE ITALY

Dad—Salvatore a.k.a. Turi, or Sammy Bonpensiero—was a Sicilian fisherman who went into the Army but was rejected due to bad knees; while my Mom—Amanda a.k.a. Mandy—was an American "Rosie the Riveter" at San Diego's Ryan Aircraft. That's how I remember them back when I was a boy. With the postwar mid-40s a time of progress and hope, my father dreamt of the future. Employment was tough to find, especially for Sicilian family men who could barely speak English. Dad pressed to pool the family's savings and, with a bank loan, buy a fishing boat. Dad believed that when things got tough, at least the crew and their families could be fed—survivalists all. That's what they did and, prior to christening our new boat, "Giuseppina," after his dead sister, they moored her about six blocks from my grandmother—Nana Maria's—house. We bought a nice house at Union and Grape Street, one block from my Dad's mother. In those days, the family stuck together.

✱ ✱ ✱

It was the forties, just after the war and our small yet comfortable 700-square-foot, two-bedroom duplex became a partnership between Dad's sister Patrina and her husband Joe D'Acquisto—also a fisherman.

I remembered those times fondly. They were good times, and vendors sold fruit and vegetables by cart or truck on your neighborhood street as they sang out praising their wares. The sound of glass bottles clinking marked the arrival of fresh milk, cream and butter, left at the door by a man dressed in white.

Our neighborhood was friendly and we children religiously attended school and church. Few people owned cars, so street traffic was light. In the streets, we played stickball, kick the can, and hide and seek. Not much ever changed, even the weather.

Some called the Italian district in San Diego "Wop Town." The respected Moniker, "Little Italy, "with its trendy shops and upscale restaurants, wouldn't occur for decades.

Our ghetto-type community was just a few blocks east from the embarcadero where the fishing fleet moored—the economic backbone of the Italian/Sicilian neighborhood. Many of the houses, including my grandmother's, were built at the turn of the century or the early twenties. Many were shoddily constructed.

New to the neighborhood, I didn't know much, but on the walk to school one of my pals mentioned that we were lucky to live in "WOP-TOWN" because only Italians could live there. I knew two neighborhood guys who lived down the block and they were Mexican. A couple of Portuguese families and one black kid also lived in the neighborhood.

When I got home from school that afternoon, I saw the garage door open and knew Dad would be sewing net. I approached, said hi gave him a hug.

"Dad, can I ask you a question?"

"Sure. What-cha wanna know?"

Dad, some of the guys today said that we live in "WOP-TOWN" and I didn't hear you or mom call this area

The Niputi ...the Nephew

"WOP-TOWN" when you bought our house. You said it was near Nana's, that's all.

"Well, that didn't take long," he said, smiling.

"Joey, I will tell you a story so you'll understand. Your grandfather was a Sicilian and when he arrived in America, he had no travel papers—no passport from Sicily. They cost a lot of money and our family didn't go to school much in Sicily so few of us learned how to read and write. Many countries were the same. So, when people left the ships, the immigration cops gave them a document and stamped it W.O.P. This meant they arrived 'with-out-papers.' With that stamp, they could now legally enter America and be entitled to apply for a job. Your grandfather found no shame in that.

"Many people from a lot of European countries also came to America and got the same WOP stamp on their arrival documents, but the WOP name seemed to stick only on the Italians."

"What did they call the other people, Dad?"

"Some were Krauts, because they were German and ate sauerkraut like your mother. Others were Czechs from a funny-named country I can't pronounce, and everyone called the Jews Kikes. But, I never understood that one."

What Dad said made sense. I also realized that if grandfather was a WOP, I was a WOP, too. Then I shouted. "Dad, I'm a real WOP like granddad!"

He laughed and said, "Some people may not like you saying WOP. They have no pride in who they are."

"Okay, Dad, I'll watch it." We walked into the house and I kissed Mom. It was just about dinnertime when I decided to ask Dad if I could go to the movies with Anthony, my pal from across the street. His parents had told Anthony and me that a great new movie just arrived in town.

"Is it a western?" Dad asked.

"I don't think so, Dad. Anthony called it a cops and robbers movie. About Sicily and the Mafia."

My father's steely eyes looked at me. "What did you say it was about?"

"Mafia gangsters, Dad. You know!"

"*Managgia.*" (Frustration.) Sammy loudly sighed. "Where did you hear that word, Joey?"

"Anthony mentioned it when he spoke of the movie and I didn't want to look stupid so I looked it up in the dictionary."

"You shouldn't use that word. Mafia is an evil word. It represents criminals, killers, and the scum of the earth. Men have been killed misusing that word. Promise me you will not use it anymore."

"Okay, I promise."

"And, son, you're not going to that movie."

"Gee, Dad, it's supposed to be good." I glanced at Mom and got her forget-it look.

"*Bastante!*" Dad said. That was his Sicilian for the decision was final. Dad didn't have do-overs.

After dinner, I went to my room and pulled down my trusty Webster's. The word Mafia wasn't a no-no word like "shit, fuck, whore or prick—" words I couldn't use and weren't even in the dictionary. I was confused.

The next day I approached Mom and asked if she recalled the Mafia conversation from the night before.

"How can I forget? Okay, what do you want to know that you already don't?"

"I just don't understand why some things are so bad while others are not, like the Mafia thing."

Mom looked at me. "You will learn that in this life everything is not black and white and simple. The Sicilians were controlled by many countries over thousands of years. Like your father, the people were suspicious of everyone. Even after their liberation in 1860, they were looked down upon and felt downtrodden by the Italians, their liberators."

"Why would they free them and then look down on them, Mom?"

"Well, for one thing, they treated them like bastard children, and for another the Sicilians created the Mafia protection racket. With its evil and corruption spreading throughout Italy, Italians were fearful and constantly reminded of where it came from."

"Was Dad ever in the Mafia, Mom?"

"No, Joey, he was never associated with them and was only fourteen when he returned to America. Joey, hear me. Don't press your father on this Mafia issue. He's not comfortable with it. He has his reasons and you should respect that."

Despite my interest in the Mafia, the message from Mom and Dad was clear. I decided to keep my mouth shut but to learn, read and study.

❋ ❋ ❋

One day later in May, just before my eighth birthday, I recalled Dad looking over at Mom just after dinner, and then shifting his attention to me. He said, "Joe, for your birthday, I wondered if you'd like to go fishing with me on the Giuseppina, the next trip?"

I was thrilled. I knew he would take me one day, but this was a major surprise and we could be out for a week or more. This was fantastic. I couldn't wait to tell my friends. I was going fishing with my father. Wow!

The following afternoon, I was out front on the lawn playing with "Terry," my Pomeranian, when Vito, one of my school chums, and a few fellas dropped by on their way to Washington School. They petted and played with Terry for a while and Vito asked if I wanted to go with them and play ball at the school playground.

"Sure, let me go ask my Mom." She said okay and took Terry from me as we departed.

When I returned about twenty minutes later, Mom looked at me and said, "What's wrong?" I must have appeared downtrodden. "Did you get hurt or get in a fight? Let me look at you."

Looking somewhat dejected, I hung my head down and shuffled. I didn't say anything until Mom asked, "Okay Joey, What's the matter? What happened?"

"Mom, when I told the guys about going fishing with my father, one of them who I didn't know laughed and said, "Sammy's not your real father." He kept saying it over and over. I got mad and left.

"Mom, what did he mean?" Sitting across from me at the kitchen table, she squirmed and paused as her face flushed and her eyes widened.

"Don't worry, it's nothing," she said. "Dad will want to talk to you about it." Mom's reply troubled me as the boy's words repeated in my mind.

Early the next morning while it was still dark Dad departed for the boat while Mom and I slept. We woke around seven-thirty and had breakfast.

"I spoke to Dad after you went to bed last night about that boy's remarks and he wants to talk with you on the boat." That was fine with me, as we left for the fishing grounds the next morning.

❋ ❋ ❋

We traveled westerly toward a place where the bottom of the ocean rose gently and became a land bank. Dad said that if tuna were around they'd stop there to feed.

The Niputi ...the Nephew

The wind was light along the way as the 600 HP diesel engine's exhaust huffed a deep growl in the background. Dad called me up to the bridge, since he never came down to the deck until the boat returned to the dock when we got home.

Dad maintained our westerly course by turning a large brass wheel connected to the Giuseppina's rudder. He talked about how we maintained our course, the rising, and setting of the sun and mysteries of the sea.

He then said, "Joey, I know you are young, but I need to tell you a man-to-man story about the Asaro, Zottolo and Bonpensiero family. It is also about you, your mother, and me. *Capisciu?*" (Understand?)

"Yeah, Dad."

"Joey, of course you know your Aunt Mary and Uncle Joe Asaro."

"Sure, Dad. I love Aunt Mary and Uncle Joe. They are my favorites."

"Good. Well before she married your Uncle Joe Asaro, her birth name was Zottolo and she was the daughter of a man named Marco Zottolo. You don't remember him. You were too small but he was from Mazara, Sicily a fishing port just around the bend from Palermo and Porticello, where I grew up."

"Really," I interjected.

"Yeah, and he was a good fisherman." Dad said. "Mr. Zottolo had several sons who were your Aunt Mary's brothers and they lived down the block from Nana Maria's. They lived in the same house with your mom and you when you were a baby."

"I did?" I asked surprised.

"Yes, you did." Sammy paused and lit up a cigarette. Then, he tossed the match into the sea.

"You remember your Aunt Mary's brother, Vito?"

"Yeah, Dad, but I don't know why Uncle Vito's my uncle or why Aunt Mary is my aunt."

"Well Joey, you know the Zottolo family. Marco was a widower whose wife Marianne died quite young and left Marco with a daughter, your Aunt Mary, and four brothers Vito, Joe, Dominic and Frankie."

"Wow, Dad. That's a big family."

"Yes it was, Joey. But, it wasn't big for long. All the men with the exception of your Uncle Vito went fishing on their boat called the *Calabria* and headed south to Mexican waters. While they were traveling, a treacherous storm blew in and the Calabria ran for protection to the bay at Cape Colonette."

"While lying at anchor waiting for the storm to calm, Joe, Frankie and Dominic decided to go to shore and get some provisions. Upon their return to the Calabria, the winds in the bay began to fiercely blow and their skiff capsized. All of the brothers drowned."

"Didn't they know how to swim, Dad?"

"Yes, but sometimes the sea can be dangerous and much stronger than men. You just can't stay afloat and sometimes you die."

"Joey, that accident was the largest single family loss in San Diego fishery history. I knew all the men who died and one of them was your birth father. His name was Joe Zottolo and he was married to your mom."

"Was he your friend, Dad?"

"Sort of, Joey, but not best friends. We were close in age. Joe was 25 and I was 26."

"So what happened to Mom?"

"Mom was pregnant with you when Joe died. You weren't born until almost three months later. She raised you with Aunt Mary and your Uncle Joe Asaro until I came along.

"Really, Dad?"

"Yeah, really. I knew your mother and, as I said, I knew Joe pretty well, and l knew you when you were just a small little boy.

"Your mom mourned for her dead husband and about two years, later I asked her out on a date and in time, I wanted to marry her and be your father. So, your mom and I got married. I loved you both. You've been my son ever since. *Capish?* Do you understand?"

"Yes. But Dad, you are my father and always will be, right?"

"Right, son. Do you have any questions?"

"Was I a Zottolo?"

"Yes, until I adopted you and changed your name to Bonpensiero."

"So, I'm a Bonpensiero, right, Dad?"

"Yes you are, son."

"So what do you say if someone says I am not your real father?"

"I tell them they are crazy. You're my dad and if they don't like it, they can come and talk to you about it."

"That's fine, son. Don't worry."

CHAPTER 4

CALL ME NIPUTI

Fathers are often the unspoken heroes of their young sons. Many boys hold their fathers in awe and wish to emulate them. This was true for my father and me. However, his job as a commercial fishing boat skipper kept him away from home for long stretches of time. When we did see each other the subject of communication was normally about work, respect, education, and the future. With Dad, the sea was his worksite and his absence was the norm. I longed to see him and spend more time with him. I learned one thing about my father: He'd tell me the truth no matter the subject or pain.

✯ ✯ ✯

About a week after I returned from our fishing trip and I was playing with Terry on the lawn, a large dark car slowed and pulled into our driveway on Union Street. A husky, bald stranger got out. He stood by the car, looked around slowly, and lit a huge cigar. He was dressed in a suit and tie and it wasn't Sunday.

No one ever drove a car like that or smoked big cigars in our neighborhood. Looking back, it was the day my life's outlook took a detour. I ran into the kitchen to tell my mother.

"Mom, there's a rich guy that just pulled into our driveway."

"Joey, how do you know he's rich?"

"He's driving a dark green Cadillac."

The Niputi ...the Nephew

"That's your Uncle Frank, your Dad's brother. You've never met him. He's here to see your father. Stay in the kitchen while they talk."

Without so much as a press on the doorbell or a knock on the screen door, Frank aggressively yanked on the door handle and broke the inside latch. He then strode in like he owned the place.

"Sammy, your brother is here!" Mom yelled out. Normally she had a sweet voice but now her tone seemed raspy, which told me something wasn't right. She began mixing a highball all the while singing and humming a little phrase repeatedly: "Gotta have a lotta ice, lotta ice, lotta ice."

"Please sit, Frank," she said, handing him the glass. "Here's your scotch and water. Hope I made it right."

Frank took the drink, casually took a gulp and dismissed her like a waitress, "It'll do," then plopped himself down in our forties-style, round-armed green living room easy chair. He tried to cross his legs, but he couldn't get one over the other so he resigned himself to sit with his legs apart, sip his drink, blow cigar smoke in the air and wait for my dad. He looked like a king holding court. Even as a kid, I could feel the tension in our home that this man's presence created.

Dad finally entered the room, saying, "Hello, brother. How the hell are you?" But before he had time to respond, Mom returned to the room gasping. "Wow! That cigar smoke is a killer and sure stinks up this room."

Frank responded, "Open the door if you don't like it. Me, I'm fine."

Dad didn't say a word but noticed me standing in the kitchen doorway and said, "Joey, come here and meet your uncle."

Unsure of the stranger in the living room, I walked in and stood near my father. I started to cough. "The smoke burns my eyes, Dad."

He ignored me and said, "Shake hands with *Ziu Chich*, Joey."

Frank took my small hand in his and immediately grinned a pretend smile. Still reacting to the cigar smoke, I wiped my teary eyes.

"Hello Joey. I am your *Ziu*– (uncle, and pronounced Zeeo.) I'm your Dad's big brother. I'll call you *Niputi*, and you can call me Uncle Frank or *Ziu Chich*. Whatever you like."

"What's a *Ni-Pu-Ti?*" I asked, sounding out the word phonetically like my mother taught me.

"It's Sicilian for nephew. Doesn't your father teach you any Sicilian?" The hair on the back of my neck bristled. His question seemed insulting to both Dad and me.

"My dad teaches me a lot, like fishing and how to sew net and also told me not to smoke. He said it wasn't good for me."

Not used to anyone disagreeing with him, let alone an eight-year-old boy, Frank spat out, "Your father probably teaches you too much!" Turning to his brother Turi–Sammy—he grinned like a Cheshire cat.

"He's a feisty one, heh?"

"Yeah, he keeps us going." Dad knew that if he didn't interrupt my banter, I would continue.

Frank downed his drink and shook the ice in the glass as a signal to Mom for another drink.

"Turi, you ought to tell Mandy to buy you some good scotch. This stuff is crap!"

"Don't drink it if you don't like it!" I didn't know if Dad was irritated or joking. But then Frank leaned forward toward Dad and said, "You probably don't have Johnny Walker or JB. It's expensive." Dad didn't reply.

I sensed that Dad was apprehensive around his elder brother. Besides, I was eight years old and wondered why I hadn't met Dad's brother before. I would have to ask Mom because I thought I knew all of our relatives.

"What's up, Frank? Our sister Grace called and told Mandy that you needed a favor?"

"Yeah, we need to talk." Dad and his brother walked to the dining room, leaving me to wonder what was suddenly different in my little world. I sensed it from the moment I first saw Frank and I was curious about this new uncle. It was how he strutted around and the tone he took with Mom and Dad. It was how he opened the door without knocking. It was how he took control in our house and, more importantly, my parents just let him. I had never seen that before in our house.

Other family members who lived nearby didn't act like this man. He never came around before, so I didn't know what to expect. My initial dislike for him soon turned to revulsion as he rattled off to Mom about what he expected her to serve at a dinner for his friends. In time, I learned that his abrasive attitude never changed. He seemed loud and had a boasting manner and I began to shun him like the plague.

It began with, "I want you to take my money and buy Booth's House of Lords Gin, Noilly Pratt Vermouth and Fernet Branca—an Italian specialty digestive. Also pick up quality cocktail olives and onions, pasta and fresh big shrimp."

"Do you mean prawns, Frank? Shrimp are small by definition."

"Yeah, yeah, the big ones and you must definitely buy 'top quality' meat for *Carne Spedini—stuffed Sicilian meat rolls.*

"Don't go buy any of that Tijuana dog meat, Mandy. My sister Grace told me you and her went down to TJ several times and bought meat. Buy prime filet from Tarantino's if he's still in business. My friends, Frank De Simone and 'Momo' Adamo, love fresh food and quality meat."

Mom then asked, "Frank, who are these men I'm cooking for?"

"That's none of your business, Amanda."

Mom bristled at Frank's tone and stared daggers at Dad. My father turned toward Frank, saying something in Sicilian. Mom's half-smile—used when angry, plus a raised eyebrow—told me all I wanted to know. She hurled some strong words Dad's way.

"Sammy, it was you who said we speak American in this house, so let's not change that because your brother Frank is here." She didn't stop as she turned to Frank and said, "My name is not Thelma. You may talk to your wife like that in your house and that's your business, but I won't tolerate it in mine nor in front of my son. I do the best I can in the kitchen and don't mind putting the dinner and cocktail hour together for you. However, we should get a few things straight. This is our house and I work my butt off alongside my husband. I'm not one of your hired help. You can't treat me like one, especially in our own house.

"Our place is small and if you bring Mary Ann it will be tight. Two, I've never made Spedini before. But if it's Sicilian, it can't be that difficult . . . I'll get a recipe from Thelma and put it together. However, what you're asking for is going to be expensive."

Frank glared at her with eyes that could kill, and must have thought: *Here was Turi's Americano wife making light of cooking Spedini and talking of expense. She ought to shut her mouth.* Yet, he didn't say a word.

I was proud of Mom for not taking his guff. I think Dad was in shock for her standing up to his brother.

Mom's Russian-German extraction and self-reliance set many back as she took charge and got things done. She didn't wait for Dad to come home from fishing so she could ask him. She survived in a multi-ethnic town in San Diego, living with those in her husband's family who spoke mostly Sicilian. So to make things easy on herself she learned the Sicilian language, much to the chagrin of the family and neighbors. She was a woman to be dealt with directly and a survivor, especially after being reared in the cold and rustic environment of South Dakota and Wyoming with a family of twenty brothers and sisters. She was a pioneer woman, kind and understanding, yet tough to the core.

She loved a lot, read much, and learned constantly. She enjoyed life and had fun living. I have memories dating back to when I was five years old and she took me to day school on her bike's handlebars, dropped me off, then rode another five miles to Ryan Aircraft, where she worked her other job. She'd then pick me up around five p.m. She was a worker, and I never doubted that Dad appreciated her abilities, admired her strength, and loved her free spirit.

Now, thinking back, I realize that both brothers were raised in a culture dominated by men, where a woman's place in the home was one of total servitude. Sicilian women were strong in many ways, but brought up culturally to defer to the man of the house. Women could not contradict or argue. To do so often warranted a backhand. They depended on their men for food, care, and shelter and, in effect, Sicilian girls were taught wifely survivor skills: cook, clean, have babies and stay quiet. The Sicilian man's home was his castle and a wife's duty was to do her husband's bidding—women were borderline chattel.

Although others may disagree, I rarely observed Uncle Frank being respectful to women, save for his wife, Thelma, and his only child, Mary Ann. Around his family of sisters, he always acted as if he was the boss and, culturally, they had to respect him as such. That was Sicilian tradition or what he learned from his father. Frank was not into anyone who disagreed with him, especially women.

"No, no, no!" Frank yelled at Mom. "I don't want you using any practice recipes for my friends. Besides, Mary Ann's not coming." He pulled his money clip from his pocket and made a big show of peeling off a hundred-dollar bill. He tossed the bill on the coffee table.

"This should cover your expenses, Turi."

"My God, that's a lot of money!" Mom said. Frank turned to Dad, ignoring Mom and her scathing tongue.

"Sammy, tell your wife to buy what she needs and make something Sicilian and make it special, with fresh antipasto, fresh ravioli and fresh fruit. You know—the works. This dinner is very important to me!"

Dad looked as pissed as Mom. He glared at his brother. Finally, he spoke.

"Frank, my wife is an excellent cook. If you're worried, *Chich*, have Thelma make the goddamn dinner. You can even invite the *Spiru* (cops). They would enjoy it. You know, brother, you've changed since you moved away from the neighborhood. Oh, and don't forget to tell Thelma to make sure it is f-r-e-s-h, and that you couldn't eat here because we only serve rotgut scotch and cheap Mexican meat just like our mother eats."

"I'll ignore you saying that, brother, and if it wasn't for the *Spiru* (Spies/cops), I would have the dinner at home. However, having Thelma make the Spedini is good thinking. I'll bring them with me."

"You do what the hell you want. That's your problem, *Frati*." (Brother) Frank, wanting the last word, ignored his brother's remark and turned to Mom.

"Mandy, make sure you create a nice, fresh salad!"

"*Buono y Bastante!*" (Good and final), said Dad defiantly. "We'll have it here!"

The exchange ended, points were made, and Frank departed. In retrospect, he probably felt good about himself. He convinced simple people to host a dinner for two Mafia heavyweights. This wasn't the first time he had used family, and it sure wouldn't be the last. *Unscrupulous bastard!*

CHAPTER 5
ONE DISH TOO MANY

Frank Bompensiero always believed he was a faithful son to his mother and father, and to his surrogate Mafia Parino (Godfather), Ignacio "Jack" Adragna, who dropped the "A" off his name and left it "Dragna." Frank was driven by a desire to achieve and he worked hard. He always tried to please his superiors. One night in 1948, thinking he was the guy to be promoted and at his egotistical best, he hosted a festive celebratory dinner at his brother's home. That fateful night, Frank would learn, by a simple slip of the tongue, that he had fallen short of his aspirations. It would be a turning point in his career. Unlike many who yearn for respect and recognition but fall short and yet continue, Frank was devastated. He took a turn for the worse. From that night forward, he would strive for only self-satisfaction. He pandered to his own personal sense of well being. In his mind, other out of town familia borrowed his services from Dragna. Hell, he was used and screwed by many, but not anymore. He felt like a cast-off whore. His new maxim became: "You ask, I give, you owe!" Frank was sure to collect one way or another!

✯ ✯ ✯

Frank arrived early on the night of the dinner. He wanted to make sure Mom had met his specifications. In his mind, you could never trust the *Americani*, and Sam's wife was American.

The Niputi ...the Nephew

True to his reputation as a "dandy" dresser, Frank was decked out. He sported a new azure-blue sharkskin suit, flaming silk tie and an imported British Indian cotton white-on-white shirt. For added panache, his initials were hand-sewn on the left breast pocket and cuffs. We all knew how expensive it was to dress like Frank. Dad welcomed him and said in his simple way, "Frank, you look good."

Mom, recalling the contentious ending the last time Frank visited, did likewise, but laid it on. "Frank, you sure are handsome tonight, all dressed up hoity-toity."

Frank smiled with arrogance and assurance. Tonight, he was certain, would be the turning point in his career. He thanked her for her compliment and then took inventory of the house. He ogled at the dinner table layout and the seating arrangements, saying, "Okay, okay."

Next, he wandered to the kitchen where he seemed to be thrilled with the aroma. Mom always put out the finest she could muster. Characteristically, he only nodded and said nothing. He wasn't one to compliment others.

"I need to go to the car and bring in the Spedini," he said to Mom. "After the guests come, I want you to place them in the oven at 250 degrees to warm for twenty minutes."

"Okay, Frank. You're the boss. I'll take it from there."

Minutes later, a ring on our doorbell signaled the guests' arrival. Frank welcomed Frank De Simone and Girolomo "Momo" Adamo into our home as he would his own.

Mom and Dad had never met either of the men. I watched the whole scene unfold like a movie where people meet for the first time and are uncomfortable. To me, it felt strange. Frank took their jackets and handed them to Mom––the hatcheck girl. Then he introduced the men to my dad. When Mom walked back into the living room after hanging up their coats, I scurried to her side as Frank uttered in a monotone, "This is Turi's wife."

Then, beaming with a wide smile, he said, "This young fellow is my Niputi Joe, my nephew, Sam's son." I wondered why he emphasized his relationship with me, since I had just met him the other day.

I looked up and shook their hands with a firm grasp as Dad had taught me.

Mr. De Simone turned to Mom. "I missed your first name."

"Amanda," Mom replied. "But that's too stuffy so everyone calls me Mandy."

Mom took cocktail orders. De Simone watched as she poured his favorite Booth's House of Lords gin. She added a wisp of Noilly Prat vermouth into the shaker and chilled the mixture while swirling an ice cube around the martini glass. She added an olive and served him first. Then she made Frank and Momo a scotch and water, and one for herself. Dad rarely drank alcohol and had his usual glass of water. Mom sat for a moment, and then excused herself for dinner preparations. She returned with small savory ravioli hors d'oeuvres that she crisp-baked and served with two types of dipping sauce.

De Simone passed his cocktail under his nose to savor the aroma of the gin. He took a sip and then swallowed the contents in one gulp.

"This martini is perfect, Mandy. Sammy, where did your wife learn to make such a wonderful concoction?"

Dad beamed and said, "My secret, Frank."

De Simone tilted his empty glass toward my attentive mother. She promptly made him another. After several cocktails and raviolis, the men were ready to sit down to dinner at Mom's beautiful dinner table. She accented it with fresh flowers and china borrowed from my Aunt Grace.

I had eaten earlier and sat in the living room. I listened to music on our RCA console radio, though I could see and hear the conversation in the dining room.

Our guests said they were from Los Angeles. Both men were handsomely dressed. De Simone wore a gray gabardine suit with a small hounds-tooth pattern in the fabric. The color accentuated his pale and lack-luster complexion. He was tall and thin, which made him appear frail and gaunt for a Sicilian. I noticed that his right eyelid drooped a bit.

He continued to pass an occasional compliment to Mom on the appetizers and drinks. But he also mentioned that he hoped she hadn't made a rich Sicilian tomato sauce. His stomach was temperamental.

"Heavens no," Mom assured him. "I've got a young one and Turi is sensitive as well. I always make sure the sauce isn't too spicy. We must keep all our men healthy. Right?"

"Yes, you must," De Simone replied.

"I think you'll be pleasantly surprised, Mr. De Simone."

"Please call me Frank." He addressed Mom with respect and praised her hors d'oeuvres selection, and now he raved about her made-at-the-table Caesar salad.

It was her version of the famous dressing from Caesar's Restaurant in Tijuana.

"Sammy and I eat there often when we go to Caliente racetrack. We know the maître d' and he gave me the recipe."

Adamo smiled and appeared to be enjoying himself, too. He was the more collegiate dressed of the three men, in a hounds tooth tweed sport jacket and tan V-neck sweater over a black shirt. He spoke in a rough and broken version of English. With his Sicilian manner, broken English and rough exterior, I knew he grew up in the old country. Today he would look like a character from a Scorsese movie.

Mom's prima piate—the first plate—was spinach and veal ravioli in a light, cream-based pesto. Frank De Simone loved it. Next, she delivered her own specialty that she called "Shrimp D' Germanese." She prepared the dish with a lemon-garlic butter cream sauce, parsley, and capers. Her guests raved about it and the salad. All diners ate seconds of ravioli and shrimp. The Spedini hadn't been served yet.

"Sammy," said De Simone, while smiling at my mother, "your wife is one bella chef. Though my law practice gets me into some fine restaurants, tonight's meal was no less than grand." Dad beamed at his brother and said, "That's my gal." Dad winked at Mom and then said. "She cooks everything fresh!"

Mom caught my eye through the dining room doorway and gave me a little conspiratorial glance. I was proud of her. And, we were both proud of Dad for poking fun at Frank's earlier rude remarks to her.

The dinner chatter went from food to social talk as Momo turned to my Mom and said, "My wife and I will be moving to San Diego soon. I'm sure she would love to have your recipe for your prawns."

My hungry Uncle Frank stuffed his shrimp into his mouth like jamming quarters into a piggy bank, but suddenly stopped when he heard Momo's comment. His eyes bugged out as his face reddened, and with his mouth full of shrimp, he began to choke. As he coughed, Momo patted him on the back and said, "Bless you, Chich!"

I didn't know it then, but this tidbit of information was a major announcement from West Coast boss Jack Dragna himself, the head of the Los Angeles crime family. Though casually mentioned at the dinner table, it carried the same weight as if it were emblazoned on parchment and Jack himself had read it from a pulpit. This news was a major blow to Frank and it showed on his puffy cheeks and by the sweat beads forming on his balding head. His face reddened as his blood pressure rose.

Momo's "coming to town" had a hidden meaning for Frank. It meant he would not be the head of the San Diego operation and had in fact been demoted. Moreover, he learned about it in his brother's house. Frank was pissed.

I could not have understood then why Frank tried to act as the congenial host. That would take years of watching people and learning about human behavior. Frank fumed as he watched his dreams of power slam into the wall the way he had done so many times with a man's head. The man with grandiose ambitions had been kicked in the balls and shoved to the back of the bus! Frank's dreams of becoming San Diego's *Caporégime* (crew captain) disappeared into air like the smoke from his giant Bering cigar.

As he recovered from his coughing/choking fit, Frank regained the strength to say, "Save room for the next course. It's *Spedini*. My wife Thelma made them especially for you."

Mom went into the kitchen and brought in the platter piled high with the Sicilian Spedini. The kabobs were thin slices of beef filled with onion, garlic, spices, and cheese, then rolled and placed on skewers and broiled. No doubt, Frank's excitement to impress influenced the amount of Spedini. Thelma had made enough to pile high on her serving platter, which could carry a twenty-five pound turkey. Adamo and De Simone looked at each other and De Simone finally exclaimed, "Madonna! What a beautiful dish. Compliments to your wife, Frank."

Already sated and filled, both guests took a small sampling as a courtesy. Frank, the hefty one of the party, scooped up three servings.

"The *Spedini* is very good, Frank," DeSimone said. "Make sure you pass my compliments to Thelma. However, I'm so full from the prior entree, I cannot eat more."

Mom's dinner was a huge success and thoroughly enjoyed by most at the table, save for Frank. He sat quietly and then started to fidget as he began to sweat profusely. His stomach no doubt was churning like a cement mixer on overload. It was time to have a smoke, a stretch, and an after-dinner drink. Frank excused himself and headed quickly to the bathroom. He did ask Mom to make him a scotch. In his absence, both Adamo and the erudite De Simone were served Fernet-Branca, an Italian digestive.

❋ ❋ ❋

Years later, I did my own digging into historical and court records about the men Frank so desperately wanted to impress that night. In less than five years, their names would be in the press and linked with Frank and the underworld. And De Simone became the scourge that destroyed Frank's reputation with his lifelong mentor, Jack Dragna, before Dragna died.

For approximately thirty-five years, Frank Bompensiero devoted himself and his services to Jack Dragna and the *Cosa Nostra* (their thing). For Frank, Dragna was more than a savior and mentor; like his father, their bond, akin to blood, was strong. His association with Jack meant everything to Frank—his family and meal ticket.

When I was a child in 1948, Frank Bompensiero left an indelible, bad-taste impression on me. I still find him stuck in the crevices of my memory. From the first and early meetings I never liked him, but I couldn't just blank him out. He was Dad's brother. Besides, as soon as I thought Frank was gone from my life for good, he'd pop up again on the front pages of San Diego's *Union* or *Tribune* newspapers. If it wasn't a new story, he'd be quoted in Neil Morgan's local column. He loved the attention.

Three years after Mom's culinary triumph, dad experienced a kidney problem while fishing and his physician directed that he seek employment "on the beach." Unfortunately, Dad's new business brought Frank closer to us, much to my chagrin.

I wondered what had driven Frank to a life of crime. I wanted to know where it started and what put him on the dark road that led to the wrong side of the law. I also wanted to know why my father was so different. Besides, I knew the adults were secretive and kept things from us. But it took me years to piece together the puzzle.

The family elder, Uncle Frank came around on rare occasions, not weekly as purported by some. The rationale of the blood family was simple: Maintain pride and respect in the family name at all costs. To them it was all about Bompensiero allegiance as the family clung together. Frank, however, gave his allegiance to another family as well—the Familia Mafia, not that the Bompensieros would ever admit that.

CHAPTER 6
SICILIAN FAMILY SHAME

After years of hearing stories about the positive and wonderful heritage of their family, several of the young and inquisitive Bompensiero offspring began to wonder why the family left Sicily and headed for America. If Sicily was so good, why leave? Maybe the history was not as wonderful as they said. One hundred years later, some rumors leaked and some of the brood got suspicious. The research began and now, no one could unwring the bell. In 1860, when Garibaldi rescued Sicily from the Spanish king, things began to change for the better in Sicily and formal records were kept. The island and its people became a part of Italy with all the laws, administration, and bureaucracy that comes with people being provided newfound civility. And, for the searchers, it became obvious why the Scuola (School), now-Bompensiero, family departed their homeland to begin a new life in America.

✴ ✴ ✴

It was August 21, 1893, and the dewy mist hung like a foggy blanket across New York's outer landmass. The morning sun finally broke through and warmed the air as the *SS Cashemire* chugged westward toward Brooklyn and New York Bay.

Immigration records revealed that the brothers Giuseppe and Giovanni Bompensiero were aboard the steamer and must have stood on the deck breathing in the morning air for the first time in days. They felt refreshed after their grueling voyage in the bowels of the ship, after sailing from Naples sixteen days before.

The Bompensiero brothers departed Porticello, Sicily, in a hurry. Brother Giovanni arrived in the dead of night from his home and banged on the door until his brother Giuseppi answered.

"Frati, I have decided to join you on your trip to America."

"Why do you want to go with me now?" Giuseppe asked.

"We talked about this weeks ago."

Giovanni appeared nervous and agitated, but to Giuseppe it made no matter. He would enjoy his company. However, Giovanni shunned eye contact with his brother as if he were hiding something. Just then, Giuseppa, their mother, and a light sleeper, entered after the sound of Giovanni's rap on the front door.

"Did I hear you say something about your wife and the boys, Giovanni?" she asked. "Are they leaving too?"

"No, Mama. Just me. Not to worry. Rosa supports me taking off to get a new start for our family. Besides, in America, I can get a good-paying job."

"The ship leaves at dawn," said Giuseppe. "We'd better be going."

Giuseppe grabbed his packed valise.

"Mine is on the stoop," said Giovanni. They kissed their mother and were on their way.

Like many others who left Sicily, Giuseppe sought freedom from the backward social castes and the grinding poverty of Porticello. He planned to make his fortune and return to Sicily to marry his intended, Anna Maria. (Maria or Nana.)

Once they were aboard the *SS Cashemire*, and the ship had left its moorings heading for the open sea, Giovanni had a talk with his younger brother and revealed the truth for his hasty departure.

"Giuseppi, I am going to say this once and no more. My wife was a *Mensa Butana y Mensa Spousa*—half whore and half wife—when I married her. Last night when I got home, she started acting like a *butana* (whore), pulling up her dress and teasing like the bitch she is. I got angry and we fought. I choked her."

"You choked her? Are you *pazzo?* (crazy). How is she?"

"*Tu, si cafoni*" (You're a fool, brother).

"What the fuck are you saying?"

"I told you, *I choked her! Idda morto* (She's dead). I carried my sons to their grandmother and told her that Rosa wasn't feeling well and would pick them up the following day by noon. I know the old bitch. Once I didn't show, the next day she'd head over to the house and find her daughter dead. She'd call the Sicilian *Carabineri* (the police). I decided to leave with you so I wouldn't have to answer any questions."

"Giovanni, you crazy bastard. You killed your wife and then tell your mother all is well and the family bids you adieu. *Tu si crentino!* (You are a cretin!)

Giovanni would say no more.

✼ ✼ ✼

Now, as they stood on the deck, they could see the fog break and Lady Liberty's image began to beckon impoverished souls to America's shores. This euphoric experience was short-lived, however, as the word of job scarcity spread through the ship.

Before they gained approval for disembarkation, however, the passengers all had to answer a list of twenty-nine social, political, and medical questions asked by the government's immigration inspectors. By today's standards, the questions were intrusive, repulsive, un-American, and very politically incorrect:

"Do you have American relatives? Are you an anarchist or a polygamist? Do you have any money? Do you have a job? Do you have any debilitating handicaps or disease?"

Arriving without passports or papers, the Bompensiero brothers were given entry identification documents stamped with the imprint W.O.P. This signified that they landed "without papers." Little did Giuseppe or Giovanni know that in time those three letters, like the mark of Cain, would identify Italians as "WOPs," and a racial slur to the rest of Americans. Others would be marked by similar societal prejudice and bias: the Mexicans as wetbacks; the Jews as kikes; the Polish as Polacks; and the Orientals as Chinks.

The W.O.P. stamp was the final step in the immigration approval process. A murmur of hope and encouragement spread through the gossip line for new arrivals—"Wisconsin has jobs!" They all wondered where or what was a "Wisconsin." Like a herd, they followed in line and listened to anyone whom they could understand and help them find their way.

Initially, the brothers were happy to go to Wisconsin, where jobs and fellow Italians were plentiful. However, they were ignorant about life and the climate and when a cold blast of Arctic air dropped temperatures below zero and snow began to fall, they hovered over an open fire and longed for the warmth of family.

After awhile, Giuseppi broke the silence by recalling the family they left behind. He spoke of their father and grandfather and the family name change. It happened years before and lessened the hidden jibes behind their back once the name switched from *Scuola*—(meaning *School*) to Bompensiero. However, the name change did nothing to hide the shame of their father's crime. Nor did it hide the hurt they felt for their dead brother. They would never be spared from shameful memories of a father gone awry.

✯ ✯ ✯

Had the fates been kind and given them parents of a more genteel class, they might have been schooled and learned of things other than fishing and hard work in the fields. However, this was Sicily and it had been a burdensome place for thousands of years.

"Papa raised us to be fishermen," said Giovanni. "That's all he knew." The brothers looked at each other over the fire and shivered and found it difficult to speak badly of their father, or discuss negative things, especially since Franco passed, mysteriously.

"You know, Giuseppi, there were times that Papa acted like a decent man."

"Yeah, Giovanni, when he was asleep. The rest of the time, he was Franco Scuola; doing anything, he damn well pleased. Hell, he was sick with pride. We were all afraid of him, and with good reason." Giovanni paused to poke a stick at the fire.

"I'll give you that Papa was proud, bullish and a stubborn man, but in spite of his faults and reputation, he loved his sons as much as any man on earth."

"Yeah, he loved us," said Giuseppi. "But all I can remember was his repeated backhands."

"He had one helluva temper. That's for sure," Giovanni said.

"Remember when we were kids on that Sunday after Mass when that man came out of the shadows in the alleyway? Christ, Papa grabbed the man, overpowered him, and stabbed him in the heart several times before he could scream. Then Papa walked on as if nothing happened."

"Giuseppe," Giovanni said sternly, "that was the man who cursed Papa many years before. He should have been satisfied with the broken fingers Papa gave him back then, but no! He had to go and hire a *Strega* (witch) to conjure a spell on our whole family. We were all screwed and ended up with bad luck and we didn't catch fish for weeks.

"Sure, Giovanni, make excuses," Giuseppe said, frowning. "All men needed courage to survive, but they didn't end up with our father's bad attitude."

Giovanni shot back defensively. "Managgia, poverty was everywhere in those days. We were ignorant peasants. So, what's the difference now? The church still owns 50 to 65 percent of the land. Besides, they never fed us anyway, pious cocksuckers!" Giuseppi said.

"There were no jobs, we were starving, and we were Scuolas who, like everyone else, were peasants. Women and children were treated like slaves. Girls were happy to become betrothed at an early age and leave home. Everything children learned came from the family. It was their spoken book-- the Bible, their way of life. What Mother and Father said was gospel, and they only told their children what they wanted them to know, nothing more.

"In Casa Scuola, there were no stories about the woes of the time, only stories of family members, and in each and every story, family members were always brave and honorable.

"Giovanni, do you remember the stories Papa told us of Grandfather *Pietro Scuola* teaching him the ways of the sea? He knew what his future held for him."

"I can see Papa now, short, muscular, and solid as the rocky cliffs that rose above the Tyrrhenian Sea," Giovanni replied, his voice turning dreamy. "He must have been wild and untamed; like the land steeped in the pagan traditions of an ancient world. He was proud and superstitious, a reckless spirit who came from a crude and unforgiving society where violence ruled and forgiveness was left to the priests."

In only ten years of heaving fishnets from the sea, Franco had learned how to survive by working from dawn until dusk. At seventeen, he requested permission to marry and received approval. To have sons and daughters to carry on the family name was what Franco lived for.

"Look at us," Giovanni said with a shake of his head. "I'm twenty-six with two sons and you at twenty-four are not even married."

"I plan to marry Anna Maria Tagliavia as soon as I save up passage money to return home. Remember, we were thirteen when we were betrothed.

"Papa raised us to be fishermen. That's all he knew."

"Yes, and then one day he took us fishing, and when we returned we never saw Turi alive again. We lost Salvatore."

"Lost my ass, *frati*. (Brother.) He was just a boy of eighteen and full of piss and vinegar. Our father killed him! Don't you remember?"

CHAPTER 7

DEATH BEFORE DINNER

Life is precious and lonely. It has been so ever since man found himself with a partner. With the loss of that partner or any other of his kind, he becomes alone; for it is true, that man is a social animal. I know of no culture on earth where death by any means: act of god—storms, earthquakes, unborn baby, act of war, tragic accident, suicide or by violent murder is accepted as commonplace. We are a species that innately wants to find or be assured that around the next breakthrough, we'll find life immortal. The word death conjures a very traumatic, emotional response in the mind of man— no matter how it occurs. There are those, however, who have performed atrocious acts that are considered evil in any culture: One might be killing one's own son while enraged and losing one's legacy for all time.

✼ ✼ ✼

As I recall, Giuseppi said, the water in Porticello Bay was calm and the *Batellas* careened easily onto the sandy shore's bottom. All was well. The trip was good. They caught fish, split off to market the fish and to do their chores.

"I think of that day often. It was also the day Pietro vowed to depart and left for Spain. I planned to leave for America.

We had just landed the *Batella* on the shore. Pietro jumped from the boat to secure the site and began to ready our fish for market." Giovanni's voice trailed off.

"I was the first one to get home," Giovanni said. "Papa looked tired and bedraggled when he entered and hung his coat on the rack near the door. I can still smell the garlic, onions, and spices blending in tomato sauce as Mama prepared the pasta for our evening meal.

"Papa slumped in his chair. He seemed preoccupied. He picked at the fish scales clinging to his forearm, but he couldn't remove them. His fingers were trembling—."

"Basta, enough!" Franco had cursed, slamming his fist down on the arm of the chair.

"Don't worry, Papa," said his daughter Giuseppina. She was a pretty girl, named after her mother Giuseppa. All in the family referred to her as Giuseppina (Little Josie).

"I'll get them for you, Papa." She loved her father and he doted on her in return. Using her neat short fingernails, Giuseppina pried the scales from his forearm. Franco smiled. His daughter was one of his few pleasures in life.

The evening meal was like a religious ceremony in the household. While his wife and other daughter continued to prepare the evening meal, Franco put his head back against his chair and closed his eyes. When Giuseppa placed a dish of crusty bread in front of him, Franco acknowledged her attentiveness with a slight smile. Ripping the end off the warm loaf, Franco dipped the bread into a plate of olive oil and red wine vinegar. This was one of his favorite treats.

"*Cena sciariari buono*" (Dinner smells good), said Franco. "It will be ready soon?"

"*Si y Grazi*," (Yes and thank you), said Giuseppa.

Minutes later the whole family, with the exception of Turi, sat at the table. Franco sat at the head with three of his four sons to his left. Turi's space nearest his mother's seat was vacant. After Giuseppa served the meal, she sat directly across from Franco near the kitchen.

The Niputi …the Nephew

The *primi-piate*, this night as always, was pasta—spaghetti with a touch of anchovy pesto sauce lightly covered with *Regiano Parmeseani* and sprinkled with freshly chopped parsley. Once each person at the table had a plate and a portion of the food, Franco said a short *Benedizione* (a blessing), had a bite or two, and then smiled at Giuseppa, indicating he was pleased with the meal.

Giuseppa broke the silence of hungry eaters.

"Why is Turi not home for dinner?"

Everyone looked at each other and shrugged, except Franco. He continued to eat slowly, chewing his food deliberately as he stared into nothingness. He appeared to be in deep thought. No one at the table replied to their mother's question.

"Hasn't anyone seen my Turi?" Giuseppa asked again. Giovanni, sitting near his father, joked.

"He's probably out chasing a girl down a Porticello alley." Then, like an angry mongrel growling a warning at an intruder, Franco turned, addressing his son.

"You are foolish! You speak as if you are on the street. You show no respect for my table or your mother and sister."

Giovanni's eyes dropped to his plate in shame and fearful of what could occur. Franco's left arm swung out and his open hand smashed into Giovanni's cheek, knocking him to the floor.

"Say something disrespectful at my table again, and you will suffer the consequences! Capisciu?" — (Understand?)

"Si, Papa." He rose from the floor.

The family fell silent. Franco went back to eating. He had no interest in telling his wife what happened on the way home.

✻ ✻ ✻

It was while Pietro and Giovanni took the fish to market, Franco and Turi stayed behind to secure their fishing belongings, then departed for the house. On the short walk home, Franco and Turi got into an argument. The reason for the argument was buried with Franco. The confrontation between father and his eighteen-year-old son happened near *Ziu Carini's* front stoop.

✻ ✻ ✻

"Franco, something must be wrong," Giuseppa said. "I can't believe my son would be late for dinner. He would not do this to me. I am worried about Turi."

Franco slammed his hand down on the table. "*Basta'mi spousa!* (Enough, my wife!) Don't worry! Turi is out in the street where I left him."

"What?" Giuseppa cried out.

"Why is he outside? Was there an accident? Is he hurt?"

Franco said nothing. A sense of foreboding overcame Giuseppa. Her heart must have constricted in fear. She felt faint. She turned to her husband and asked, "Why isn't Turi here, Franco?"

Franco stood up from his chair, leaned over the table, propping himself on his fists and stared indignantly at his wife. "Your son is not hurt. *Iddu morto!* (He's dead!)" Giuseppa screamed. The family, in shock at their father's words, looked at each other.

"What savagio bastardo killed my son? Oh Diu, oh God!" Giuseppa wailed. "Who did this awful thing?" she said with a vengeful hiss, though in her heart she feared she knew the answer.

"Your son Turi disrespected me!" Franco shouted. "Capisciu?" (Understand?)

Franco resumed his seat at the head of the table, calmly picked up his fork, and continued to finish his supper.

Giuseppa recoiled as if she had been slapped; her tears caught in her throat, as her heart knew the truth. Knowing her husband's vicious ways and temper, she had seen him in action, but this—this was evil.

She turned to Pietro, her eldest son. "Go find my boy and bring him to me."

The boys rose from the table almost in unison; Pietro, Giovanni, and Giuseppe left the house. They didn't travel far as their neighbor, Ziu Carini, stepped from his doorway as they walked past.

"Come, your brother Turi is here," he said.

"Turi and your father argued over there." He pointed a few feet away.

"Whatever Turi said must have wakened the devil in Franco. Your father unleashed a mighty backhand to your brother's head and he fell, cracking it on the granite stoop. Then your father grabbed Turi's throat and squeezed, cursing God and humiliating the unconscious Turi with more threats of violence. Finally, your father rose and left Turi in the street. I carried him into my house. Boys, it is a sad day when I had to watch your *Malatu papa* (sick father) kill his son. God will punish that evil man."

"Our father has done the unspeakable," said Pietro, "and yes, God will punish him. But for us, we must grieve and console our mother."

✳ ✳ ✳

"You know," said Giovanni, "our father had it tough as a boy. Poverty was everywhere in those days; most were ignorant peasants. There were no jobs, our name was *Scuola*—School, and like everyone else, we were peasants. And were starving. Women and children were treated like slaves. Girls were happy to become betrothed at an early age and leave home."

Everything children learned came from the family. It was their unread Bible— their way of life. What Mother and Father said was gospel, and they only told their children what they wanted them to know, nothing more.

In Casa Scuola, there were no stories about the woes of the time, only stories of brave and honorable family members.

"Do you remember the stories papa told us of Grandfather Pietro Scuola teaching him the ways of the sea?"

"I remember," Giuseppe said. "But, none of that justifies his action with his son Turi."

When the word spread, the townsfolk called Franco *mala bruta*—crazy animal, because no normal man would kill his own son. The police disagreed after hearing Franco's story. They said Turi's death was accidental, that it resulted from Turi's stupidity and disrespect to his father. It was a family matter and the head of the house had settled the issue. It was, of course, a matter of honor. Case closed.

✻ ✻ ✻

When the police ruled Turi's death as a family matter and a deed of honor, Giuseppa realized that Francesco would escape punishment and her son's death would never be avenged. Her love for her husband turned to hate. She wished Franco dead.

As his wife turned away from him, Francesco became distraught. Within a few weeks, he became ill and died of an undetermined illness. At his funeral, the town criers whined over the loss of a son and father within weeks of each other, while behind her heavy black veil Giuseppa smiled, knowing she had avenged her son's death. The community that had lived with Francesco's evil nature viewed his passing as a good thing. All knew that God had reached down from on high and settled the score.

Several months later, a stranger visited Porticello. His name was Bernardo Bompensiero and he had come from Brindisi, another town on the mainland. He was known as a respected landowner. A hardworking and prosperous man, Bernardo had never married and, in his senior years, the loneliness of his large empty bed became a hollow partner. He sought companionship. In time, he met Giuseppa, now a widow, and began to court her.

There was also the matter of his considerable property. Under the new Italian law, if he died without male heirs the state would take everything, so Bernardo and his attorney devised a plan. Giuseppa and Bernardo would marry and Bernardo would adopt her sons, thus securing the Bompensiero holdings.

Franco's sons Giovanni and Giuseppi agreed that a name change would be beneficial, a way to shun the notoriety and town gossip. They would like to get Pietro's position, but he had already departed to Spain. Freedom from Franco's dark shadow persuaded them, and again Giuseppa and her sons could walk proudly in the world without shame. In time, and with the passing of generations, Giuseppa and her children believed all would be well.

The townsfolk of Porticello whispered that Franco's downfall was the sin of hubris, extreme pride, the greatest crime of the ancient Greeks. After six hundred years of Greek control over Sicily, hubris had wormed its way into the Sicilian culture. Some viewed hubris as man's tragic flaw, rooted in the worst aspects of humankind. The family always feared that, if true, the ugly head of hubris would infect some future Scuola offspring—and it did.

✱ ✱ ✱

My grandfather Giuseppe, the young man who came to America with his brother Giovanni, was a proud man who faced many challenges. He was fortunate to father two sons and four daughters before he went to his grave. He was unaware that one day his firstborn son, Francesco, named after his grandfather, would carry an evil trait.

No matter that the family name was changed from Scuola to Bompensiero, it did not alter his son's blooded character. Though the adopted Bompensiero surname was a variation of the Latin root language and could be defined as "Good Thoughts," the name fell short of Bernardo Bompensiero's legacy. However, the kindly, generous man from Brindisi gave all and died long before Frank Bompensiero tarnished his name and placed it among the annals of villainous men.

CHAPTER 8
BAPTISIMA
...AND THE EVIL BEGINS

Though born on American soil and baptized a Catholic of Sicilian immigrant parents, Frank returned to Porticello, Sicily when he was eight years old. His father Giuseppe was suffering from incurable facial cancer and wanted to return to his homeland to die. In Porticello, Frank lived as an impoverished peasant, becoming, in time, a juvenile thief and a robber. After neighbors complained about this thieving, his mother could take no more humiliation and tossed him out to return to America. He sought the warmth of his Uncle Giovanni's house in Milwaukee, Wisconsin. Soon the dark times of Prohibition met young Frank with a boozy "hello" and he ran afoul of the law. It was there that he experienced his second baptism as he killed a bootlegger. The police sought him for murder, and later he would again be baptized into a secretive Sicilian society— the Mafia.

✱ ✱ ✱

My grandfather, Giuseppi Scuola Bompensiero, immigrated to the USA and, after working and saving for several years, returned to Porticello, Sicily, in 1901 to marry his betrothed, Maria Tagliavia, who was now twenty years old. They had first been betrothed when she was seven by her father, who confirmed the marriage contract with a handshake and hug, and again when she turned thirteen, in accordance with their custom. However, Maria never met or laid eyes on her husband-to-be until the day they were married.

The poverty in Porticello was worse than Giuseppi remembered. The tides of recession dragged across Europe and jobs were nonexistent. Only the wealthy few could afford to have their children educated. As much as my grandparents loved Sicily, they realized that it was not the place to raise a family. Following the wedding, the young couple quickly decided to return to America. In the summer of 1901, Giuseppi found work as a laborer in Milwaukee. Four years later, their first child was born. They named him Francesco after Giuseppi's father.

Eight years and three children later, Giuseppe and his family returned to Porticello, Sicily just after the birth of my father, Salvatore Sam *(Turi)* in 1913. He was three months old when they left.

Eight-year-old Frank did not take well to leaving America. Later, he admitted to me that he hated living in the poverty and destitution of Porticello. He said that the beaches were dirty and roads were rough cobblestones. Moreover, he hated the *butanas* (whores) who yelled to the men on the streets from their balconies. Even worse, he hated what he called the *bicausu*—the outside crapper. "Damn, it was terrible!"

Frank despised work that he considered "dirty," like fishing, working in the rock quarries, or in the fields, or the construction trades. These were the only livelihood options available to young village men with little or no skills or education.

His father Giuseppi, once a strong and sturdy man who had made his living as a fisherman and who had been a good provider, was now feeble, bedridden and dying.

Maria, a good and faithful wife, tried to make his time on earth comfortable for her ailing husband. However, he impregnated her two more times before he died. The first to be born on Sicilian soil after they returned was a daughter named Josephine. Then, without skipping a beat, Maria had two more gifts from her dying husband, second came *Santha* (Sainte—Thelma). When Turi turned five years old, his mother Maria gave birth again, this time to *Patrina*—her last child. Deeply religious, she viewed Patrina as God's gift provided by her dying husband.

Maria did her best to supplement the family income by becoming a wet nurse for the rich. But the burden of caring for her dying husband and raising her children in poverty plagued her. She sent Frank to the streets to work for food. When eight-year-old Frank started bringing home a little money and vegetables, Maria turned a blind eye. Over the ensuing years, Maria's neighbors complained about her son Frank's thievery. The pressure became overwhelming. She finally addressed him. "I can't take the scandal any more. You have to leave the family. Return to America and get yourself a real job and with your Uncle Giovanni's help you may grow into a real man."

Frank was shocked and angered by his mother's attitude, especially after he had faithfully helped feed the family for over six years. Yet, he secretly yearned to return to America. Even though his father was failing and the family would have to find their own way, he was happy to be free from family obligations, especially since the family didn't appreciate what he had done for them.

✳ ✳ ✳

Seventeen-year-old Frank arrived in New York City aboard the *Dante Alighieri* after being in Sicily for almost nine years. He now felt as if he were a foreigner and an immigrant. In fact, his English was barely understandable.

It was 1922 and he thought himself a man. Though he had some money he had saved for himself, he decided to jump on the first flatcar heading west from New York. After two weeks of hopping trains and running from the yard bulls, he recognized "Milwaukee" on the side of one train and hopped it. He arrived in town as winter approached and slowly made his way with his knapsack of treasures toward the Third Ward.

The Third Ward was an Italian ghetto and not much better than New York's Harlem, but it was a welcome sight for Frank as he made his way to his Uncle Giovanni's tavern.

Unlike Porticello, things in the Third Ward had changed: they had improved and looked much better than when he left. As he tried to find his uncle's house, he remembered a time when, as he spoke with his father, calling Milwaukee "Shitsville."

His father replied and said, "Chichu, you don't remember one winter when the water and sewer lines froze, cracked and fouled our water supply. Mama didn't know when it happened and cooked a pot of greens using the bad water. It gave the whole family the shits. Then he said, "To this day, I don't eat no boiled greens!"

At least in the ward, on occasion, the Italians and Sicilians were often inspiring and humorous. Most times, though, they bitched over the hard life they lived. Frank also recalled the times being tough, although not as bad as Porticello, where one thing was sadly absent—hope! Years later it became very clear to me that those were the same conditions that created industrious entrepreneurs as well as lazy, vicious criminals. Sadly, Ziu Chichu Bompensiero fell into the latter category.

Frank finally found the tavern of Uncle John (*Giovanni*) Bonpenser (a variant of "Bompensiero"). In America, Giovanni changed the spelling of his last name to "Bonpenser" shortly after he arrived in Milwaukee, hoping to delude the Sicilian police who were looking for him. The name change spelling must have thrown the police off.

On the way, Frank also recalled a warning his father Giuseppe gave him as a boy.

"Figghiu, my brother Giovanni is marked, like Cain. He has murder in his soul. He is a hard and dangerous man." Then he told Frank of how Giovanni killed his wife just before the two brothers left Sicily for America. Thus, it was that family members concealed the *Scuola* curse and only spoke about it in hushed whispers if at all. Evil, like water, finds it own level.

✳ ✳ ✳

Frank liked America and the opportunities he saw from its street action. He naturally gravitated toward those people with money. In Milwaukee, he found easy scores. It was sure better than robbing a villager for a paltry five-lire note equal to twenty-five cents in American money.

Although his sister Grazia (Grace) resided in Milwaukee with her aunt Mary Ann, he hadn't seen her in years. Frank probably wanted to see her, but he needed to concentrate on taking care of himself. Had he bothered to check in on his sister he might have discovered the despicable conditions under which she labored.

Before the family left for Sicily, Maria decided to leave her two-year-old daughter Grace, born in 1911, with her elder sister, Mary Ann, who hinted that she could sure use some company and help around the house and would love to raise her. Maria assumed that living in Milwaukee with her sister would be much better for her favorite daughter.

She thought that Grace would have a nice place to eat and sleep and her own family to care for her. Maria never knew what evil motives her elder sister had in mind for her daughter. Grace was raised in abject servitude and suffered as a slave in her aunt's house. Later, they would all learn the truth. Grace was forced to sleep on a mattress in the damp, cold and dark cellar of the house. She had also been beaten and worked like a mule. She had been fed so little that, after Maria returned to Milwaukee fourteen years after her husband's death, she did not recognize her own daughter.

Grace suffered from the effects of chronic malnutrition and never recovered from her earlier sufferings. Maria felt terrible guilt for leaving her daughter behind. She vowed in her heart to make it up to Grace. Maria and her sister Mary Ann never spoke again. However, Maria faithfully cared lovingly for her daughter Grace until Maria passed from the earth.

Frank, the loving brother, kept his distance, not even inquiring about Grace when he got back to Milwaukee. He finally got a job in an auto parts supply house. He, however, had no fondness for what he thought was stupid, boring work. Over conversations with me years later, he'd characterized it as more of a personal matter. He hated his boss.

"That fucking piece-of-shit Kike Jew bastard! He'd call me a stinking, garlic-smelling WOP! I shoulda killed the cocksucker. The last time he called me a Wop, I could have killed him. But I decided to quit. I've hated Jews ever since!"

Frank went back to his Uncle Giovanni and asked to work in his tavern. His uncle couldn't refuse, and gave him the janitor's role of sweeping floors and other jobs as assigned. Frank was grateful and vowed to pay his uncle back. However, with Frank, saying and doing were two different things.

"But, you know, Niputi," he said one night sixty years later, "when one door closes another always opens." Frank liked sayings like that. He told me how things changed for him one night in an alley.

"One night, it was after closing and I was headed home. I saw some *poltroon*—a hick—tossing his drunken stomach into the alley. I was going to pass him by, but then I see a pistol butt sticking from a belt holster and decide it would be an easy score. I could take it, sell it and make a buck. I could pay back my uncle in the process. So, I stroll by like I'm passing him and then kicked him in the balls. He grunted like a pig, rolled over, and puked some more. Then, I grabbed the gun took off," he said, laughing.

But Frank quickly decided that using the gun would be more profitable than selling it. He had big plans that included making some real dough by knocking off a case of booze or two. With a gun for protection, he had power. Although Frank had used a shotgun in Sicily, he hadn't used a handgun. He watched a silent film about war, *The Big Parade,* several times and learned to shoot a gun by watching the actors. Now armed with his own handgun, he thought he had a good chance to score since Prohibition was ongoing. Frank wanted a piece of the action.

About a week later, while sweeping the floor, Frank said he overheard a couple of Irish "Micks" in the tavern talking about a booze run. Frank was clever and played stupid about the conversation.

Normally, the two Irishmen wouldn't be caught dead in a "Dago" joint, but their activities were private and they didn't want anyone listening—especially other Irishmen. Frank spoke only Sicilian around the tavern, so the men talked freely. While Frank worked cleaning a spot on the floor near them, they referred to him as a WOP and he didn't let on that he understood.

The men heard him speaking Sicilian to the barkeeper several times as the barkeep spoke it in return. The men never perceived a threat. "That dummy's no problem," said one. "He speaks that Wop stuff. He doesn't understand English."

Frank smiled to himself and listened intently. He understood their plan and knew when and how he would intercept them to steal the goods. He planned to arrive at the drop-off point before the two Irishmen. He'd take all the risk himself and split with no one except his uncle.

Plans, however, sometimes go wrong. Frank wound up shooting the truck driver, who died. Frank realized he was in over his head and ran to his Uncle Giovanni's and told him what happened.

"*Figghiu* (son). do you respect me?"

"Sure, *Ziu!*"

"Your mother sent you here because she couldn't take care of all the crap you caused in Porticello. She must have been crazy with the pressure of your father dying and having your brother and sisters to raise. Then with you stealing and all the neighbors yelling at her. *Capisciu?*"

"Yes, Ziu!" Frank replied.

"Only because of your mother am I helping you. Don't fuck up again! You must listen and be respectful."

"I will."

"The guy you killed was a bootlegger and the other one got away. But he saw you and they have long arms like the *polpi* (octopus). *Tu Thesda Di Merda* (You shithead), you used a cop's gun. "You didn't tell me about that, *Chich.*"

Frank was shaken but told his uncle the truth.

"Do you still have the gun, *Chich?*"

"Yes, *Ziu.* You want it for repayment for all your help?"

"Hell no, you'll need it more than I do. Now, the Micks and the cops will send the *Gane* (dogs) after you. If you don't leave town tonight, they'll find and kill you. I don't want your mother blaming me for your stupidity."

Frank finally became terrified.

"I have an old paesano in Los Angeles—*Ignacio Dragna.* They now call him "Jack" and he is a man of honor. That means he is death in a suit. Capisciu (understand)? He is from the old country and a *Caporégime* and, like others, he rose in the family when his boss, *Giuseppi Adrizzone,* the head of the family, died. Jack took over as the Capo. Now, he runs things." A look of bewilderment on young Frank's face made his uncle realize that he didn't understand what death in a suit, or man of honor really meant.

"*Chich,* what I meant to say when I said he was a 'man of honor' was that he is *Mafiusa* (Mafia). *Capisciu?*"

"They have their own rules, their own way of seeing and handling things. Nothing gets in their way. When you get to California, keep your mouth shut and do what you are told. If not, you will die.

"When you get to Los Angeles, call this number and say, 'Giovanni from Milwaukee told me to call.' And, goddamn it, Frank! Be respectful! They play rough. If they don't believe you, they will kill you."

"Si, Ziu," said Frank as his eyes widened and the impact of what he had done and what lay before him finally sank in.

"Don't say anything more. Just do what I tell you. You have a whole life ahead of you. *Capisciu?*"

"Si, Ziu."

"Good. Do you have any money?"

"A few dollars."

"Here, take five more. Spend it wisely."

Frank packed a small sack with clean shorts and a couple of shirts. He took his jacket and added a hunk of bread, some cheese and salami.

CHAPTER 9

KILLER ON THE RUN

I can only imagine that the trip to California had to be treacherous and frightening for the eighteen-year-old Bompensiero, who spoke little English and could read less. He spoke of it after one too many drinks as we dined in our almost nightly foray after his release from prison. He relayed how he lay in a flatcar rumbling down the tracks like a hobo going from one pigsty town to another. He ducked cops and yard bulls as he jumped onto the next flatcar, fleeing west. Sleep was next to impossible because thugs often tried to overpower and rob the ragtag patrons of the "boxcar express"—men with little more than the clothes on their backs, seeking a better life on the run.

✹ ✹ ✹

Sicily had prepared young Frank to adapt to whatever life threw his way. However, a week of jumping the rails from one fetid railcar to another had never been what he expected. Frank's natural bravado and his weapon helped him out of more than a few dangerous tight spots. He learned to run and hide, but he did not like it. Filthy, hungry and exhausted, his fears drove him—fear of falling asleep, fear of attack and, ultimately, fear of death. Later, that too would fall by the wayside.

After a run-in with a couple of men who threatened him, Frank learned that flashing his pistol gained him a huge advantage.

"What's a kid like you doing with a gun?"

"None of your fucking business. But I've buried one already, so leave me the hell alone or you'll be next."

Riding the rails from Wisconsin to California became the catalyst for developing the paranoia that would dog him all his life. Frank would say, "In those days, my gun became my only security. I could never trust anyone. Besides, *they* were always watching!"

Figuring out his location and switching trains became a challenge and Frank fell several times while jumping trains. He was sore and limped a bit. His Uncle Giovanni told him the trip might take seven to ten days and also scrawled the letters for "Los Angeles" on a piece of paper. He hoped the nearly illiterate Frank would recognize the letters when he saw them again. Frank, no dummy, continued to look for the two words on every rail yard sign he passed.

Forgetting much of what he learned in the three school grades he attended almost twelve years before, he found an old magazine with a map of America on the back. He used it to practice the words and look for familiar cities. Once he saw a sign with the word California he knew he finally had crossed the border from Arizona and his insecurity and inability about signs improved as he became more attentive. He was nervous about missing the Los Angeles station and jumped from the train as it pulled into Redlands, California, a farming community east of San Bernardino. Frank easily made his way to a gas station and found a pay phone. He pulled the last bit of change from his pocket and dialed the number from the crinkled paper his Ziu Giovanni gave him.

The voice on the other end sounded young.

"*Pronto?*" (Hello)

The Niputi ...the Nephew

Frank replied "Hello" a couple of times. When he failed to get a reply, he reverted to Sicilian.

"*Haiu bisognu di parrari cu Ziu Ignacio.*" (I want to speak with Uncle Ignacio.)

With that, the phone changed hands and another man answered.

"*Pronto! I'o Ignacio, Ma Giboy?*" (This is Ignacio. Whadda'ya want?)"

"Scuzza, Ziu, my Ziu Giovanni from Milwaukee gave me your name and told me to call on you for help. I killed someone."

"*Como si chiamma?*" (What is your name?)

"*Lo chiamato Chichu Bompensiero, Ziu.*" (My name is Frank Bompensiero.)

The silence on the other end of the phone made Frank wonder if he screwed up by saying he killed someone. Finally, Ignacio Dragna shot back.

"How old are you, Chich?"

"I was born in 1905. It is now 1923 so—.

"Dragna interrupted, "I asked your age! Not if you knew mathematico. "*Tu Para Siciliano?*" (Do you speak Sicilian?)

"*Si, Ziu.*" Frank stuttered and replied in Sicilian, "*Lo sunu ottanta-simo.* (I am eighteen years, *Ziu.*)

"Your answer was better, especially in Sicilian. But that is good and bad!"

"Why is that, *Ziu?*

"Good because you are old enough to work for a living; bad because in California you can get the death penalty for murder. Don't you get it? You are a killer! But, that's okay, *Chichu.* I'm going to take a chance on you because of your *Ziu, Giovanni Bompenser.*"

Frank told Dragna the name of the Texaco gas station and the number on the building where he'd wait.

"*Si, Chichu*, stay near the phone and out of sight."

"You got off the train too early! It'll take over an hour to get there so I'm sending two of my boys to pick you up. They'll be driving my black Studebaker. *Capish?* (Understand?)

Not waiting for an answer, Ignacio continued, "Are you clean or have you had a chance to wash? Are you hungry?"

"I'm filthy and hungry. I've been on flatcars on a train for almost ten days."

"Chichu, listen to my men. They will get you cleaned, dressed and fed. Don't forget, Chichu, stay around the station so they can find you."

Frank felt a sense of relief.

"Thank you, Ziu."

In that first encounter with the Mafia's West Coast chieftain, Ignacio "Jack" Dragna, Frank finally felt a sense of belonging. It would be the emotion that tied him to Dragna until the day Dragna died.

Frank later recounted to me what happened when Dragna's men found him sitting on the curb next to the phone booth.

"I fell asleep—the first sleep in ten days. Then in the fog of sleep I woke to a car's engine sound and this black Studebaker pulls up and two men get out. They were clean-shaven and dressed for church and it wasn't even Sunday! I musta looked like a bum!"

One of the men said, "*Buon giorna, Tu Si Chichu?*" (Good day, are you Frank?) When I heard Sicilian I stood up and nearly cried! Then the man said, "You smell like a cow!" I was embarrassed and looked down at my pants after being in a cattle car for a few days. I had manure and foul-smelling hay stuck on my trousers. I smelled so rank that over time, I got used to the smell.

"Si, Si. (Yes, yes.) After ten days, I thought I was becoming a cow." The men laughed at my humor.

They took me to a local store and bought me fresh clothes, but they would not let me change clothes. They headed for the local YMCA, where I got a hot soapy shower. Food was next. They stopped at a local restaurant and had coffee as they watched me eat and eat—like a half-starved man."

Later, after sitting in front of Ignacio's Los Angeles card room, Frank attentively listened to his soon-to-be-mentor.

"Your life is *merda* (shit), but there is hope. Your hope, *Chichu*, will be me in the form of papa who will teach and guide you. But, for me to help you, there is an old saying that I use. Have you ever heard of *Yaigyo*?

"No, *Ziu*. Is it Sicilian?"

"No. It simply means, 'You ask —I give and you owe. *Capish*? Understand, that is my method of business. Frank nodded.

Always remember, YAIGYO.

"*Si, Ziu. Io capish.*"(Yes, Uncle. I understand.)

"Good. So, who did you shoot? Do you even know? I want all the details."

Frank told Dragna the story. He didn't spare details from stealing the gun from the drunken cop in the alley, to overhearing the Irish gangsters talk about the booze delivery. He explained what happened when he tried to rob the trucker.

"Ziu, when the trucker stopped to offload the booze, I jumped him and pulled my gun. But he wasn't alone. His passenger was lying down in the seat and it was dark and

I couldn't see him. The passenger attacked me and in the scuffle I fired the gun twice and hit the driver. The gun noise scared the passenger and he took off."

"Good for you that they weren't Sicilian."

"*Perchi?* (Why?)"

"If he were Sicilian and connected, you'd be dead and so would your *Ziu Giovanni* as well as your entire family. They can be ruthless. Can't take chances with the Sicilians, eh? We carry the vendetta for generations."

Dragna let him sweat a little before he offered his help.

"I've got connections and can probably fix it. But, it's going to cost you for a long time, Chichu. To pay me back, you must be committed to our cause and you and I will be joined at the hip. That means that once you make a commitment, there is no going back. When you join, it's for life. I will use you until I die and then someone else will use you. Capish?"

"Si, Ziu."

"In this business, *Chich*, we are *familia*. Our cause binds us. And, it is forever! You could say it is a *Cosa Nostra por vita* (Our thing for life)."

For Dragna, enlisting the young man into the ranks of the *Cosa Nostra* required an absolute commitment. Dragna had to follow tradition, which meant he had to be sure that Frank understood what it meant to join them. Frank had to comprehend what he was committing himself to.

What followed was an intense line of questioning. If Frank faltered at any point, Dragna would send him on his way or have him disposed of. Frank relayed the conversation between him and Dragna as follows:

"Chichu, I don't think you really understand the meaning of Mi Cosa Nostra. So I'm going to explain it, again. It means, My Thing, and it's all about the way I oper-

The Niputi ...the Nephew

ate as compared to someone else. That's it, simple, heh? *Tu Capish?* (You understand?)

"*Si, Ziu Dragna.*"

"You don't mind following orders, do you?"

"*No, Ziu.* Not from you." Dragna looked at him long and hard.

"There could be others who will give you orders, but you will always be mine and under control of my family—no other. There is only my family. Mine! *Capisciu?* (Understand?)

"*Si.*"

"*Chichu*, my boys said you smelled like dead, four-day-old cows. Do you feel better since you showered and ate?"

"*Si, Ziu.*"

Dragna kept his eyes on Frank. All traces of friendly banter were gone. He leaned toward Frank and whispered what Frank now understood to be the prelude to an oath.

"*Chichu*, you have come here asking for my help and it is expensive. So, I must repeat that it is *"familia por vita."* (Family for life.)

"*Si, Ziu.* I'm sure." He had already heard it many times.

"Fine, *Chichu*, we start now. I will call you *Figghiu* (son). You can call me *Ziu* Jack or *Ziu* Dragna when people you don't know are present. When I call and ask you to take care of something, I want it done. No excuses. *Capisciu?* (Understand?)

"In time you will earn your way and make money and most importantly, be respected. That also means that if someone has to disappear, you will take care of it without question. We will teach you. *Tu Capisciu?* (Understand?)"

"*Io Capisciu!*" (I understand!)

"You know, *Chichu*, this may all sound like silly questions, me asking if you understand and you replying and me saying something else and you repeating. However, it is very important and the life and death vow you are going to take to be part of my family. In Milwaukee, you are a criminal and a dead man running. It will take me some time to square away the beef with the booze guys. You used a cop's gun to kill a man, and the cops don't like that. They will be looking hard. They want you, so you will have to hide."

"I still have the gun, *Ziu*."

"Good, give it to me. I'll get rid of it. That way, if they catch you, they won't have evidence and the case will be harder to prove. I know your uncle. He is someone who cared enough about you to send you to me. I will honor that. Now, I doubt that you had much schooling, be it in Sicily or a *La Merica* (America) but there are those who, like the old Greeks, pushed *Baptisima*. Hell, I like your attitude, Chichu, and to think you already conducted your ritual washing for the rite of admission to our society by killing that trucker. You got spirit. In time we'll see what we can do for you."

"We tossed your clothes because they stunk, like you did, big-time. Now with a shower and new clothes, you'll be a new man. You'll also march to the rules of my house or you won't ever march again. *Capish?*"

"Absolutely, *Ziu.*"

"Well, *Chichu*, I guess you can say you are now one of my *soldata* (soldiers) and will be baptized again soon. But, it will take time before you earn the rights of my family. Do you know that in the old days they used to call martyrdom a baptism by blood. They would stick a knife into someone's throat and *finithu* (finished). He was baptized a martyr." Dragna laughed.

"Frankie, you've got to hide until this quiets down. You have to go underground where no one will know if you are dead or alive."

"I've have *cuscinu* (cousins) in San Diego. But I don't know where that is."

"Will they take you in and can you trust them?"

"*Si, Ziu*. They are blood, my *Ziu Pietro's* sons Matteo and Giovanni. They are fishermen and have a house there. I think they will make room for me."

✱ ✱ ✱

And so it was that Frank heeded Jack Dragna's advice. He went south and moved in with his cousins, Matteo and Giovanni Buompensiero, brothers who earned their living as fishermen.

My Uncle Matteo's son Pete recounts the days that Frank stayed with his family.

"Frank lived with my father Matteo and *Ziu Giovanni* for almost two years. He hid in their cellar, and my father said that Frankie used to say that their cellar was a good place. That it was much better than the family home in Sicily. It was better especially since it had an in-house toilet."

Frank's exile to San Diego became his proving ground. Among family, he felt safe. He paid his way by working—in the dark of night—by robbing, stealing and mugging, the only "work" he knew. After eating with his cousins, he'd sneak down to the wharf where he could scope out merchandise and people. There he would choose a mark or steal something to make a quick buck in trade.

He hid from any strangers who came around, and when Jack contacted him from L.A., he'd head north on a train or in a car and pay his debt.

During his first eight years in California, Frank Bompensiero sharpened his eyeteeth at the feet of the Los Angeles Mafia capo Jack Dragna. In Los Angeles, he would do whatever he was told to do by Dragna and received a stipend for his obedience. He also learned to intimidate. Paid to kick ass and do errands, he also stuck a revolver in someone's mouth to get their attention. It worked and he was fond of saying, "Sometimes they were so scared they shit their pants."

"Not a bad job," Frank would say as he talked to me over dinner years later.

Frank's exile to San Diego allowed him to travel a bit, make good on his promise to Dragna and drop back into his cellar hole when needed. Under Dragna's tutelage, he became a good Mafia soldier. In essence, that meant keeping his mouth shut and doing whatever he was told. Living with the Buompensiero brothers allowed Frank to survive and, of course, he promised to pay his way.

Matteo and Giovanni thought that meant Frank would help them in their commercial fishing business. However, as mentioned earlier, Frank didn't like smelly work. It did not fit into his self-image. He didn't go fishing, but took a crooked path. In all the photos taken of Frank near or at the waterfront, he was dressed like a businessman with shirt and tie—never as a fisherman or in work clothes. He did not socialize with the Buompensiero brothers whom he lived with, but on several occasions took them to Los Angeles to meet his associates. If you knew Frank as I did, you realized that his purpose was to flaunt his lifestyle while gaining respect among his Sicilian family relatives.

In February 1927, two things happened that changed Frank's life for the better—or worse. First, he fell in love with Santha (Thelma) Sanfilippo. Second, his mother, brother and sisters arrived from Sicily.

CHAPTER 10

A THIEF AND MORE

Young Frank's formative years in Sicily from age eight to seventeen no doubt prepared him to adapt to any environment. Some might argue that he was coerced to steal and rob in order to support his family. I think not, because hundreds of other children of Porticello never elected to take the easy road as did Frank. His own brother was one of them. After returning to America and fleeing Milwaukee for California, Frank chose the crooked path offered by Jack Dragna. He could have gone on to San Diego, lived with his cousins and obtained some form of employment. That was not to be. He now worked for and owed Jack Dragna. When his mother, brother and sisters arrived in San Diego in 1927, he was "in the chips." He had a fine car and nice clothes and once again was "respected." Seven years had passed since his mother sent him packing. Time appeared to soothe Maria's forgiving heart for his past indiscretions. Besides, her Figghiu-D' Oro (son of gold) was a successful businessman and she was proud of what her son had become.

✴ ✴ ✴

To supplement his income, Frank decided bootlegging would be his sideline business. He needed cash; his lifestyle demanded it. Besides, how difficult could it be if women were distributing wine and hard stuff right next door?

Frank still had a lot to learn about making money—and about women. He didn't have a clue how to start, but he was young, brash and fancied his very attractive neighbor, *Santha* (Thelma) *Sanfilippo*. However, the Sanfilippo family (Lorenzo and Filippa, a.k.a. "Pippa") didn't want Frank sniffing around their daughter.

In 1927, Frank got an unexpected shock as a passenger train arrived in San Diego with his mother, Maria, brother Turi and sisters Grace, Thelma and Patrina aboard. He hadn't heard from them in years and didn't know that his father had died three years before. Frank hadn't seen Grace since she left to live with their Aunt Mary Ann fourteen years before, and he didn't recognize her. She appeared weak, frail and withdrawn. He wondered what had happened to her. His brother, now fourteen, had grown to be a strong young fellow. Frank was thrilled to see his mom and family again. The only one missing was Giuseppina. His mom told him she would be forthcoming as she married Nino D'Acquisto and would be arriving as soon as they got established.

The dutiful and lonely Frank helped his mother immeasurably when she arrived in San Diego, and Maria knew her prayers of protection worked for Frank. He was no longer a waif, thief, robber or mugger . . . If only she knew.

She believed in her heart that God had taken care of Frank, her firstborn. Poor illiterate Maria was torn between her ancient Sicilian pagan superstitions and her Catholic faith. She eventually went to her grave believing that her Franco was a good boy. To her, Frank was the biblical prodigal son reborn, and who could argue with the Bible? Maria never learned that her son was a stone-cold killer.

About a month after they moved in, Giuseppina and her husband arrived and moved in with her mother. They now had one big happy family.

In no time at all, Maria, a shrewd opportunist, sought to make a match (as was the custom) between her daughter Grace and eligible batchelor Joe Corrao. Joe was not only a fisherman but also one of the property owners of the house Frank had arranged for a rent-to-buy agreement from Thelma's brother and mother. All were happy except for Filippa Corrao-Sanfilippo, Joe's sister.

Frank also pushed to obtain an engagement with Thelma Sanfilippo, but Pippa and her husband, Lorenzo, refused to bless the proposal. They didn't like Frank or what he did, and they didn't want him making moves on their daughter. However, when Frank left town on business and her brother Joe went fishing, Pippa approached the sheriff and concocted a story about Maria not paying the rent and obtained an eviction notice.

Before Maria and her children were told to vacate their dwelling, Joe Corrao's boat had engine problems and returned to port. Upon hearing that her intended arrived back in port, Grace rushed to the wharf to meet Joe. She told him what his sister had done. Joe, aware of the initial agreement, became furious and resolved the issue. However, a week later when Frank returned, he played the heavy and called a family meeting, indicating he would talk to Filippa. As titular head of the family, he could lay claim to resolving the issue. The bad blood between the two families would never be resolved. Tina Corrao, who lived in the house as a little girl, recalls her family dancing a jig in the kitchen the day Filippa Sanfilippo died. "Pippa was a real bitch."

***

Frank decided he had learned enough to set up his own business, but as usual, Frank had little knowledge about the bootlegging business. But that didn't stop him, because he needed money to marry Thelma. In this case, a little knowledge would prove to be a dangerous thing.

Frank knew he didn't need anyone but Jack. On his next trip north, he spoke to Dragna and received his blessing to come out of hiding and to create his own bootlegging operation in San Diego.

From about 1924 through 1927, Frank continued paying his dues to Jack, but by February 1927 he moved into an apartment in the 2000 block on Columbia Street near his mother. He couldn't wait to meet the demands of the Italian neighborhood's drinking population. Jack Dragna would be his sole source of procurement—that was the arrangement. As Jack said, obtaining the booze wasn't difficult, keeping it in a safe location while making it available to customers was the challenge. Frank took that to mean he would have to upgrade his apartment to create a way to hide his liquor.

When the two fishermen who lived in the unit above him departed for a trip, Frank hired a couple of plumbers to install wall-to-wall tanks in the ceiling space between floors of his rental—an ingenious idea. The plumbers also ran booze pipes from the tanks to a lavatory on the ground floor of Frank's apartment.

With a switch of the hot- and cold-water valves, Frank was able to shut off the water. Pure wine, whiskey or gin would run down the line from the overhead tanks. He paid cash to the plumbers for their services and promised residuals in the form of wine to keep their mouths shut.

No one knows much about Frank's travels in that three-year stretch, though it's safe to say that between his San Diego booze sales and his trips to do work for Jack Dragna, he had his hands full. As one of Dragna's soldiers said, "You can be sure that Jack used Frank, his favorite mule, quite often."

At some point, Jack decided that Frank had paid his dues. Dragna honored Frank by bringing him formally into his family fold and making him a Mafiosi. Frank swore to the *Omerta Code*, took part in La Familia's ritual and became known as Jack's hit man.

By Jack bestowing the rank of *soldata* (soldier) and making him a "man of honor," Frank truly believed that he had arrived. He was now a made man with full family membership. To Frank that meant he was untouchable. He had formal responsibilities and privileges. Now, at the mature age of twenty-four, Frank had money, respect and power. Now he could marry Thelma.

Unfortunately, Frank didn't have the wisdom to see that honor and shame are opposite sides of the same coin. He would never be honored. His legacy would be nothing more than that of a thug who brought shame on his family's adopted name, Bompensiero.

With his station in life assured, Frank said to hell with everybody and he and Thelma eloped in 1929. He was twenty-four and she was eighteen. In short order, Thelma became pregnant and Frank's idyllic life appeared to be headed in the right direction.

But Frank's brilliant bootlegging plan had one logistical drawback—he hadn't considered the impact that increased street traffic would have on his business. Eventually, the booze police got wind of the activity and started investigating. On May 15, 1930, the police found his Little Italy apartment of illegal booze and as the *San Diego Union* newspaper reported, "Frank Bompensiero was headed for the big house."

However, while out on bail awaiting trial, Frank and his wife moved in with his mother Maria, the Corrao and D'Acquisto families, including their children, and his brother Turi. Twelve people slept in the three-bedroom house. Frank and Thelma dreaded the commotion and likened it to feeding time at the zoo.

Frank's sensitive wife couldn't handle the turmoil and wanted to spend time together quietly before Frank went off to prison. Frank made a few apologetic gestures to his mother about needing more privacy before he had to leave town on business and found a place in a quiet neighborhood in Kensington.

It would have been prudent for Frank to keep a low profile while awaiting his fate, but that wasn't Frank's style. He was a made man, a *soldata*, and always pressed for action, so within weeks, he robbed/purchased or whatever, forty-eight bindles of opium and buried it in his Kensington yard. Frank was arrested in short order as two young boys had spotted him through the fence and notified the police.

Though he was not at the residence, the authorities also arrested Frank's younger brother Turi (Sammy, my father, who lived with his mother in WOPTOWN). They thought Sammy had been in on the drug deal, but they released Sammy later because one of their young witnesses said Frank was alone when he buried the drugs. Besides, Sammy couldn't speak English very well and was a minor.

Just before the trial began, an assistant district attorney notified Frank's attorney that the charges were going to be dropped. The evidence (forty-eight bindles of opium) disappeared from the police security/evidence rooms. Word on the street was that someone in the department was paid off to "misplace" the evidence. This is but one of many unexplainable occurrences in the strange relationship between Frank and the San Diego Police Department.

Frank fancied himself a clever, seasoned criminal, but history proves he was shortsighted in the business and planning end of the operations—something he would never, ever learn. Although Frank's business operations usually floundered, he made out every once in a while, but that was usually due to the influence of Jack Dragna, war or a growing economy.

On one occasion, Jack wrangled Frank a job as a heavy on a floating casino called the *Montefalcon*, anchored in Los Angeles harbor. It was a gambling nightspot for L.A.'s rich and famous, and Frank's job was to learn about the operation and report on the action. He earned some green for passing the info to Dragna, and it wasn't long before Dragna, Filippo Sacco, a.k.a. Johnny Roselli, and a few others came aboard and robbed the casino.

They got away with the table cash and, though later arrested, they were released. This, according to official records, was due to either Fourth Amendment search and seizure laws, or insufficient evidence. Again, did someone get paid off?

In April 1931, Frank's sentencing on the Prohibition rap finally came down. Though given a three-year term in McNeil Federal Prison, he served less than two years.

Frank's absence troubled his mother and, to protect her from the truth, Turi and his sisters told her that her precious son of gold had gone off to "college" to learn more about American business. He could be gone several years. Maria may have suspected, but whatever truth she knew, she kept in her heart. The family would never openly admit he was in prison.

Frank's reputation as a seasoned, good-for-nothing criminal most likely influenced the judge. I say that because Frank's sentence was stiff compared to others who had similar offenses but were slapped on the wrist. For example, Grace Frontero and Frank's mother-in-law, Filippa Sanfilippo, were both professional bootleggers. To their credit, the women were much better at the game than Frank ever imagined, and more clever. Though eventually busted, they received shorter sentences or served no time in jail.

Grace Frontero was the best around. A shrewd and effective businesswoman, she did a lot of planning before she jumped into the booze business. I tell her story based upon the input from her grandson, Samuel Frontero, who says it reflects an interesting time in San Diego's history.

Grace's maiden name was Giacaloni. She became Frontero when she married a young fisherman. A tough gal, Grace ran the show in her family and was a fiery example of a comely yet intelligent woman. Dark-haired, short and wiry, she was the schemer and the aggressive one.

With the guts and determination of a man and the brains of a brash student, she planned and set up her own illegal booze operation. Watching the whiskey police in operation, she knew she'd be out of business in no time if they found her still and if she sold openly.

To ensure the survival of her business, Grace built three stills. She ran them and hired family members to run errands and do the hard work. She was a good planner, manager and thinker. She considered all factors: manufacturing, distribution and the local sale of wine and whiskey. She even planned an escape route. Grace told her husband about her enterprises; he was content with Grace handling the business affairs.

She began her venture with a ten-acre farm that she purchased for next to nothing in El Cajon. Her sons and other relatives planted vegetables and sold their truck farm goods at the local open-air market. The whiskey police followed the "dirt scratchers" from farm to market and back to the farm. After concluding they were barely scratching out a living, they left them alone.

If they had looked inside the dilapidated barn, past the cooking stove and canning operation, they might have found Frontero's still, running twenty-four seven, dripping out hard liquor in a cellar just beneath the floor.

Grace also created a small basement still in a rental bungalow she owned on Jackdaw Street in Mission Hills. A family member rented the house and watched over the still. Her third still was located in another rental home on Columbia Street.

Eventually, the police tagged Grace's operation. She was sentenced to three months in jail.

When her husband received word of his wife's arrest, he came in from his fishing trip and pleaded with the San Diego Police, claiming that his poor, ignorant immigrant wife was just stupid. She couldn't speak English and only followed his orders.

Instead of Grace going to jail, her husband received a three-month sentence for violating Prohibition laws. He served the term in the Santa Barbara state prison while Grace kept the other two stills dripping out booze and stashing the cash while her husband enjoyed his holiday from work with free food and board. The police may have been the characters the Hollywood's Keystone Kops were modeled after. America was a good country!

Grace's grandson, Sam Frontero, says, "She was one hell of a granny." He wished he had known her better. "She was one shrewd and smart lady and her daughters spoke highly of her."

Sam told me that when Prohibition ended, Grace sold her mechanical still and possibly her grape presses to Matteo Buompensiero, my father's first cousin, who wanted to make wine in traditional Sicilian style.

✳ ✳ ✳

Frank was released from federal prison in 1933 and Thelma was relieved to see her husband again. She carried the burden of the lonely housewife and mother for almost two years. But Frank resumed his crooked ways almost immediately. His wife and the family knew Frank had not been rehabilitated.

Faced with a wife and daughter to support in dire times, Frank returned to the Dragna family operation as the only way to survive. Though Prohibition was over, the Great Depression was in full swing. Twenty-five percent of all workers and thirty-seven percent of all non-farm workers were unemployed. Some people starved; many others lost their farms and homes. However, Frank found people to hustle, items to steal and places to rob.

Frank had learned nothing from his stint in "prison college" and resorted to the mother's milk of his youth—thievery. He held up a drugstore, a movie theater and robbed a high-stakes poker game in San Diego. The players were known businesspeople with big wallets. That meant they had power and connections. However, the police weren't called. Why? One of the players was a cop. While there is no record that the armed robbery ever took place, years later Frank brazenly boasted about the robbery to

Dad and me. "We split twenty five hundred smackers," said Frank. "Not a bad day in the business world."

It would be easy just to accuse Frank for all the ongoing crime. But that would not be the case in the nation. Crime in the streets became rampant as "survival" was in the air. Homeless vagabonds jumped freight trains crisscrossing the nation to find a better place, while stealing along the way. Dispossessed middle-American farmers, "Okies and the like," stuffed their possessions into a dilapidated Ford Model T and migrated to California. They hoped the posters flaunting plentiful jobs were true. But they weren't.

Although the U.S. economy began to recover in the second quarter of 1933, the recovery largely stalled for most of 1934/1935 and times were tough for the Italian colony in San Diego as well. In 1934, the fishing industry was in trouble and the lack of fish in local waters affected men's ability to feed their families. Then a string of strange occurrences broke out on the waterfront. Net connectors on boats were misplaced, couplings weren't where they were supposed to be, and tools disappeared.

All the small-boat skippers were concerned. Peter Corona, in his book *Little Italy, The Way it Was*, highlighted people, places, things and interesting points about San Diego's WOP Town, and made slight comment about the Sicilian/Italian criminal element in San Diego and the country. He refers to the *Manu Nera*, the Black Hand of Napoli, and pays lip service to the Mafia, a term that was not used in the homes of Little Italy. Mafia was a concept of Sicilian origin, and many feared that if you doubted, the boogieman would get you. Corona relayed the story of his father and an attempted theft aboard his boat, the *Buoa Viaje* (Good Voyage).

Knowing times were tough and crime was on the rise, Joe Corona, Peter's father, wondered if someone was stealing from his boat. The Italians were humble people and mostly proud and honest. He also knew the loss of anything on their boats endangered their means of family survival.

One night as he tied up his boat to the dock, Joe Corona decided he was a good fisherman and would catch a thief. With his loaded 12-gauge shotgun cradled in his arms, the skipper crouched down in the dark directly across from the deck where anyone coming aboard would land. No doubt, his double-ought magnum shark rounds would stop a thief, assuming he shot an intruder.

Morally, he worried that the culprit would not be a shark, but a man. Joe was not a killer. Over the quiet beating of his heart, Corona heard a faint sound that grew louder, the sound of someone breathing hard. Then he heard the rustle of the tarp on the deck being pulled back. The skipper lifted his weapon and his flashlight and aimed both at the sounds. Shocked by the blazing light from the flashlight glaring in his eyes, the blinded culprit cried out, "Oh, shit!"

Joe Corona stood up not more than four feet from the man and no doubt said something like, "Kneel down or I'll blow your head off like the dog that you are!"

There was no wavering in the skipper's voice. The sound of steel hammers being cocked added to the perpetrator's fear. He didn't know if he was going to be blown away, and the fear almost made him piss in his pants. He had no god and would not pray anyway, though his hair stood up on the back of his neck. The young man was a ruffian and already had a bad reputation both in San Diego and from those who knew him as a teen in Porticello. He lived in the neighborhood, was a married man with a broad smile and hearty welcome during the day, but by night he was a common thief.

The elder Corona pressed charges against the twenty-nine-year old. The man's mother pleaded for an hour with Mr. Corona and the city police, hoping for her son's freedom. She vowed that he was a good boy and that his father had died and others led him astray. If they let him go, she promised he would not bother the community or the fishermen community again.

Corona's super travel and family log speaks of one young hoodlum in delicate terms so as not to offend living family members and to protect the innocent. I doubt that Corona's omission was due to any fear of reprisal. Rather, I think it more likely that the erudite author and California education bureaucrat chose the high road rather than delve into the muckraking reality of naming names of family friends.

In the end, the elder skipper Corona bowed to the pleadings of Maria Bompensiero. Being the gentleman he was, he did not press charges, but had Frank swear that he would never steal from those in the Italian colony again. For once, Frank upheld his mother's word and stole no more "in the neighborhood."

One would think that luckily walking away from another felony would convince Frank to think clearer and take the straight road. But, by twenty-nine years of age, Frank was too far gone to change. So he accepted his mother's support and took Corona's decency in stride as "good fortune" and, if you will, permission to continue with a no-one-can-touch-me attitude. Frank could never see the future. He only thought of what he could get away with.

Although Frank kept his word about Little Italy, elsewhere he continued robbing, stealing, extorting or disposing of someone. Whatever his Mafia capo Dragna asked of him, he did. Frank had help along the way. Emotional and financial help came from his family, mostly from my father, his brother Sammy, who always saw the good in his brother despite glaring evidence to the contrary.

Frank also had an unwitting cohort in the San Diego Police. They were inept at obtaining and retaining evidence. The SDPD often failed to follow proper procedure and of course they couldn't admit that some officers were on the take.

Police corruption stories were rampant in the 1930s and, if you looked at the cost of trying to police a population that was drinking, selling booze or making it, you could understand why. Everyone wanted a piece of the pie.

A noted law officer, Eliot Ness, became a local cop busily rounding up bootleggers in southern Ohio following his stint with the FBI. He went for easy marks like Philippi Giuseppi Milazzotto, another Sicilian who dabbled in wine and spirits. Slam bam, Ness arrested him and tossed him in jail while the final minutes on the clock of Prohibition expired. So, too, did it go with racial bigotry, stereotyping and nationalism. The public was suspicious of the tactics, but it became the social norm. WOPs were tagged as Mafia criminals, Germans were Nazis, Mexicans were lazy wetbacks, and Jews were cunning, sly and rich. Finally, the Thirty-third Amendment repealed Prohibition and guys like Milazzotto were stuck in jail.

Frank prospered from 1935 through 1950, as he became the third partner in the Jack Dragna-owned bar on Third Street and Broadway in San Diego known as the Gold Rail. Of course he told everyone that the bar was his, but his name was documented as being partner number three on the liquor license.

The Niputi ...the Nephew

After settling in and spending a few years getting his feet wet as a bar owner-operator, a gift from Jack Dragna, he and a few associates decided to take over San Diego County's juice and bar supply distribution. The Vita-Gold Juice Company was created. It only lasted for a short time as the word got around that the boys were using the strong arm: Buy juice from us or else?

The SDPD came to the rescue. Though this event happened with Jimmy Fratianno who was not affiliated with any liquor business in San Diego or any other place, Frank got him involved. More than likely, he kibbutzed with Jimmy at the La Costa resort during one of their occasional meetings and he mentioned to Jimmy that they could corral the whole of San Diego's bar supplies market--like a clean business for a change.

One day, Dad came home for dinner around six and when Mom had offered me some fresh-squeezed orange juice to hold me over until dinner, he busted out laughing. We both looked at him because that was not something he usually did. He went on to explain that his brother and Jimmy "the Weasel" Fratianno thought up a way to force everyone in the bar business to buy orange juice and bar supplies from his newly conceived hustle, Vita Gold.

Hell, with crazy Jimmy, he probably accosted each bar owner with a gun and threatened them. The word got out and the police shut the two down in a hurry. Jimmy left town quite unexpectedly.

"What about Frank? "asked Mom. "Are they going to arrest him, too?"

"I don't think so," Dad said. "When I talked to Frank today, he just laughed and blew it off like it was nothing. Go figure. According to Frank, Jimmy was the arm twister when Frank wasn't around. My brother got lucky again."

PART II
LOYALTIES & LIES

CHAPTER 11
MANHATTAN MISSTEP

Major and minor events happen in life when you least expect them. In my father's case, his lifelong fisherman's occupation came to an abrupt end while at sea. He experienced a malfunctioning kidney and when he saw a urology specialist he was advised that his fishing days were over. At that time, his employment options were slim and none. After not hearing from Frank for months, he arrived on the scene. He suggested a solution to his brother's problem. Like a drowning man, my father grabbed for it— hook, line and sinker. The results of his decision set the stage for life-changing pressures—stress, public notoriety and future financial disaster.

✱ ✱ ✱

The pre-afternoon sun caused Turi to squint as he steered and avoided the marker buoy near Point Loma and the harbor's entrance. Several seals barked as the *Giuseppina* slid by while another larger seal splashed into the water.

Turi pulled down the brim on the gray and blue-striped crewman's cap, shielding his eyes for the moment. At five-foot-six inches, he stood facing the oncoming wind and spray. With his suntanned craggy face and muscled arms, he stood straight and looked tall standing behind the Plexiglas windbreak. His four-day-old beard stubble made him look older than his thirty-five years. Strands of gray peeked into the edge of his sea-weathered skin. But to him, the sun's warmth felt good after a cold night on the vessel's "traveling watch."

Faced with a questionable future, he reminisced about his past. Knowing he was fortunate to be born in the USA, he hadn't felt like an American as yet. Just after being born, he was taken to Sicily to his parents' home and raised in the Sicilian culture until he returned to the States in 1927 as a fourteen-year-old.

In San Diego, he lived around his fellow Italians near the waterfront. The remaining family then returned to the USA, where opportunity awaited. And, in his mind he was already a man because he had worked to help pay for his family's sea passage to America. Since he had never been to school, Turi primarily spoke Sicilian, his native tongue. It took him years to learn passable English because the language spoken at home and by his crewmen at sea was Sicilian.

Many hours at the helm tired him as he contemplated his future, since his days on the water were almost behind him. His body had given out. Too many years fishing tuna on the big boats and pulling net on the small boats caused his kidneys to give out and his doctor forced him to quit fishing. He had to find a new line of work. The news staggered him; the blood in his urine had ruined his life and he could no longer work the sea. What was he to do? The freedom and responsibility to set a course roaming the seas and find elusive tuna allowed him to be the man he wanted to be, the skipper of his own boat with a crew of family who loved it as well.

Armed with his strong convictions and keen desire to succeed, he had worked hard and become successful. The *Giuseppina* became one of the top small boats in the San Diego fleet and provided him a good living.

With a wife and son to support, he needed to find something else, but he couldn't read or write. When he arrived in San Diego at fourteen, he was placed in third grade with nine-year-old children. Then the teacher tried to make him sit in a semi-enclosed children's desk, but he was too large. When they tried to force him, he pulled a knife and was expelled.

✱ ✱ ✱

Today, after a marginally successful fishing trip, Sammy alone on the bridge thought about the *Giuseppina*. It had been his home away from home for years, and although he wasn't ending his fishing days on a high note, he found solace knowing his seven-year-old son, a fledgling fisherman, did well on his initial trip to sea and that his crew was safe.

With a confident left hand, Turi slowly moved the brass steering wheel making subtle adjustments, then with a deft hand on the throttle he steered the vessel into San Diego Bay and he headed for the marine dock across from the Civic Center.

He and his brother-in-law, Joe Corrao, discussed plans for the next trip. Joe then made a ship-to-shore call on the "KOU" marine radio band to his wife, Grace, knowing that she waited nightly at the kitchen table for a KOU phone call when the Giuseppina was out at sea. Finally, the phone rang and the KOU operator came on saying, "We have a marine service call from the M.V. *Giuseppina*, would you accept the charges?" Grace always accepted and would take an order for the next trip's food supplies.

Turi was not about to waste time waiting for any ship supplies, especially when fish were biting. It was blue fin tuna season in the local Pacific waters and, as always, the sea beckoned him. This was their livelihood and with ten crewmen aboard, the skipper had to ensure food supplies were ordered, refueling occurred and the boat was ready to return to sea that day. As usual with fish biting, he was possessed to get his share and his crew knew it. He would not be deterred from the call of the sea and headed the boat out of the harbor. Turi enjoyed fishing and enjoyed memories of his childhood fishing with his father. He longed for the work and the sea.

Unlike his older brother Frank, who opted for a life involving little to no physical work, Turi enjoyed hard work and relished in the sweat equity of his labors. To him it was the awesome feeling of achievement he found in accomplishing a task. For one who had nothing to look forward to except work, he learned to love it. Yes, he loved his family and brother in particular, though he never would understand Frank's aversion to work. Yet Turi always deferred to Frank as the titular head of the family after their father died. That was the Sicilian way.

He remembered his mother sending Frank back to America, just before his father died. Turi was nine years old and was devastated by his departure but looked forward to the time when they could be together again. Turi never understood why his mother sent Frank away. In the Sicilian family, things unsavory about the family were not discussed. In fact they were shunned and tossed on the dust heap of time.

Turi was unaware of Chichu's activities in Porticello. Frank was a ruffian and troublemaker and spent much time stealing from vendors and people on the streets. His mother ignored his behavior as he provided *Lire* to support the family. But eventually she too said no more, and turned Frank out.

The Niputi ...the Nephew

Turi was a traditionalist who respected family customs. As a youth working next to his father, he was continually reminded that the only thing he had in life was family, their values and pride. He learned *Io Sacchio nienti* (I know nothing) when asked for information by others. His family-values protocol was always honored.

"Turi," his father would say, "live and work each day as if it is your last and always be proud of who you are and what you do." Turi lived by his father's words.

✺ ✺ ✺

As they tied up the *Giuseppina* to the dock, he knew that today's routine would be different. He would have to tell his wife about Dr. Plumb's diagnosis and that he had to quit fishing. He had no choice. The urologist found albumen and blood in his urine, and the strain of his labors were killing him. He had to stop doing what he loved.

After several weeks on the beach he continued to weigh his options. Though he found a laborer's job working at the county sewer system for the WPA, he longed for something more. When Frank got back into town, he called. Turi hadn't heard from him since Frank had requested an upscale dinner for a few of Frank's special friends. Frank did mention that the dinner went well, however. Turi waited as Frank spoke, hoping that he would thank Mandy, who did all the work. But that was not to be and Frank continued controlling the conversation.

"I just visited Mom's," said Frank, "and Grace told me you had to quit fishing. Why in the hell haven't you called me? It's been weeks."

"It's been longer than that Frank," replied Sam. "The last time we saw each other was when Mandy cooked dinner for De Simone and Adamo. That was almost a year ago."

Accepting no responsibility for his actions or lack of contact, Frank just said, "Goddamn, time really flies! I've been busy with *Mi Cosa Nostra*. You know Jack sends me all over the place."

"No, Frank, I don't know how busy Jack keeps you. I fish for a living. I'm also gone quite a bit of the time."

"Yeah, I know we're both busy, but why didn't you call me and let me know you had a liver problem?"

"Kidney, Frank! Kidney problem! I didn't want to bother you with my medical crap. Besides, I knew you were out of town."

"Yeah, I know it's a helluva life. So, what's with this friggin liver problem, brother?"

"It doesn't matter, Frank. I am out of the fishing racket. That's it."

"Well, listen brother. I've been around—you know, in and out of town, *La Spira ascoltatore!*" (The spies and snitches listen) he quickly hissed. Frank was paranoid about snitches listening to his conversations. Ironically, he was the biggest mouth around, always bragging or letting something slip during of his rants. He lived his life that way. Always concerned about being tapped by the police, he warned whomever he spoke to on the phone: *Sensi recordade.* (They record our conversations).

"Turi, we are *familia* and need to help each other when one of us gets in a jam."

"Yeah, Frank, I hear you but I didn't wanna bother you. Who knows where you are or what you're doing?"

"Okay, okay. So, what are you gonna do?"

"Well, I'm no barber or pizza maker, that's for sure. The only thing I know a little about is booze." They both laughed aloud thinking about Prohibition.

"Frank, I don't know anything about the liquor business. I've been running the *Giuseppina* for quite a few years and we've done good. Mandy and I have equity in the boat and are saving to buy a house some day.

"Frank, when you left Porticello for Milwaukee in 1922, I was sickened. I remember you bringing us food and Lire, but then Mom said you had to leave and make your fortune in America. Then Papa died and you weren't there and you didn't come to his funeral.

"Frank, leaving was bad enough, but we didn't hear from you for years. Someone told us you were in San Diego with the Buompensiero brothers, Matteo and Giovanni. Mom, the girls and I didn't get here until the spring of 1927. Hell, we didn't have money enough until we sold the upstairs floor of the family house. Frank, when I got back I was a real foreigner. I couldn't speak American."

"You mean English. Don't worry, neither could I, Turi."

"Frank, when we got to San Diego, the government made me go to school and didn't give a shit that I couldn't speak the language. They put me in the third grade and some teacher tried to force me into one of those kid's chair desks and I pulled my knife. That was it for school. They threw me out."

"Well, Turi, you learned a lesson. This is not Porticello, where they don't have schools. So you went to the sea school of hard knocks and made it work for you. Now, you'll have to find something else, so your body won't give up on you. Maybe the liquor business is it. But, things are different in the San Diego liquor business. The *Spiru* have their fingers in the cookie jar. So, you have to be connected to obtain a license.

"In San Diego, the boys play favorites, but you gotta pay the man one way or the other. The guy in charge of licenses on the State Board of Equalization is in our pocket. We call him "Wild Bill" Bonelli. My contact with him is his Liquor Administrator boy, Charles E. Berry. He only deals in cash, if you get my drift."

"That's not going to help me, Frank. I've got no connections."

"You'll be fine, *frati*, I guarantee. Don't worry, I'll find a place for you in no time. When Mom told me of your sickness, I put the word out. There's a joint over in Coronado called the Colony Club. You might be interested in it.

"Some Italian family named Schiutto owns it. They were shoemakers before. The word on the street is they were having difficulty generating business. The stupid cocksuckers probably thought if people had *scarpi* (shoes) on they'd walk right in and make the owners *strunzs* (turds) of money. The Schuittos don't know their ass about making money in the liquor business. They're now trying to find a buyer and I think I can get the joint cheap."

Turi knew Frank spoke with authority, he was street smart and had been with the Dragna family's Gold Rail bar after the war in 1948. Frank always knew what he was talking about. If Frank thought they were trying to find a buyer, and if he felt I could get the joint cheap, he was probably right. Frank knew everything and he could read.

"You might have to change the name for the license transfer. No fucking blue sky for those *Mamzer* bastards-(In Jewish slang.) They've even hired a business broker to handle the transaction, but he's in my pocket, so don't worry about him. We'll pay him nothing.

"Turi, drive over and at least look at the place. See what you think. Then call me and I'll get the wheels in motion."

"Thanks, Frank. I'll take a look and call you."

Sam and Mandy took a ride across the ferry that afternoon. Driving into Coronado, they felt relieved that possibly they'd be able to get a new start in a business that would work. They drove to Orange Avenue and found the Colony Club. It was in a wonderful location and on the main drag. Sammy thought, *What a joint it could be.*

It was early in the afternoon when they went in and decided to have a cocktail. Although Sam didn't drink, he decided to have a scotch and water with Amanda. The place was dark and it took several minutes to adjust their eyes to the surroundings.

Sammy looked at Mandy as they sat in a table in the corner. There they could see the whole joint. First, it was dark. Second, it was filthy. And third, he knew he and Mandy could make the joint clean, bright and airy, a place where people would love to come. It wasn't long before their small talk became more of an agreement on what could be done with the place. They both liked what they saw and felt it was a good opportunity. Ergo, it was a done deal and work was needed to put it together.

They walked around the restaurant some and returned to their seats as Mandy finished her drink. Sammy's was still half full. He just wasn't a drinker. Although he partied a lot as a young adult, he never drank much but was a great dancer and enjoyed the dance halls throughout San Diego. Turi was a workhorse and he recalled loving to dress up and take Mandy to town to dance. He enjoyed clean shirts, sports clothes and the action like most others. However, his life had not been centered on nightlife, except on special occasions. Sammy felt more comfortable with getting into the bar business, where he didn't have the physical stress and strain on his body with the sea life.

Then an older gentleman approached the piano and began to clunk on the keys, but he wasn't very good. Not only did he hit a couple of bad keys, but his personality sucked and Sammy thought, *this guy would have to go along with the name of the joint.*

They left and when he got home, Sammy called his brother.

"*Chich?* Turi! Mandy and I just got back and want the Colony joint in Coronado."

"Okay, Frati (brother), I'll start the ball rolling. I'll call you soon." The next day, Frank called while my dad was out and told Mom to write down the number of the business broker and to make an appointment. He would handle the deal.

"Oh, Mandy, tell my brother not to worry about this guy pressing him for money or taking you for a ride. I've told him Sammy's my brother and to be nice, or else. Just remember, if the S.O.B asks for anything, tell Sammy to tell the schmuck: Frank's going to take care of it. Leave it at that."

That night at dinner, we sat as a family of three and Dad excitedly shared his plan to enter the liquor business and open his first business in Coronado. They would move fast, trying to get a lot of the prelim work out of the way.

CHAPTER 12
LEARNING THE BUSINESS
...NON-DELIVERED PROMISE

Dad was a smart man who knew what he didn't know, beginning with his failure to learn how to read and write. There was no pretense with Sammy. He'd keep his mouth shut and seldom if ever questioned anything his brother Frank told him. When it came time for Frank to teach his brother the bar business basics, Dad learned from the workers in the trenches, a bartender and cocktail waitress. On the first day he attended his brother's teaching session, Frank was virtually a no-show. That pleased Sammy as he and the bartender, I'll call him John, became friendly and he taught Dad the basics of mixology, back bar setup and how to recognize the bottles—Dad had good cognitive and recognition qualities. He also could be creative when it came to making money and use of his innate Sicilian bravado, which he used to create his own checks and balances scheme.

✳ ✳ ✳

Soon after my father signed the documents placing the business under his name, he and my mother started implementing the changes they planned and even hired a couple of the *Giuseppina's* crewmen to come and help with the heavy lifting and painting. In no time, they shaped up the Colony Club, and Mom and Dad came up with the name, the Manhattan Room.

Frank knew that in the bar business and dealing with cash, most people dipped their fingers in the till. *He would, so why wouldn't anyone else.* He himself was a thief, an accomplished one who hadn't been caught. He also believed that most of the employee-bartenders and cocktail waitresses working in "his" bar, the Gold Rail, were thieves. The bar (which Frank claimed to own) actually belonged by liquor license disclosure to Jack Dragna's two sons. Frank was a minority partner on the license.

Frank said a few hours working at the Gold Rail would save Turi a lot money. Frank would check Sammy out and show him the ropes. And also teach him how to keep his employees honest.

When Dad showed up at the Gold Rail, Frank was on the phone, busy, and told his day bartender to show his brother around and teach him the bar setup. Dad spent one day at the Gold Rail learning how to set a good back bar of liquor and bartender basics. When Frank failed to return, Dad didn't go back the next day, and Frank never called.

Dad was satisfied, however, with the information garnered from John, Frank's bartender. Dad was affable and got on well with John, who showed him how to pour and mix cocktails and some of the tricks owners used to cut costs with the size of shot glasses.

When Dad returned home after his training day, he told Mom that he had an idea how to ensure he could keep bartender theft to a minimum. He recalled that the biggest problem with being a thief was accounting for the liquor you either poured or failed to pour and maintaining the corresponding accuracy of the cash in the till. You couldn't take in money from a customer and not put it in the till. Someone would notice, no question, and bam! You'd get caught.

To carry out the theft, you had to maintain an accurate cash count in the till by using something to count an item, like toothpicks or small, seldom-used glasses. The bartender created the value of each item. One item could equal ten dollars accumulated. This allowed the thief to keep a tally of how much booze he poured versus the cash in his register till. Prior to checking out of the work shift, the boss would pick up the till tray, count the cash, subtract the starting bank and know exactly the day's income. However, he'd never know the percentage of booze that left his inventory because of sloppy pouring, cheating a customer or over-pouring.

Dad knew the key to theft was a cursory daily bottle inventory check. With his method, he established the base line bank for the shift, so the cash checked in at the close of shift measured against the inventory consumed and the register tape provided him his base margin of security.

Dad reached back to his fishing days to come up with a way to measure his liquor consumption. It was similar to how much fish weight amounted to a boat's fish well. Each well carried X amount of fish, dependent upon size of fish. This equated to so many tons. Dad surmised that if he could measure the amount of booze in a quart, the standard back bar bottle used in 1950s, he could use a stick to measure the bottle before and after a shift and know how much cash should be in the till.

That also depended upon the size of the shot glass used by the bartenders. State liquor regulations allowed owners 1/8 ounce of spillage (because accidents do happen) when pouring drinks. This state also assumed that bar owners used a one-ounce shot glass. If a bartender used a 5/8-ounce shot glass, in theory you could save 3/8s of an ounce of booze, which went to your pocket as cash.

Dad whittled on a rectangular stick about fifteen inches long. He then marked up one side with lines representing one ounce of liquor in a quart bottle. It only took the time filling an empty quart bottle one shot glass at a time and marking a black line on the stick for each shot. It worked. Though a mechanized version came out to weigh and then measure a standard shot, dad relied on his method for years.

Dad also knew he had to increase the Manhattan Room's business, especially for the afternoon trade after the offices closed. Although the Manhattan Room had a piano bar, they hadn't had a piano player since Dad bought the place. Dad wasn't about to pay some jerk to sit there and plunk the keys while drinking up the profits.

Mom placed an advertisement in the local paper for a piano entertainer. Several days later, a handsome young man came through the door and asked Mom for the manager. He was responding to the advertisement for a piano player. I guess I walked into the Manhattan Room just after Mom said, "Great, there's the piano bar. Have at it." I knew something was different as the delightful sounds of upbeat music filled the air.

Dad, in the office, also came out to check the back bar. He heard the music and walked over to the player, where I stood listening. He interrupted the young man and said, "I'm Sammy, the owner. You're hired. When can you start?"

The young fellow laughed and said, "I'm Val and thank you. I can start today."

Dad said, "You're on the clock. We'll talk money later." That was Dad, the decision-maker in action.

Dad called a carpenter friend of his and asked him to come in and elevate the first round of tables beyond the piano bar. He believed elevating the tables and boots

The Niputi ...the Nephew

surrounding the piano bar might be just the trick to lure in early dinners and thus increase the consumption of liquor.

Val was a handsome young man with a giant smile and wavy black hair. He made the piano talk and I was intrigued. I had never heard music like that before. Val's music was alive with melody and the way he played was especially light and airy. He was wonderful, and at a young age. And my mother sure liked him.

It was almost five o'clock and the seats around the piano bar were already filled and the tables close to the piano bar were also filling. Dad was helping the day bartender mix drinks and smiled as he saw me. If this business continued, we'd be full by six p.m. and have a good day. I looked at Mom and she smiled.

"He's good, isn't he?" she said. "Unfortunately, he can only work three days, Monday through Wednesday. He plays at the Coronado Hotel on the weekend. But they don't pay enough for him to make it. Dad figured we could help each other and it's working."

"You aren't kidding, Mom. He's unbelievably talented." Then, I got an idea and immediately planted the seed. "Boy, after listening to him, I'm ready to give up my accordion." *There, I said it. Now I waited to see what would happen.*

According to Dad, liquor was the only way to make real money in the business. In food, Dad said, "The killer was the free stuff and it started with salt, pepper, sugar, catsup, tomatoes, lettuce, and vegetables. They would start to go bad and if your cook or chef improperly planned or guessed wrong on the dinner crowd, you ended up taking it in the shorts."

He was hard over on this view and practiced this philosophy throughout his life. Although I'd pull his chain and ask how the drive-in's, Mexican joints or Italian restaurants made it. He'd reply, "How the hell do I know. I don't know that stuff. But, I learned that from my brother." Later when I became old enough to really understand the business, I found that his point was right if you knew nothing about food, preparation and marketing a good quality product.

Yeah, you could sell leftovers the next day. And yeah, if you included everything that an owner had to pay before the owner saw a profit in the price of a steak dinner, it would cost you a bundle, and that was in 1950. For him it was all in the liquor, and he vowed to only open businesses that didn't have food, unless the liquor license came into play.

In a couple of weeks and with a little advertising the word spread about the Manhattan Room's great entertainer. Soon, we were getting a lunch crowd and the weekends were even picking up, even though Val didn't work those evenings. Dad had him in for the lunch crowd. Val would then leave around five to go change and prepare for the Coronado Hotel's dinner crowd.

We even started getting a classier crowd of customers.

Dad got my Uncle Joe, the Baron, to come over and show our cook what was what in the Sicilian kitchen. During my ten or so years on the *Giuseppina, Uncle Joe* was a whiz with Italian spices and really knew his way around the galley. He used to take our food supplies, add spices and such and turn it into a delight to eat.

Dad introduced him to our head chef, saying, "Chef you're great, but my brother-in-law Joe has a few tricks I want you to learn and incorporate into our menu!" It was not a request but an order, and the chef knew it.

All appeared to be headed in the right direction. Dad told Mom and me that we were finally making money, and he felt relieved since we had so much tied up in the place. However, Frank hadn't been around for months, which was always fortunate from my perspective. I didn't like him. Even as a kid, I noticed he was arrogant, brash and controlling, always trying to push Dad and be a big shot with his foot-long cigars and Cadillac cars. Besides, I just didn't like him.

Frank returned to San Diego a few months later and stopped by around twelve-thirty on a Wednesday and noticed that the place was clean, bright and looked one hundred percent better. He felt good and proud that his brother Sam was able to turn the joint around. Then, he heard the piano kick in and some laughter coming from the piano bar.

He looked over and saw the young piano player and several of his no-doubt buddies giggling and humming along to a light and bubbly refrain. Frank listened for just a few moments and watched, and there it was, the touchy-feely and too much verbal expression, he surmised from the onset. *Those fucking queer cocksuckers. That's all my brother needs is for these bastards to make his place a queer joint. Once that starts, it's all over.* He noticed that the piano player was smiling and laughing the most. *He must be the fucking ringleader.*

Frank asked the bartender, "Where is my brother Sam?"

"He's in the office, Frank." Without hesitation, Frank strode behind the kitchen doors and headed for the office, where he found Sam working numbers on a calculator.

"Hello, frati," he said in a gruff voice. "We've got to talk. I'm glad to see you're working the numbers, because it won't be long before there are no more fucking numbers to worry about. I told you I would cover your back and my first official act of doing that is today. Look, Sammy. I left you alone for a couple of months and you've done a great job of cleaning the joint, changing the menu, and bringing in the crowd. But then you go and fuck it up by hiring that faggot out there playing the piano.

"You, brother, are going to lose it all."

"What are you talking about, Frank?"

"That dickhead queer you've got beating on the ivories in the piano bar, that's what. Are you crazy, hiring a fucking queer? You've got three queers sitting around him giggling and playing footsie with him right now."

Sam looked at the clock, got up, and headed for the dining room. Frank followed. As soon as he and Frank got through the doors, they both noticed the cocktail waitress taking orders at the piano bar. She was dropping off several drinks and was taking additional orders. At least a dozen customers were drinking and singing around the piano bar. The piano player, with an air of mischief in his smile, joined them in song as he played along.

Sam turned and headed back to his office. "Do you see what I mean?" said Frank.

"No, I don't. I see a piano bar full of customers drinking and several others at the bar. The reason why they're here is that piano player. Ever since I got him, he's doubled, no, tripled our business and we're making money. Before that it was shit."

"Sammy, if you don't fire that queer, you're asking for trouble. I've been around the liquor business my whole life. I guarantee you'll be the only Bompensiero queer joint operator in this or any other city. Besides, you are giving the family a bad name. Brother, I'm telling you. I ain't coming back until you call and say he's gone."

"Yeah, thanks, Frank. I'll think about it and make my decision."

CHAPTER 13

ALONG CAME THE MAN

Anyone who knows San Diego will tell you that Coronado is a quaint and beautiful town almost surrounded by the sea. Small upscale yacht docks, giant wharves for aircraft carriers, a semi-retired population and low crime rate. Capped off with beautiful weather, and the turn of the century Hotel del Coronado made it the celebrity spot in San Diego. And June Jordan, Coronado's chief of police, was going to keep it that way. Shocked when fellow San Diego police, the sheriff and the FBI teased him about his new policy of allowing criminal elements into his sacred cottage-like village and its latest newly renovated nightclub, Jordan retaliated. A man of justice, he didn't waste time ensuring that "his" turf was purged of those with questionable reputations. And as Dad found out, the chief of police had what the Sicilians called Forza (power) and he would not be dissuaded by the facts.

✳ ✳ ✳

Dad was operating the Manhattan Room with his bright new renovations, a good bartender, pretty good home cooking and the new piano bar musician who drew a crowd every day and night he played. Dad had a winner in the musician. People came from miles around to have lunch and dinner and, especially, to hear the Manhattan Room's pianist.

Then one day several months later, around four o'clock, fate raised its ugly head in the form of a visit from the local police chief, June Jordan, who dropped into the Manhattan Room to speak with Dad.

Apparently, Jordan had attended a local monthly luncheon and get-together with the county sheriff, area police chiefs, local FBI agents and some Navy Shore Patrol representatives. It was a gathering of the local law enforcement officials and they took this opportunity to shoot the breeze about crime in the San Diego area.

Most areas in San Diego always had something cooking in the crime pot, with the exception of La Jolla, Del Mar and Coronado. Those were the prime and fairly wealthy communities where police budgets and their inherent "Rich Guy" power base provided more than enough support to deter crime. These were the elite areas with extremely low crime rates as the police had a handle on everything.

When the speaker called out Jordan, who almost got whiplash responding to his name, those at his table paid attention along with those in the audience. "June, we thought you'd be interested in knowing that you may have a new player in your neighborhood and it isn't a new yacht or aircraft carrier," the speaker said. Those in attendance laughed. "In fact, your new resident isn't really a lowlife, but happens to have some heavy baggage following him too closely, we think. His associations, however, could begin to bring you into the fold of crime."

"Who knows?" said the speaker. "You and your Hawaiian-shirted boys might have to start to work for a living like the rest of us."

"What in the hell are you talking about?" questioned Jordan.

"You've got a joint at 1107 South Orange Avenue. I think it's called the Manhattan Room or something like that."

"Yeah, I know the place," said Chief Jordan.

"Possibly you didn't know that Frank 'The Bomp' Bompensiero, a hoodlum with a hard rap sheet and Mafia connection, has been seen hanging around that place for some time now. I'd keep an eye on the place if I were you, because we are."

With that, the rest of his fellow chiefs started to laugh and chide him.

"Well, I appreciate the heads-up and I'll look into it," said Jordan. That was the start of a downhill slide for Dad's new business, but he didn't know it. And, it would get worse. He just couldn't see it.

Later, when Jordan got back to his precinct HQ, he thought about his being blindsided by the Feds. Yes, he was embarrassed. But more importantly, he was concerned about the crime implications. What if this Bompensiero character had something up his sleeve besides his crooked arm? Why didn't Jordan know what the hell was going on? He fumed and then had his secretary contact the SDPD documentation center. "I want everything they've got on this SOB—everything, dig deep! I don't want some flimsy rap sheet. Get the details, sealed or not. If you run into any headwinds, call me and I'll get hold of their chief."

"You got it, boss, I'll make the calls. You'll have it this afternoon."

That afternoon, like clockwork, June Jordan peered over the documents. Then he saw it. Frank had been caught red-handed with his fingers around a cookie jar of 48 bindles of opiates, buried in his backyard. He mused, then fumed as he read on and realized they never brought

Frank to trial. *Wait a minute. Sonofabitch. He hated to be caught short.*

Now, his eyes on the street would pay. Chief Jordan reflected on his back door into Tijuana. Drug traffic had been a minor player up till now in Coronado, but that didn't mean it would stay that way. He'd stay leery and would bide his time. Maybe, little old Coronado could catch a big fish and gain himself a feather. He would talk to his guys.

"Hell, chief," one of his three detectives said. "My wife and I just visited there the other night after work. They hired a new piano player and we had a great time. The guy is a fantastic entertainer who also plays at the 'Del.' We decided to stay for dinner and loved it. The new owner changed things around, opened it up and cleaned up the place.

"He hired a new chef and menu. Wow! The place looks great. Quite an improvement, I'd say. My wife had sea bass smothered in a special sauce with garlic, capers, parsley and onions. Man, it was out of sight. Me, I had sand dabs. The best I ever ate. It was pan-fried in olive oil, butter and capers, touch of lemon and sprinkled with parsley. It was absolutely delicious. Some kind of Sicilian sauce, the waiter told me."

"What the hell do I care what you ate or how it was prepared?"

"Chief, I'm just saying that the Manhattan Room seems to be operating as a straight place with some upscale Italian food. It has good ambiance with a great piano player. You ought to try it."

"Yeah, Sicilian sauce all right. Well, don't like it too much, just yet. I've got a hunch. Well, at least you're right about one thing."

"What's that, chief?"

"The WOPS can't do without their Dago food."

Shortly before six, Jordan called home and said to his wife, "Be ready by six-fifteen. I'm taking you somewhere special to dine tonight." She was thrilled. He was in his civilian attire. Minutes from their home they turned onto the main drag and stopped near the Manhattan Room. He told her, "I want your opinion on this place, honey. I've heard it's good."

"Let me at it," she said.

A nice crowd was already at the bar and the sound of laughter and music seemed to be coming from a happy gathering around the piano bar. Jordan hadn't been to the joint in months, knowing the last owner ran a dive. It was dirty then and he wouldn't take his staff there for a lunch of dog food. Now, as they were seated in one of the booths, he looked around and the cocktail waitress came over.

"Can I help you tonight?" she chirped, almost in tune with the music.

"Yeah, a Manhattan for the lady and I'll have Dewar's and soda, thank you. And by the way, is the place under new management?"

"Oh, yes sir. The Schiutto brothers sold out a couple of months back and now Sammy Bonpensiero owns the place. He's done a great job and we love it. In fact that's him sitting in the booth on the other side of the dining room with his brother. Frank, his brother, is the one with the big cigar."

June Jordan killed three birds with one stone that night. He had a good meal, made his wife happy, and decided that the Manhattan under its current management would not be around Coronado within thirty days.

The only one who didn't see any of this coming was my dad. It would take him years to learn about the power of notoriety, the press and the machine that in time would run over him. This was all for supporting his brother. "Guilt through association" became his mark of Cain. Although they were not in business together, didn't frequent the same hangouts over the years, didn't have the same friends, or socialize outside of the intimate family, their name and occasional appearances together would cost my father dearly.

The following day, Jordan entered the Manhattan Room around noon. It already had a lunch crowd and June looked around for Sammy. Not seeing him, Jordan approached the bartender, flashed his badge and asked, "Is the owner around."

"He's in the office, sir. Just go right through those drapes, the office is down the hall."

Dad and I were sitting in the office and I could see a man approaching.

"Is Mr. Bom-pa-Cero here?"

"Yeah, come in," said Dad.

"I'm June Jordan, the police chief of Coronado, and I wanted to introduce myself."

"Glad to meet you Jaa... June," said Dad.

"I'm Sammy. Is your name like the month?"

"Yeah, Sammy, like the month. But, I don't care about my name. I'm only interested in yours."

The chief's quick reply made the hair on my neck stand up.

"Well, June like the month, this is my son, Joe."

"Hello, sir," I said, extending my palm. Jordan shook my hand.

"How are you, young man?"

"Fine, sir," I replied.

"Sammy, can we talk in private?" said Jordan.

The Niputi ...the Nephew

"Anything you have to say can be said in front of my son. He's my partner.

"Okay, your choice," said Jordan.

"Look, Sam. I don't know you from Adam, but I pulled a background check on you to ensure that you were on the straight and narrow when the ABC license came across my desk for review. You came up clean. In fact, some of my boys have visited your joint and tell me you run a straight operation. You've been a fisherman from what I gather for at least twenty years. Then you had to quit for some medical reason and seriously, Sam, I don't care what you do for a living now, but the reality is this: Sammy, I don't want any Bonpensieros on the Coronado side of the bay, and that includes any related Mafiosa thugs."

Dad interrupted. "What the hell do you mean, Mafiosa?"

I remembered the word from my conversation with Dad years before. I looked at Dad and his hazel eyes were ablaze with blood and fire as the older chief cast derogatory words at Dad.

"Look, Mr. Jordan, I am American-born but Sicilian by blood and birth. I don't know what the word Mafiosa means, let alone being accused of being or associating with one. You've got your goddamn nerve calling me Mafia!"

I stood quietly and then heard the word again, "Mafia" and my dad had said it *Now I would learn more.*

"Now, Sam, don't get your balls all bent out of shape. I did not call you a Mafiia, but you sure as hell hang around with one. It's your brother, Stupid!

"Sam, in this country if you look like a turd and smell like a turd, you are a goddam shit. No ifs, ands or buts, I guarantee. And your brother Frank is a turd, like it or not. He is a convicted felon. He's got a rap sheet as long as your arm. Though he hasn't been convicted of any of the serious felonies, we know the SOB is crooked.

"We know he's killed before. Hell, after he got to California, he became a member of Jack Dragna's family and started burying bodies. We can't believe how ignorant you WOPs are. All on our side of the fence know who the players are. Just ask your bigmouth brother Frank. He's been caught on tape telling more tales than you will ever know.

"We know all the players from Dragna and his sons in L.A. Along with your brother and the Adamo, Mirabile and Matranga family in San Diego. Frank is on the FBI's watch list and has been since he snuck into Los Angeles and lived in our lovely town. Then the dumb S.O.B. gets nailed for drugs then Prohibition violations. We know it all.

"Sammy, you're hanging with a known felon and Mafiosa, brother or no brother. How in the hell do you think I knew about him over here? The San Diego police chief and the FBI told me. He's been in scrapes with the law all over the states and his last Fed stint at McNeil Island doesn't sit well with me.

"You want some advice for the long term, stay away from Frank. He's been in trouble and will be in the future. If you hang with him, he'll drag you down. Get smart, Sammy. You have been told. Now, it's up to you. However, if he shows up here, you are going to get busted. No threat, just a warning.

"The city, state, and federal police are on his tail. We know he's a crook, a thug, and a killer and as soon as we prove it, he's going up the river again. So now, close up your joint and go back across the bay and play footsie with your big brother. But, for damn sure, keep him on his side of the water and out of this place. And don't try to tell me he doesn't come around. He was here last night sitting with you in a booth. Hell, even your waitress knew who he was. She pointed him out. By the way, you have some good food and the piano player is great too. It's just too bad, Sammy. He's not welcomed on my island."

Sammy just glared at the chief. He knew the chief was right.

Even though Sammy didn't mess with Frank's friends or businesses, it didn't make any difference to the cops. June Jordan taught him that. Now, Dad felt as if he were just a pawn in a game between his brother and the law. And he was in line to be screwed. The cops didn't give a fig for him. They just wanted Frank, and this troubled Dad as he thought about his brother.

"If that's all you got, chief, I have a business to run." Sammy knew that the fuzz were onto Frank and they weren't going to get off until they nailed him.

After Jordan left, I looked up at my Dad and he put his fingers to his lips—meaning quiet. He said very little except, "I could do nothing but stare at that cop. His mouth did all the talking and I realized my dreams for a nice joint in a classy neighborhood were dead." We never spoke about the chief's visit or his telling Dad about his brother and the Mafia.

The Bompensiero brothers had a close Sicilian heritage. Their relationship was thick and steeped in paganistic support for one another. His brother always watched out for Sammy, and now Sammy had to warn Frank. Dad also needed some brotherly reassurance. That's about all he could do.

"Frank, this is Sam. Meet me at the wharf." It was convenient to meet on the finger piers where they normally parked the *Giuseppina*. Once he told Frank what the chief said, Frank's reply was, "Fuck him, that low-life rousting cocksucker. It's a free country. We know our rights. They have no reason to hassle you."

"Well, Frank, he doesn't give a shit about what you or I think. He says he was going to get with the ABC and his local Health Department rep and put the kibosh on my operation. He flat-out told me that you were being tailed and watched and the state and fed cops were just waiting for you to screw up, so they could put you away again."

"As I said, Sammy, fuck him and his on-the-take motherfucking brothers."

Frank was easy with the words and threats, but he didn't give a damn about collateral costs. He never had to pay. To him, they were just minor details, and he never gave a damn about what his activities or his presence cost his brother or the family.

June Jordan was a man of his word and, within a short time, Frank was seen at the Manhattan Room and the chief's men starting hanging around and causing a ruckus over any infraction of police, health or issues involving boisterous clients. The rousting had begun and with that, it wasn't long before the customers backed off. Then, the Health Department gave a D card to the kitchen, and the Alcohol Beverage Control agency suspended the license pending a sale.

Sam spent almost all of his ready cash to get into the Manhattan Room and now he was in effect going to be shut down. He was worried and might have to go see his sister, Grace. She and her husband, Pedu, were always there to help.

"Don't worry about the lease and all that bullshit *frati*," Frank said. "The landlord will waive the lease, I guarantee it. I also have an idea that should make you better

The Niputi ...the Nephew

off than you were in Coronado. Some property just came available and I can get you on the lease and it doesn't have a liquor license."

Frank never said how he was going to do it, or how he was going to get Sammy a lease. But it was obvious that he would cajole, threaten, beat, or kill someone if they got in the way of his objective.

"The joint I've got in mind is down at around Union and Broadway. There may be two joints for the price of one. I'll check my sources and be back in touch shortly. Don't worry about anything, brother. I'm working on it.

"Stop down to see me at the Gold Rail and we'll go take a look. This will all blow over soon. You have to get the lease and file a change of address with the ABC. You can make book on it."

Sammy needed some reassuring from his brother, and Frank did make him feel better and more confident than he had after his discussion with chief Jordan.

Frank talked with authority and knowledge. "Look, Sammy, don't worry. I pay for grease, which makes things happen with [1]the State Board and the upstate ABC hierarchy.

Dad almost apologetically admitted to me later what I already knew. "Joey, my brother can read, write and knows a lot of stuff—much more that I do." He was almost and I felt sad for him. It was more important to him than it was to me. There was no doubt that if anyone tried to put the arm on Sammy or his operations, Frank would lend support. Hell, everyone knew Frank was a "made man," whatever that meant. So no one would screw with him—he was a killer. Dad unfortunately admired and respected his blood brother's faux knowledge.

Frank was tied to Momo Adamo, the San Diego Mafia boss, and they all reported to Jack Dragna in L.A. In fact, Frank was tighter with Dragna than Adamo or Mirabile. Besides, Frank and Jack went way back and he gave Frank a piece of the Gold Rail, so to speak. Sammy understood that if it weren't for Frank and Dragna's relationship with William G. Bonelli, a California bureaucrat with long fingers, Sammy wouldn't be in the liquor business. So, in his mind, he owed his brother in the old-fashioned way. You ask, I give, you owe!

As I think back now of the nice young man, our piano player, he always had a bright warm smile for everyone, no matter what Uncle Frank said. And in time, I learned that Frank was wrong almost all the time. But his influence and actions had a major impact on my family.

Oh, and you've probably heard of our gay piano player. Dad told him he appreciated his talent and the business he brought into the Manhattan Room, but brotherly pressures required he let him go.

You might know the musician by his sobriquet, Mr. Showmanship. He really didn't need the Bonpensieros to promote him. He left on his own and, in a short time, the young man we called Val, short for his middle name Valentino, left for Los Angeles and became an overnight sensation. His talent became known for its world-class acclaim under his surname. Liberace.

CHAPTER 14

CORSAIR IMBROGLIO

In November 1952, Eisenhower was elected president and, after his inauguration, he headed to Korea to find a solution to their internal conflict. Princess Elizabeth assumed the crown upon the death of her father, King George VI. The Netherlands held its last two executions. In the Western Hemisphere, Wernher von Braun published, "Man Will Conquer Space Soon." In San Diego, Sam Bompensiero's business interest drew increased scrutiny as his brother Frank's ugly reputation grew. However, not to be deterred, Dad found a hot dog stand on Broadway to convert into a lounge. This time, he had a creative backup plan. His new venture would cater to underage sailors and other minors. Sometime after he opened and was refused a liquor license, his brother Frank called with another opportunity he supposedly created—the swank Algiers restaurant. However, amid a lot of hullabaloo, grand opening and operational mismanagement by Frank at the helm, the Algiers became the Chuck Wagon Restaurant. Dad continued to look for a liquor license and I tended bar in our minor joint and experienced two events that affected my future thinking .Oh, and Dad, true to his word, bought me a dream gift for my birthday.

❋ ❋ ❋

Six months before my sixteenth birthday, I had a driver's learner permit, and one night I turned a corner on a neighborhood street while driving Dad's new 1953 Cadillac. With the pavement slick, I skidded into a parked car. The car belonged to a San Diego police detective. He stormed out of a house, asked for my driver's license and almost fell over when he recognized my surname.

"Any relation to Frank?"

"Yes, he's my uncle. My father is Sam." With those last comments, Dad arrived on the scene and inquired about my health after the accident. The policeman asked Dad what business it was of his. My father introduced himself. "So, you're Frank's brother. I've always heard about you."

"What the hell does that mean. I don't know you and am only responding to my son's call for help. Look officer, if you have a beef with my son or me, arrest us. You can then deal with my attorney. If not, call a uniform and take down the accident information and we'll get on our way."

"Fine," said the officer. The uniformed police showed up, they questioned us, took our insurance and my driver's permit information and we left.

"You're getting your own car. My car was new and I don't want you driving it anymore," said Dad.

A couple of weeks later, Dad surprised me with my first car, a 1951 Chevy hardtop. Dad then asked my cousin Tony to spiff it up--customize it. Wow! It was a beauty outfitted with French-styled molded headlights; Chrysler taillights, new grill, and side moldings, and fitted with tuck and roll upholstery. Then, Tony added 20 coats of burgundy mist metallic paint, to catch the eye. With Tony's hard work, the Chevy and I made the December 1956 issue of *Hot Rod* magazine.

That was the best part of my year. However, there was much more coming, fueled by Uncle Frank's unwanted newspaper notoriety. A cloud of suspicion and association

The Niputi ...the Nephew

unfortunately followed my father as we tried to build a new home in Point Loma.

Dad, encouraged to leave Coronado by the police chief, crossed the bay and found a great location on Broadway and Union Streets. It was a block up from the USO (United Service Organization) building, which housed many young sailors when on the beach.

Dad hired designer William "Bill" Moffat to create a Barbary Coast motif and Bill Tarditti, a carpenter/contractor, to build it. Moffat recommended that Dad spruce up the adjoining hot dog stand and cut a service window into the bar area to generate food sales inside the bar. Dad agreed and hired a cute little lady to operate it. She called herself "Cookie," although I suspected her actual name was far more exotic and reflective of her Oriental heritage.

Dad selected the name of the joint—*The Corsair*—from a list of names suggested by Moffat, and from day one, the place was a hit. He kept the prices affordable for young sailors. The near beer flowed and hot dog sales took off as Cookie put out a mean hot dog!

When the ABC and vice squad received his application for a liquor license, they laughed, but still dropped in to see what Sammy had going, knowing he would go bust not serving alcohol. They weren't barmen or business people but simple bureaucrats, and it pissed Dad off for them to think he wouldn't make the business profitable.

Just about this time, Frank called with good news about a forthcoming liquor license, but it had some strings. Frank was tied up in another of "his joints," a swank nightclub and dinner house on El Cajon Blvd. So he made a deal with the savvy Kahn family and was ready to go, but he needed a little help in the bar and kitchen area.

A.J. Kahn and his sons, Irving and Yale, were Jewish. I point out Jewish only because, as a rule, Frank was a bigoted man who seldom had any couth regarding another person's heritage unless they had power and could do him harm. For some reason known only to Frank, he didn't like Jews.

A.J. controlled the roost in town and his sons performed as professionals, leading the charge into the business world as required for being successful. I believe Irving was an attorney and Yale was a hardened and excellent entrepreneur, similar to Nate Rosenberg.

The Kahns had significant holdings in the food, cocktail lounge business, and entertainment. They had commercial real property surrounding Horton Plaza and their holdings were eventually expanded into the Chuck Wagon Restaurants on Midway and Rosecrans and one at El Cajon Boulevard and Sixty-third Street in a prime spot that once held the Algiers Restaurant, which Frank liked to term his business.

Ownership of the Algiers was questionable at best. Dad and my uncle Joe Corrao invested money in the restaurant and worked there as well. Dad managed the bar, where he had a full crew of two bartenders and several cocktail waitresses. His brother-in-law Joe worked the kitchen, with its crew of waiters, cooks, and dishwashers. Frank came and went, looked around, counted receipts and grabbed the cash on his way out. One day, he had taken so much that no bills were paid.

Typical of Frank, he considered paying the bills as some other schmuck's job. Frank wouldn't get dirty paying bills. Where the money went, no one knew. I would submit that Frank, no doubt, had his hand in the register and failed to pay vendors. I watched him doing that a dozen times over the objections of my father.

The Niputi ...the Nephew

One day, the Algiers was open and the next day we were closed, with Frank's crybaby mouth blaring to all, including *San Diego Evening Tribune* journalist Neil Morgan. Frank said, "It was the public's fault. They didn't like Sicilian Steak." He always need a ruse. His comments were also alluded to in Judith Moore's novel, "A Bad, Bad Boy."

I can assure you that, as one of two broiler men who worked behind the full view barbeque cooker at the Algiers from the day it opened, we had no such animal (Sicilian steak) on the menu. The menu's entrée list, according to my copy, offered a Filet Mignon, New York steak, top sirloin and prime rib. On the seafood side, we offered lobster, abalone steak, salmon and trout. No pasta or ravioli or anything Sicilian ethnic. That was it. We also had a Caesar salad created tableside by Gino, our captain-waiter, and a small dessert menu. Nothing else. So, if Frank claimed that to his daughter (Judith Moore's source), he was doing his normal mouthy thing. However, even though Maryanne had eaten at the Algiers, she went along with her dad knowing it was untrue.

Frank's lack of business acumen in the nightclub and entertainment arena is worthy of note because it relates to later comments comcerning his involvement with the Matranga brothers. Years later, Joe and brother Gaspare requested Frank's help in getting a Teamsters Union loan.

I was privy to that transaction and will address it later in the story which speaks to the failed La Mesa Bowl enterprise. Their transaction was clouded and still is due to misinformation generated for news in the dailies.

Back at the Corsair, Dad kept the prices affordable for young sailors. He charged fifty cents for a four-ounce cola or fizzy citrus drinks, and a dollar for a near beer. Near beer, with less than .5% alcohol, was ruled legal for underage drinkers under the Volstead Act.

Dad gambled on near beer to entice the underage crowd. It did, because he added something extra. He brought in a bevy of hot teenage girls who lit up the place. He hired pretty girls with short skirts and liberal attitudes. He knew how the briny days at sea made young men feel. They wanted to see young women, and our young girls played waitress, played pool, took a playful slap on the butt and Dad paid them with a cut from pool and pinball machine money.

The Corsair's concept hadn't been tried before and it seemed weird. Dad had this notion about sailors and as a former seaman thought he knew the heart of a young sailor.

There were always plenty of seventeen- to twenty-year-old sailors waiting in line to put a quarter in the slot and cozy up to some young thing. And, Dad kept the Corsair filled with the teenie boppers. It was legal and they wanted to shoot pool with the boys.

The sweet smell of dime-store perfume was a definite draw for a homesick sailor lonely for any companionship that didn't reek of dirty socks and jocks.

Dad told Bill Moffat, his designer, that the Corsair had to be built to convert from a no-booze to booze operation within a day. Dad's initial idea was a winner. It worked and made money without any threat from the ABC.

The Corsair became a real sailor hangout, whether they were underage drinkers or not. They really loved the atmosphere, the food, and the games, even though they couldn't buy hard liquor. On occasion, however, you'd find them spiking a few drinks from a bottle in their car, and then head back in to hoop and holler. The Corsair was an innovation and Dad's brainchild. It was the product of his life perspective: "You do the best you can!" And he did.

The locals considered Dad a smartass because his no-booze operation worked. Although he couldn't get a liquor license, he tapped into the hot market of the under twenty-ones who had change in their pockets and were ready to party. As a teenager, I tended bar and it was a rare night when the place wasn't packed. I asked Dad casually one night why the sailors keep coming back?

"Simple," he said. "The Navy boys are hot-blooded young men who have one thing on their mind—girls. They can pretend they are in a bar with booze. They fall 'in heat' daily and as long as we keep the girls turning over, they will be back, just like the hungry tide rolls into the shore, hungry and often."

The downside was that the Corsair had more Shore Patrol and beat cop visitors than any other joint in town. Young guys were more aggressive, as they argued over the pretty girls and coyotes alike, or the games, or whatever ticked them off. I learned that early on, as Dad allowed me to play like a bartender at the Corsair, the first and only time I worked behind one of our bars. We hadn't been open very long and one of the youngish bartenders didn't show up. Dad didn't care and opened anyway and did the bartending until he got a break to call me at home. He asked if I could come down to the Corsair. He needed a hand. When I arrived it was about 3 p.m. and Dad was behind the bar serving a couple of near beers to two uniformed sailors.

"Hi, Dad. When did you get behind the bar?"

"When my day guy got sick and had to go home. That's why I called you. I've got to run to the bank and do a few errands. Can you cover the bar for me for a couple of hours until the night shift guy shows?"

"Sure, Pop." I'd been waiting years for the opportunity to get behind the bar and this was a chance for me to get my feet wet. Other than the two guys sitting at the bar, it was quiet. I wiped down the counter, checked and then restocked supplies for the night shift. Dad had showed me how to work and shut off the carbonation system for soft drinks, our support bar and where we kept our free treats. The two sailors drank up and headed for the draped door.

"You should be set, Joey. The two new waitresses will show around 3:30. Have 'em fill out time cards."

With that, Dad left. I put a few quarters in the jukebox. About five minutes into my first solo shift, a young guy pulled back the drape from the door. Aside from giving the place a warm nightclubby feel, the drape kept the sun out. He strolled over to the bar and perched himself on a stool.

"Welcome," I said, smiling. "What can I get you?"

"What have you got?" he said.

"Near beer, cola, orangeade and a clear citrus fizz, similar to 7-Up."

"How much?"

"Near beer is a dollar. All soft stuff is fifty cents."

"Are you shitting me? A *dollar* for a BS beer and fifty cents for a cola I can get anywhere for a dime?"

"That's the price set by the boss," I said, feeling a little uneasy.

"Well, fuck the greedy bastard and his hold-up prices."

He reached into his black leather jacket and pulled out a switchblade. He punched a lever and it popped open—bam! He grabbed the handle and stabbed the blade, piercing the new bar top and gashing the surface.

"Hey, what the hell are you doing?" I yelled at him while leaning over the bar to show him I was serious. "Put the goddamn knife away and get the hell out of here before I call the cops, asshole."

As most experienced barmen will tell you, leaning toward an assailant holding a knife is foolish. He grabbed hold of my shirt and pressed the blade to my neck.

I think my mind went blank.

Just then, the door drape swung away and sunlight flooded the room as Dad came through the drapes and noticed me with a knife at my throat. He assessed the situation and closed the gap between himself and the wiseass in what seemed like a microsecond. With his eyes full of fury, Dad slammed his fisherman's calloused meat hook fist upside the guy's head. The force stunned him, knocking him off the stool while the switchblade clattered to the floor.

Dad didn't stop there. He was all over him. He grabbed him by the throat and raised him to his feet. The guy was taller than Dad, but height didn't seem to give him an advantage.

"You dirty son of a bitch! Try to kill my son?"

Dad pulled one hand away from the assailant's throat and swung his right clenched fist in the guy's stomach. The guy let out a gut-wrenching grunt and started to puke. Dad sidestepped the would-be attacker's vomit and plowed a hammer-like fist into his jaw.

"Cocksucker!" Dad spat at him as the now-unconscious tough slid to the floor, a crumpled mess lying in his own vomit.

Dad, his face flushed, took a deep breath, and stopped.

"Joey, give me the bat and call the cops."

Minutes later the cops arrived, followed by an ambulance. Dad and I gave them a briefing while the now-cuffed ruffian was loaded into the ambulance.

After the police left, Dad and I stood on either side of the bar. No words had to pass between us to verify how close we had both come to either being killed—or killing in self-defense.

Years later, I would remember the incident and how lucky I was to have a father who would come to my aid without reservation.

"It's a good thing I had to come back and get my keys," Dad said, looking around. "Or I don't know what I would have found here."

I nodded, still a little shaky and trying to shore up my voice.

Dad shot me a sideways glance.

"Best not tell Mom," he said.

I nodded.

"No problem, Dad."

I found my voice and felt a tightening in my chest that felt like pride.

"Thanks for being my father and protector." However, what happened that day at the Corsair haunted me for a long time. Whenever I saw a switchblade knife it reminded me of the creep with the knife in his hand, pointing it close to my throat.

✹ ✹ ✹

Dad would go on to own several more bars in San Diego. However, the Corsair launched the careers of several of his employees. One of them turned out to be a new family member. Larry Matranga blew in from Detroit to seek a change of pace from his dad's dry-cleaning business. In San Diego, he had two uncles, Joe and Frank Matranga, who were in the liquor business and ran their own bars. Joe decided he wanted his own bar and built "Pal Joey's" in Allied Gardens. He ran it until he retired and passed it on to his son Larry, a former San Diego Marine officer who ran the place until he died circa 2011. He was a cousin to the Detroit Larry Matranga that Dad hired.

Young Larry Matranga learned bartending at the Corsair and then at the Kings Club, working for Nate Rosenberg. He eventually married my cousin Tina and they bought into a bar called Patrick's. Unfortunately, it burned down. Never say die, Larry and Tina found a location for another tavern down from Croce's in the Gaslamp District. The family, including son Mario, enjoyed the business and operated a hell of a San Diego's blues and boogie joint called Patrick's II. It is still operating on Fourth Avenue and F Street. Christopher, their eldest son, didn't care for the liquor business and chose to become a steel man.

CHAPTER 15

TRAVELS WITH LEO

Marilyn Monroe, the blond bombshell, married slugger Joe DiMaggio in 1954, and the King of Rock and Roll, Elvis Presley, created a new craze in music. He was also banned from entering San Diego two years later. The United States launched its first nuclear-powered submarine, the Nautilus. President Dwight Eisenhower warned America that we should not get involved in the disputed Vietnamese political muddle. Surprisingly, I would become involved some years later. The Corsair, non-liquor "bar," had recently been converted into an on-sale liquor-licensed bar. Things were popping, and Dad introduced Mom and me to Leo Patella, a fisherman and a new partner in a Third Street bar called The Spot. Leo, like Dad, loved westerns and horses and they went in partners again, buying a riding horse. Leo became my best adult friend.

★ ★ ★

It wasn't long after the Corsair's success that Frank called Dad with information that his pal, "Charles E. Berry," from the state's local tax board had told him that a liquor license might be available soon. In these early days in the liquor business, Frank had the contacts to get liquor licenses in San Diego. No one knew how, but he was known to have an "in" with someone "important." The word on the street was, "If you needed a liquor license, go see Frank." Dad and I never discussed how Frank got the licenses.

The Niputi ...the Nephew

When asked, Dad would say, "Who knows? He has friends and I don't question it. He gets them. That's all I know."

Frank always told Sammy what was and what wasn't a good deal, and my father believed him. But this was about a food joint and Dad didn't like it. Frank was always the one who had pounded into his brother, "Stay away from food." That's what he believed.

To Sammy, the possibility of getting a license was long overdue. But this was something Dad couldn't grasp. Although many people believed Frank was knowledgeable about the liquor and restaurant business (maybe because he ate and drank), most people in the actual business knew better. They took his antics with a grain of salt, but kept their mouths shut.

When the Algiers was taken over by the Khans, Dad fortunately still had the Corsair operating. So several months later, when Frank got back into town, Dad asked Frank about the liquor license he had spoken about. Frank said he would check and mentioned that if it was a go, there was a greasy spoon called "The Spot Café" on Third Avenue near Broadway. It was a small dive, but maybe his brother could make something of it. The place had a reputation for serving burnt toast, broken yolks and rancid coffee to drunken sailors after the bars closed. Dad intimated that since the joint was a dirty dump, it was a good thing for us.

Dad would use the run-down condition as a reason for the landlord to sign a lease with a good tenant who would clean up the place and improve his property. Dad was a good salesman. He got a lease and put in a new cocktail lounge, Dad's first liquor-selling club on the San Diego side of the bay. He dropped "Café" from the name and the new hot joint on the local bar scene became "The Spot."

Frank and Dad discussed going into a partnership, but after Coronado and the most recent Algiers fiasco, Dad was gun-shy. But he agreed that a partner for The Spot might take the heat off any future encounters with the local politicos. Frank recommended his wife Thelma's nephew, Leo Patella, whom Dad knew to be a fisherman. In fact, Dad as a young fisherman had fished with Patella's father.

Both Dad and Frank thought that Leo would be a good addition to the operation. Besides, Leo had never been in trouble with the law. His reputation was solid and he was "clean." No police record. They knew Leo could stand the scrutiny of an investigation.

It wasn't long after that that Leo came to our house for dinner at the Union Street house. I was about fourteen at the time and Leo was about 29 years old. Leo was a big man, especially to me—still a runt. He stood almost six feet and was thick and muscular. He weighed in excess of two hundred and fifty pounds. At first glance, he was intimidating, but his warm personality and great sense of humor made him an instant success in our family. Leo fit right in. For Mom and Dad he was another son. For me, he was a big brother.

He was interested in what I was doing in school and what I liked. I showed him my room, model airplanes hanging from the ceiling and the related treasures a budding teenager collects. He thought my prized baseball glove was great and we played catch on the front lawn after I told him it took me almost an entire summer of picking strawberries on my knees in Oregon to pay for it—a whopping twelve dollars.

For mom, Leo was everything Frank wasn't. He was a nice, clean-cut young man and looked like a football lineman. He was nothing like his cantankerous, mouthy mother Anne and her similarly inclined daughter, whom Mom and I both disliked as much as a bout with diarrhea. Leo was a simple, happy guy and not a push-you-around braggart and loudmouth like his uncle Frank.

Once established in the family, Leo joined Dad on the liquor license, helped build The Spot and bartended. When I visited the bar on business, we got to talk and, on his days off, we'd take off to the desert. On occasion, we went to Nogales and then took the back roads into Tijuana, Mexico on roads others only talked about. But, in time, Frank's old bureaucrat buddy Barry's antics with liquor licenses began to smell and someone started a quiet investigation.

"Hey Joey, wanna go to Calexico? We can go and have some great Mexican food, maybe come back through Tijuana?"

I'd pile into Leo's big blue Chrysler sedan and we'd head for point's north, east or unknown. We always had great adventures.

From 1952 through 1959 Leo and I were family. But after Frank went to prison in 1955 and college sucked up my time, we traveled less and less. In time, we drifted apart. However, we spoke often enough and I always had a soft spot in my heart for Leo. He was my big brother and I could always go to him for advice.

One day during a ride, I wanted his advice about a conversation I overheard at the Corsair one night. I mention it because it speaks to *Ziu Chichu's* character, some of his notable friends and what their views were on life and reality. It also spoke, at least to me, of the dirt-in-your-face attitude of Frank Bompensiero. Leo listened as I told him the story.

"Leo, this happened back at the Corsair when, at the end of the month, the sailors were broke. Dad knew the place would be dead, called and had me shut the Corsair down around midnight. I happened to be operating a night shift and he mentioned that his brother needed to meet a couple of men at the Corsair. Just as I started to hang up, Dad asked, "Is Bill Biaggo there yet?"

"Yeah, Dad. He's sitting in a booth reading the paper."

"Good. Get rid of stragglers and tell Bill to clean up."

Biaggo was simple, quiet and kept to himself. He was old school Sicilian and Dad once said he was "connected." Dad gave him a job to help him along. Bill barely spoke English. His bosses probably liked it that way. With Bill, you gave him a hammer and pointed him in a direction and he would go pound. That was all I knew about him. And there was something else. Dad once said that Bill would "die before giving up anything or anyone."

Bill was in his early seventies at that time and I always wondered what he had seen and what he had done throughout his life. Years later, while doing research, I found Bill's name multiple times in reference to those who were on the FBI's watch list.

As the sailors left, I came out from behind the bar and locked the door, turned on the lights and told Bill to scrub down. Dad came in minutes later and went to the office, and Uncle Frank strolled in. He gave me a nod. I returned the nod and pointed toward the office. He barely got to the office when a rap at the door announced that Frank's visitors had arrived. I knew the men as Joe and Gaspare Matranga. I had known them for years and wondered what was up and why they needed to have a meeting with Frank and at our place.

The place was quiet and I could hear the conversation blasting out of the office like it was on speakers. No one in that group ever spoke softly, especially Frank.

The Niputi ...the Nephew

Joe Matranga started. "Look, Frank, I've come down on behalf of my brother Gaspare, who has a slight problem to resolve and he's a little uncomfortable discussing it. I knew that you'd be the one to handle it."

Joe Matranga was the family member who spoke for the brothers, and it was only right in the Sicilian culture for him to address a distasteful subject, especially for his younger brother. Joe was married to one of the Detroit families and knew his way around. Although not what you'd call a heavyweight in the close-knit society, he wouldn't make a move in San Diego without talking to Joe Adamo or Frank first.

"*Que cosa* (What's up), *Gaspare*? You brought your brother, Joe. "*Tu si scandatu?* (Are you afraid?)" Frank asked.

Gaspare was hesitant in his reply and stammered as brother Joe took up the apparent jabbing challenge. "*Nudu scantha.* (He's not afraid, only uncomfortable.)"

"Okay, what in hell is the beef and I'll see if I can fix it." Frank sounded annoyed.

"Well," Joe started, "this young guy, a bartender, works for Gaspare at his joint in Chula Vista and he's been drooling all over Gaspare's daughter. She's very attractive, you know."

"Yeah, ain't they all!" injected Frank.

"Gaspare is worried that his daughter is getting too involved with this guy."

"So, why don't you fire him, Gaspare?"

"Well, Frank, it's a problem. My daughter has been coming down to the joint and sitting at the bar while he's working and when he's not mixing a drink, they act like lovebirds, with him feeding her more bullshit."

"Oh come on, Gaspare, he's probably like all of us. He's trying to get in her panties!" More laughter. Then Frank said, "Is he serious about your daughter or do you even know?"

"I don't really know, because I haven't spoken to him about it yet."

"How long has been this going on?" asked Frank.

"Several months, Chichu."

"Well, he sounds just like the rest of the horny, fucking sailors!" Frank laughed.

"It's not funny, Frank," said Gaspare. "This is my daughter, my blood. What if it was your daughter?"

"Well, it ain't my daughter. And if it were, I sure wouldn't have waited for two months to figure out what to do. I see this as a family matter between you and your family. Not something that needs my attention. If you're asking for advice, that's something else. Gaspare, I would have talked to my wife and daughter about this thing she's doing. But, of course that's up to you. Hell, I can't tell you how to be a man and run your own house. I'm guessing, but maybe she already told you that she's in love. I don't know. But, it all depends on what you plan to do. Hell, you may already have a bambino coming down the road."

"Tell me!" Gaspare grumbled. "Hell! That's just what I'm worried about."

"Well, you've got to live with it so, tell this *strunza* (turd) bartender where the fuck you stand and what you expect. Don't come crying around here *Senza Cologne* (without balls) and wondering what the fuck you should do. Hell, you came here wringing your hands, Gaspare. You know that you aren't going to do a fucking thing. You think I don't know you want me to do your dirty work? What the fuck," Frank said, raising his voice. "So, who is this bartender?"

The Niputi ...the Nephew

"He's nobody. I think he's a sailor who was looking for a night job and he looked pretty good and has a nice personality, so, I hired him."

"Yeah, a nobody who now has you by the nuts!" laughed Frank. "Why is he working two jobs?"

"What do you mean two jobs, Frank."?

"Look, Gaspare, quit fucking with me. You said he came around looking for a night job. So it makes sense he's doing something during the day. So what is it?"

Gaspare stammered, "I think he's in the Navy and has a kid and needs the money."

"You think? You are a lying *strunza. You've seen him in uniform, haven't you?* You haven't spoken to him about your daughter. Yet, you think he's married with a kid and needs the money. You cocksucker! Who do you think you're shitting? You don't even give me that information and play like a dumb fuck! I don't appreciate it and now it's going to cost you, big-time. I could have helped you, a favor so you could owe me – but no more. What do you want me to do, rough him up, break his legs, or feed him to the sharks for trying to fuck your daughter?"

"Frank, you don't have to be so crude."

"Crude! You, Gaspare, are a *mala minciada* —(sick prick!)"

Frank paused for a minute. Then, he said, "Because you bring me this as a family matter, I'll honor that and say, it's your call. So tell me what you want."

"Well I don't know, said Gaspare." I've never encountered this kind of thing before."

"Yeah, *tu pezzo merda*—you piece of shit! You can't make a decision and your daughter's a virgin, too!"

The room became silent. Dad walked out, shaking his head.

Then Frank spoke slowly, "Gaspare, the call is yours. Make up your mind but remember, this is a YAIGUO thing." (You ask, I give, you owe.) "You got that, Gaspare?"

Then Frank yelled out from the office. "Sammy, is the *Giuseppina* at the dock?"

"I think it came in yesterday, our sister Grace called and said they had a small load and will probably unload today."

"Good. Call the skipper and tell him I need a favor. I may want him to take us out to the islands tomorrow night. We won't need a crew, but we're going to do a little fishing. Oh, Turi, tell him not to pump the bilge after they unload. I want to save it to draw the *pesce gane* —the sharks."

The meeting broke up soon after that as I scurried from behind the office door. We closed up and went home. On the way home, Dad asked me if I could hear any of what went on in the office.

"I heard it all."

"Joe, realize that my brother, your uncle, is *pazzo* (crazy). He gets involved in all that shit because of what he has become over the years. Ever since he was a kid, left home, and was tied up with Jack Dragna, he had been operating the same way. That is what he does and the local people know it. He has balls and will do just about anything to ensure his status rises and people respect him."

"Pop, are you telling me that they would toss some guy to the fucking sharks because he was trying to nail some chick who wants it? Hell, I chase girls all the time."

"Yeah, maybe, but it depends on whose daughter you are chasing. You know that because I've taught you when to back off and how to treat the women and their parents. It is all about *respecto*—respect, Joey. That's the thing!"

Dad and I never spoke of that night again. But I was reminded of that incident a few years later when I was a student at San Diego State.

Dad received a telephone call from a man whom Dad knew well and had fished with over the years. He asked me if I were dating a young Sicilian girl from the neighborhood. I said, not really. But I ran into her on campus one day and we enjoyed a cup of coffee together and we spoke of meeting for dinner and possibly a show. She was delightful and friendly and I thought maybe we could hit it off. However, I had a reputation for running around, or most likely he was concerned over a Bompensiero dating his daughter.

"Well, her father is concerned and asked me right out if I knew what your intentions were regarding his daughter."

"Well?" When I didn't immediately reply, he asked again.

"Well, Dad, we just met. I've got a long way to go in school before I get serious."

"Well, tell her good-bye now, son!" I did.

Messing with girls outside the Sicilian ghetto was okay, but within the ranks, it was a no-no. I took Dad's advice.

What I heard that night at the Corsair when Uncle Frank met with the Matrangas would stay with me for a long time. Until then, I'd never given much thought to issues of respect—from the Sicilian viewpoint. I was an American kid growing up in the mores of the 1950s. I was free to date and met many girls both in my job and at school. It was about having fun—and we did. What I learned that night at the Corsair brought me up short. It was suddenly a new twist on life.

I mulled over the events on the drive home that night Finally, I asked Dad if Uncle Frank killed people just for the sake of it.

"Not if you ask him, but then, no one asks."

He was quiet for a while, then he said, "But, you are right, son. What he does is crazy."

"Do you have to kill people to gain respect? Dad, I respect you but you haven't killed anyone, have you?"

"No, son, I never have and never will. My brother and I differ when it comes to the way we see life. But, he is still my brother and I respect him for that, not for what he does."

"Pop, it's not important that *Ziu Chich* is involved with that shit. It's just that he involves the whole family in his thing by just being there. It's like we had responsibility for meeting the Matranga brothers at the Corsair and hearing all that crap."

My father shook his head. There was no response. He knew I was right and could do nothing about it except cut his brother out of his life. That was something he could not do.

Nothing more was ever said about the matter and I never asked if the *Giuseppina* went out for a short fishing party to the islands or if five people went out and only four returned. It was none of my business. I intended to keep it that way.

But the incident continued to eat at me and I found myself spilling the whole story to Leo Patella. When I finished telling Leo what happened, he looked over and seriously said, "Joey, now you know why I don't like *Ziu Chichu's* business. You have to forget this. You'll be fine. Just keep thinking the way you do and do like the three monkeys—hear no evil, see no evil and say no evil. And, Joey, remember the *'say no evil'* part. Don't ever forget it!"

I understood.

However, forgetting the implications of what happened that night at the Corsair wouldn't leave me. It must have showed because it wasn't long after that Leo and Dad came up with another idea. Perhaps it was simply a diversion to help me move on.

I don't know how the subject ever got around to the western era of America, but Western movies were Dad's passion and Leo's. Then one day, the subject became horses and Leo said he was thinking about buying one. Dad was all for it and wanted to go in together and share the expenses.

"You and Joey can go riding and play like 'riders of the purple sage.'"

And that's just what we did. At the time, we lived in a seven hundred square-foot duplex and had one forty-eight Oldsmobile sedan. We were hardly in the social strata to be considered in "the horsey set," but Dad and Leo—two fishermen—were hell-bent and determined to buy a horse. And not simply to buy shares in a racehorse like many of the guys did to show off, but a saddle horse—to ride. At heart, Dad was just a cowboy!

Leo and I scouted a few horses and finally bought a big gelding, a golden palomino-pinto. Most pintos were black and white or brown and white, but ours was gold and white. We named him *Treasure Boy* and stabled him at Balboa Park Stables.

In those days, among Balboa Park's most popular features were its horse stables and miles of bridal paths that wound through the wooded landscape. The stables are long gone now, as are the bridal paths.

When not in school at San Diego High, I would walk from our home on Union Street a couple of miles to the Balboa Park stables. There, I'd find Treasure Boy standing quietly off to one side of his stall chewing on some sweet alfalfa. He was quiet and lollygagging, no doubt resting after a walk, trot or jog with Big Leo aboard.

We often referred to him as *Pancho Villa* Leo Patella because he really got into the part of playing the Mexican bandit. He'd invariably wear his fancy Tijuana-purchased sombrero and a brace of single six .45-caliber pistols on his hips and even a bandalero of cartridges across his chest. When asked by other horseman where he was going all duded out and carrying all of that armor, he would laugh and say, "You never know when you might run into trouble on the trail, *amigo*. So I go prepared."

There was never a question in anyone's mind when Leo was going off on a ride because he and Treasure Boy dressed the part. He purchased Mexican riding regalia for Treasure: an authentic Mexican Latigo hand-woven bridle and reins, open treed saddle and gaudy colored blanket. He also got himself a red, yellow, green, black and blue serape to cover him in case it got cold or rained.

In no time, he'd be out of the barn with Treasure prancing and skittish to step out and get on the trails. Ol' Treasure must have felt relieved when I showed up with my seventy-five pounds ready to ride bareback versus *Pancho Villa Leo's* heft, and toting an arsenal.

Leo and I had a ton of fun with that horse. Once, I even rode in a big San Diego parade as part of the "Fiesta del Pacifico," down Broadway, passing *The Spot* and *Kelly's* and Uncle Frank's *Gold Rail*. Dad and Leo had a gathering of well-wishers assembled to see me and Treasure Boy go

The Niputi ...the Nephew

by. I was in costume as a shirtless Indian boy with headband, trousers, moccasins, natural tan and body paint. I used Leo's Mexican bridle and attached feathers to it for show. Treasure Boy looked great with painted hands and skulls on his palomino front and rump. I rode bareback and he proved his temperament by behaving well.

All was good until a couple of months later, when Treasure and I were on a trail ride up by Roosevelt Junior High School. We were resting and Treasure was grazing near a stop sign when a trucker stopped and yelled out, "Nice-looking horse." Then he revved his engine and hit his air horn. Treasure became scared shitless and flew sky high, bucking for tomorrow. He went into his fastest gear and "took hold of the bit."

With Treasure at full gallop, I hung on for about two miles and couldn't rein him in until he sideswiped a telephone pole, whacked my left leg on the pole, and finally careened off into a busy car-filled intersection near the merry-go-round. I fell off. Treasure stopped and I grabbed a rein and stumbled along with him in tow back to the barn, a mile away. I had a cracked kneecap, so Dad put an end to my riding days.

✱ ✱ ✱

After almost a year and a half of operation, the Navy and the local cops complained to Alcohol Beverage Control (ABC) that the Corsair caused too many babysitting problems policing the minors. They were always in a fray over some young thing. Skirts do that to horny, teenage sailors. The blue-suit cops said, "It was worse than any four bars servicing the adult bar population in San Diego." That's what the local authorities finally realized and what helped Dad in eventually obtaining a California liquor license without the help of his brother.

Neither Leo nor I enjoyed the liquor business, but he and Dad had to make a living. Although my father enjoyed the business, Leo never did. It wasn't something he or I wanted to do forever. Besides, our Uncle Frank was always on the news. It seemed that just as things would die down, we'd be broadsided and had to face the next blast of gas from the media.

We often talked about Frank and his way of life. Leo always said the same thing: "What are you going to do, Joey? There's no way out. He's family."

Leo was right, of course. It was a fact that hung on us like an ugly shroud. It was something you just learned to live with. While I had dreams of a career in the Air Force, Leo was formulating another plan of escape. I marvel now at the tenacity he had to hold on to his dream.

About the time Frank was sent to San Quentin for bribery in 1955, Leo met a young Italian girl from Cucamonga, California. Her father had a winery in that region that was founded by his father years before. Leo and Rosalie married in 1954. Leo and the Mandala family visited our Del Cerro home several times in early 1960. I lost track of them after I departed for the Air Force and for many years was totally out of touch.

During their marriage, Rosalie and Leo had two sons, Sam and Frank. They were named, of course, after Leo's Dad on one side and Rosalie's Dad on the other.

In later years, the U.S. Department of the Treasury officially deemed the "Cucamonga Valley" an American Viticulture Area, or AVA. To me, this conveyed a long-deserved recognition to the Mandalas and to the vintners of one of California historic wine-growing regions.

Today Rosalie, whom my parents cherished as Leo's wife, turned eighty in 2013 and is happy with sons and grandsons who carry on the fine Patella and Mandala name.

I recently spoke with her and it was refreshing renewing acquaintances after almost fifty years. Unfortunately, I learned that Leo became a diabetic at a young age and over a six-year period suffered greatly before his passing in 1975. I resided in Europe at the time. He passed on quite young at only fifty-one years old. This was just five years after Dad died.

Leo worked with Dad until December of 1960 when the police-conceived retribution raid nailed down Dad's liquor businesses. After that, he went back to fishing until he had to quit due to poor health.

True to his own philosophy, Leo's underlying principle of living held true: "Hear no evil, see no evil, but most of all – speak no evil." Leo figured that if he went fishing, he wouldn't be around to testify in court against his uncle. Leo signed on as a crewman on the next tuna clipper heading south. Leo was a good man and I'll always remember my pal *Pancho Villa Leo* riding down the pine-covered trails in Balboa Park under the Cabrillo Bridge—a gentle giant of a man and a good friend.

CHAPTER 16
HOUSE ABOVE THE BAY

In 1954, the State of California exercised the "right of eminent domain" and cut a swath through Little Italy like Sherman's March to the Sea. Hundreds of families had to move. Mom and Dad found a lot in Point Loma and bought it, intending to build their dream home. Their nemesis came in the form of a prominent and influential local radio station owner named Fred Rabel, who just happened to own the house adjacent to our newly acquired property. Along with the commercial music and entertainment Rabel provided his listeners, he used his radio station and political connections with the city fathers to harass us, delay our home's construction and incite John Q. Public against people they didn't even know. As I later discovered, the media were insatiable when they were out for blood and hungry for a front-page story. They seemed to delight in dragging our family through the mud. Journalistic principles to not print unsubstantiated word of mouth be damned—my family was convinced their editors were motivated to print the salacious for the sole purpose of satisfying their readers' insatiable appetite for crime and criminality. Oh yeah, do not forget increasing readership, selling advertising, and making a buck.

✳ ✳ ✳

Along with thousands of other San Diegans in 1954, my family lived along the Highway 101 corridor skirting

San Diego's majestic bay. "Eminent domain" was the operative legal term that fostered the move to replace Highway 101— *El Camino Real*, or the "King's Highway"—with an interstate system. We were told to get ready to move because major portions of Interstate 5 would run through our neighborhood. It would begin at the Mexican border and carve its way north through California, Oregon and Washington—possibly one day to Alaska.

There was no question that it was a good thing for future San Diego development and for the state of California. However, to the six thousand families who lived within the several square miles identified for "eminent domain" clearance, it was seen as the destruction of the neighborhood and a scattering of the local primary Italian population into the outskirts of the city

The plan had been in the works for years, but was ignored by the locals. The residents were primarily involved with work, school and more work. They just went about their business maintaining the status quo—that was, until the county administrative districts sent in the topographic surveyors and marker men with their earthmovers, who took down houses that weren't being moved.

Our home was a duplex and scheduled to be moved. It stood on a lot just north of the corner at Union and Grape Street. Dad sold it to a family that wanted to move it to a lot they owned on Sassafras Street, a couple of miles north. Dad, Mom, and me—along with Dad's sister, Patrina D'Acquisto, and her husband, Joe, and their daughter, Virginia—were affected by the move.

Dad said we'd be fine and that was good enough for me. But we only had a year to find a place and get a house built before we had to leave Union Street. In those days, contractors didn't build a hundred houses at a time. Most did it as individual homes by contract, and, at most, only several homes were built.

Mom reminded me that we had to save our money for the move and with that in mind, we started driving around the bay and Point Loma looking for a piece of land. Since the time we lived in our first home on Keats Street in Point Loma, Mom knew that Dad would love a place near the bay.

From his formative years growing up in Porticello, Sicily, Dad loved the sea—it was in his blood. Whether he recalled life as a child fishing with his father, or fishing as an adult skipper on the blue pacific out of San Diego, Sammy and the sea were connected—a bond that tied him to his roots.

It took Mom and Dad almost a year to find a lot in Point Loma. While out driving one day, Mom noted a speck of dirt on the side of a hill. It was devoid of life except for chaparral, some weeds, and it was lost to local vegetation. This piece of land on the side of a hill across from the Naval Training Center above Rosecrans Street appeared to be a strip, maybe a quarter acre on the side of a steep hill. Access to the house would have to be on Udall Street. My mother took down the name of the street and approximate location and through a local Realtor friend found the title documents at San Diego County's hall of records.

The owner was a naval officer who was overseas, so our Realtor wrote him. He apparently had purchased the property while in San Diego for training and had been in Japan since 1948. He had been gone for more than six years. Dad offered him six thousand dollars for the lot and he accepted.

Dad then found an Italian contractor, Eddie De Flavia, who lived in El Cajon and had a good reputation. He had designed and built quite a few beautiful homes, and he was happy to build one to specification. When completed, the house would be large, over four thousand square feet and be built up from the ground to the street level. This was almost fifty feet above the lower ground level. The home was designed to have two fireplaces, a kitchen, a step-down living room, dining room, and three bedrooms upstairs. It would also have a stairway down to a huge den/TV play room, billiards room and another bedroom bath and washer/dryer room, all with a view of the bay, of course. Because the house would sit on a tiered foundation nestled on the side of a steep hill, there was not much land under it. The home's elevation structure was about fifty feet high. The internal basement was about three stories high, which was unusual, but it was big enough to put in an indoor swimming pool. We didn't.

It was tough getting the plans and paperwork through the county. But, in the end, the county approved the plans and construction began. Considering the engineering recommendations, huge steel and concrete pilings were required to hold the fifty-foot-high structure on the foundation. So a few of Dad's fishing buddies, along with me, a teenager of fifteen, were given jobs digging foundation channels. These were five to six feet deep and almost three feet wide. I soon learned about blisters and ditch digging.

It wasn't long before Dad's introduction to the bar business, and building his new home in Point Loma became intertwined in a melodrama that could have been aired alongside "Days of Our Lives."

The home took two years to build, thanks to a man by the name of Fred Rabel who lived at 3050 Udall Street, the corner house next to our property. Rabel owned radio stations KSON and KCBQ. And he learned that the new owners were members of a Sicilian family named "Bonpensiero."

Name verification validated that my Dad was the blood brother of reputed criminal Frank Bompensiero. Rabel then launched an all-out attack using his media contacts, political pressure, and his broadcast power to hinder, slow, and aggravate every step of our construction.

Construction was bid at $30,000, but delays, thanks to Rabel, ratcheted the cost to $38,000. But that was funny money compared to the two years of delay and impact to people's lives caused by Rabel spewing hate on the radio waves.

In the final analysis, Rabel's fear and privacy issues were his main concerns. He seemed neurotic about having someone with the Bonpensiero name living less than twenty-five feet from him. So Rabel flaunted his power and created enough heat with his vitriolic radio broadcasts to try to keep the house next door from being built. He pressed the county to resurvey the property and find any excuse to kill the construction project, including going after the De Flavia Construction Company.

For months, daily on-air announcements berated our family, claiming, "Elements of the Bompensiero family were reputed members of the Mafia, the Sicilian crime society. They were moving into the neighborhood and threatening the lives of decent Americans." He invariably would add: "The brother of notorious mob boss Frank Bompensiero was moving into the neighborhood and driving prices down."

On-air comments included the use of names such as "thugs," "Mafia," and "Sicilian dogs." He frequently punctuated his diatribe with, "Even if they are not affiliated with the Mafia, they have no right to build in a decent white neighborhood in Point Loma." Talk about racial insensitivity. It was unclear whether he meant "Sicilians" in general or "Bompensieros" specifically.

There was no question that Rabel used his media influence to pressure the city fathers and county planning department to stop the project and "toss the Mafia hoods to the dogs."

After going through six months of this kind of harassment, we finally received city and county approval of our building plan. We started to build. With the foundation laid, the framing sticks started to rise. Along with its daily KSON radio news, the broadcaster never left out an accounting of Rabel's next-door neighbor, the Bonpensiero house under construction.

That construction hit another roadblock when Rabel claimed the structure would block his view. An inspection and any irregularities needed to be resolved before construction continued. KSON's efforts, combined with the city's tactics to impede construction, proved devastating and costly to our home building project.

Finally, in January 1957, the *San Diego Union* reported that, after much deliberation, the county concluded that construction could be continued and the building permit would be reissued. A report followed by the grand jury indicated ". . . that plan changes were supposedly made on the job after the plans were submitted. Moreover, and in many instances, clashes of personalities were behind the disagreements. Inspectors could have been more alert, but at the same time, they were working under peak load conditions. There was no evidence of criminal negligence or threats."

By this time, almost two years had elapsed and the house was still a shell—three months away from completion. Dad had to find another contractor. Eddie De Flavia had to back out after suffering from Rabel's daily harangues. Eddie said, "I've never encountered anything like this in twenty years of contracting."

Eddie was a wonderful family man and hard worker, but his reputation and company were destroyed. After his company was smeared on the radio and in the newspapers, he could not financially recover. His workers could not survive and while Dad did his best to help his friend, it was too late.

It was one of those bureaucratic happenings. Those in government supposedly to help the citizenry were influenced by powerful men and their biases. The whole building and planning department could not honor their commitment and maintain department integrity. County inspectors over-inspected and held up previously reviewed and approved plans.

After all was said and done, almost two years after De Flavia poured the foundation, the San Diego influence peddler Rabel and his company gave up. Dad's attorney assured us the city would give us clearance to complete the house and we received an occupancy permit. Although within days of us moving in, another blast was heard.

This time, it was Rabel's radio station during morning and lunchtime broadcasts. They began attacking Frank Bompensiero individually about his alleged Mafia and *La Camorra* connections. Then, mimicking the radio, the *Evening Tribune* carried front-page pictures of Frank and included a picture of our house.

Later, following a broadcast, Rabel mentioned on air that he had to get away from the stress. He needed relief from the vermin and garbage the city failed to clean up in his neighborhood. He mentioned that he was flying down to Mexico with a small group of business associates for a fun trip of hunting and fishing. His mistake was mentioning his vacation on the air.

The Niputi ...the Nephew

Somehow, Frank, though in prison, heard about it and when Dad went up on his next visit, Frank unloaded about the schmuck Rabel. Dad relayed his brother's comments upon his return home.

So, Frank tells me, "Your Jew neighbor is still on the radio. He recently announced that having you as a neighbor was stressing him out and he was going to go down to Mexico for a vacation. He noted the trucks pulling up and unloading your goods. He reminded his audience that the neighborhood's going to hell with all the crooks, gangsters and Mafia moving in."

"What the hell," Dad said.

"Yeah, this guy doesn't lay off and he can't keep his mouth shut. But I was glad to hear you moved in. So, I'd love to see the place as soon as I get out of here."

"You know you are always welcome."

"Well, maybe not with that schmuck around."

Dad shook his head. "*Chichu*, you know what happens when you fight back? It is nothing but a political jungle. And this prick has powerful friends and does not want us near him. Hell, we could be living anywhere in San Diego, it wouldn't make any difference."

"This business will be handled. Sammy, you forget about it. I have contacts down south and this asshole is flying down to Mexico to go fish and hunt with his radio friends. Hell, you know, brother, flying small planes can be dangerous. Who knows if he'll ever come back?"

"Frank, what are you talking about?"

"Nothing, brother, nothing."

In June 1960, about five weeks after he was released from San Quentin, Frank visited the Point Loma house. Coincidentally, I finished my last class at State that day and drove home as usual, finding Uncle Frank and Dad walking around the front.

I had only seen Frank twice in the past five years and both times, he wore blue prison dungarees. I paid my respects to *Ziu Chich* with a shake and an embrace and joined the two as they concluded their walk around the property, including the no-man's-land (dead-end curb) between Rabel's house and ours.

"We are just finishing the tour," said Dad. Frank turned to Dad and said, "Frati, your house looks great and after almost two years it's a wonder you ever got it built. It must be almost perfect," he said, laughing. "That fucking Judah Rabel caused you a lot of grief."

Frank looked around furtively and said, "Some of my people think that the Judah has been a real pain—drawing attention to me and our friends and we don't need attention in our line of business, if you get my drift. Bad press is no good for anybody. In fact, he hasn't shut up yet. He made some comments about me being released from San Quentin. They keep hearing him blast you and me on his radio station and, recently, using our family name and linking to some Napolitano *La Camorra* crap."

"Yeah," Dad said, as if he were trying to downplay the event. "I'm just waiting for him to get tired. It'll blow over. Look, Frank, you are finally out and it cost a bundle to set you free. Enjoy it now. You are on parole. Screw this guy. But you're right about this jerk. He and his wife were both drunk on their butts. I recently heard a commotion outdoors and they were stumbling down our street and landed about fifty feet from our front door. They shouted at me to find someplace else to live. They cursed and yelled "friggin Mafia trash" at the wind and anyone else who would listen.

"Just to piss them off, I went in the house and grabbed my shotgun. When I came out holding my gun, I started aiming at seagulls overhead. Rabel got so damn scared he and his wife ran toward their house. Of course, the cops arrived and I went out and told them I heard shouting and yelling out front and got my shotgun before inquiring into the noise. I wanted to protect my property. The neighbors were drinking from an open bottle and celebrating something in the middle of the street. Apparently, they got scared and ran for the house. They must have called the police. I made a statement for the record, but no charges were filed. But I called my attorney anyway."

"Can you believe these *Americani bastia* (American bastards)? You know brother; some assholes are just evil."

"Yeah," Dad said like he was trying to smooth it over.

A few nights later, after dinner, while Mom was washing the dishes, Dad went down to watch TV and I followed him into the den.

"How are things going, Dad? You okay, business good?"

"Yeah, everything is fine."

"Joe, have you seen those neighbors of ours?"

"Not hardly, Dad. I never see them. They are behind their fence or indoors. With me at college most of the days, I'm not around so, if they did come out, I wouldn't see them. Why do you ask?

"My brother mentioned that Rabel ought to keep his fucking mouth shut about the Bompensieros or his radio waves might just disappear— along with him. No threat, just a fact. It could happen. But, you know that's *Chichu*. Anyway, I just wondered because you're around during the day more than I."

A few days after Dad said that to me, I noticed Rabel driving into his garage in the afternoon.

From then, on Rabel lived quietly across the street after until we moved, almost two years in the future. I guess he continued his life as a radio station owner-operator and commentator or found some other castle to charge.

We did have some very good times in the big house on Locust Street. Sneaky Mom started saving years before, with my contributions from my tuna-fishing earnings, and was able to increase her new furniture account.

Mom, Aunt Thelma, and her former sister-in-law, Josie Hanley, drove to the Los Angeles furniture mart and bought her furniture on a layaway plan, which was a new concept for the time. She bought gorgeous handmade furniture from North Carolina. It was French provincial design and made in cherry and alder wood.

Although the soft hand-painted flowers were removed as the years of continued moving wore down the finish, it was truly gorgeous in its natural wood state. I still have their master bedroom set and several end tables, fifty-seven years later. It still gains ooh's and aah's from onlookers.

Mom purchased a living room suite consisting of a light beige silk sofa, two matching love seats in mist green, two grandfather's chairs done in sea foam blue, with end and coffee tables to match. All tables were inlaid with Carrera marble. Dad saw it for the first time after we moved in and was awestruck that Mom had saved to pay for all the furniture during the home's two-year building period.

We had many friends over while we lived in the house. We also had several parties with over one hundred guests each time. In fact, my cousin Tina, who lived with us for a couple of years, met her future husband, Lawrence (Larry) J. Matranga, at the house, which had an unbelievable unobstructed view of San Diego Bay.

However, with Tina in high school, me in college, and Dad gone most of the time on business, Mom was lonely. The house, though beautiful, was too big and seemed empty with only her there by herself. One day, Mom mentioned moving to Dad, and he responded accordingly.

"Sell it and find us something."

Mom put the house on the market in 1960 for $275,000, a huge sum for the time, and it didn't take long before Mom got a solid offer. It was for seventy thousand cash down, and two $100,000 equity notes, one on a ten-acre commercial parcel on Kearny Mesa, bordering the proposed freeway, and the other, majority equity interest in an apartment house that Mom ended up calling "Joseph Manor."

Mom added up the numbers, what we still owed on the bay house in Point Loma and the cash flow of the other two properties. Mom and Dad thought it was a great deal. We then bought a new home across from San Diego State College in Del Cerro for $42,000. Dad also had a pool built, since he knew Mom and I enjoyed swimming and we had had to live out of a suitcase for two years while building the big house. As usual, we had the house landscaped with a lot of rock and no-work plants and no lawn to tend.

The last time anyone checked, an engineer had purchased the bay house for $1.2 million. During a recent visit to San Diego, I introduced myself to him and told him of digging the foundation when I was about fifteen years old. We both laughed when I admitted not being able to lift a shovel of dirt any more. I told him the tale of Rabel and the old days when San Diego's county planning engineers played politics and favorites.

"I know," he said. "I've seen what happened to you and your family happen to others. But, as a construction engineer, I personally inspected this house. Its foundation is solid and to tell the truth, Point Loma would have to break off into the sea before this house would slide down that hill. It was truly overbuilt."

And before I forget, *Ziu Chich's* remarks about taking care of Mr. Rabel while he was flying down to or returning from his hunting trip into Mexico appeared to be nothing more than hot air.

PART III
TEEN YEARS

CHAPTER 17
GOONS, GUYS & GIRLS

I really felt my oats in the fifties, especially in 1954, when I was changing schools from Saint Augustine High School to San Diego High School. I heard stories from the neighborhood guys of what girl action was like at SDHS. At the beginning of my teen years, I was still cloistered at Saints, an all-male school, where academics and Latin were stressed. The structured environment started to pinch. My hormones were churning. I looked for freedom, good times, big football games, walking and talking with girls, and maybe even trying out for some sports. While I fondly remember my days at SDHS, there was a dark cloud of guilt by association that overshadowed my first year there.

※ ※ ※

Dad was not keen on the idea of my transferring from a Catholic to a public high school. He was not big on sports, any sports, thus my argument about sports were ignored. Without any schooling and little background in a starving country like Sicily, work to survive was the only activity he knew, and I could understand where he was coming from. If he played any sport as a boy, it was probably chasings someone else's soccer ball down the alleys of Porticello, probably trying to steal it.

He did have one piece of sports advice that I recall and still laugh about today. When I brought up sports, it wasn't often, because there was little if any sports TV. The big names in NFL quarterbacks were Norm Van Brocklin and Y.A. Tittle, while the NBA all-stars were headed up by Bob Cousy and John Kundla, names I had forgotten. TV sports heroes were rare. However, in the ring sports, boxing and wrestling, Dad's hero was Primo Carnera, Italian of course (1906-1967), and former world boxing champion. Carnera was a seven-foot giant from Italy who boxed for years, then switched to wrestling in 1946.

Antonio Argentina Rocca, another acrobatic high-flyer, was one of Dad's favorites and, as I recall, we purchased our first black-and-white television in 1952 just to watch the two men wrestle. There were those who knew about gridiron college greats, but Dad wasn't one of them. I laugh when recalling someone mentioning Joe DiMaggio while I was present and Dad muttered, "Yeah, I heard about him, the *base-ama-ball* guy, right?"

I recall his advice to me about sports, "Joe, you might get hurt running around. You are better off owning a team." That is all he ever said about that subject.

In my sophomore year at *The Gray Castle*, I learned up close and personal a lot about sports: I wasn't big enough, fast enough or cared enough about them. I tried out for junior varsity baseball and that was a drag. They only wanted me for my wheels—team transportation to games. But along the way, I learned about guilt by association, persecution and enough about the law to realize that Uncle Frank's reputation cast a long shadow. I also learned that some police exceeded the rules to meet their personal objectives.

My uncle had not been sent to prison yet in 1955 when I entered SDSH, but the papers were filled with news about his activities and on-going trial. But, for me, I had my own weekly visit from a couple of plainclothes detectives. One was named Magdalena, a.k.a. Maggot. He hustled me out of my third-period class, took me off campus and pushed in the back of his car. There he threatened the crap out of me. Today those visits might be met with lawsuits. In the fifties things in the police department were somewhat looser.

He and his sidekick, another goon, grilled me for an hour. The subject matter was always the same, "Hi, Joey boy, how are you and the family? How is Uncle Frank?" They wanted to know where he was, what he was doing, and whom he was doing it with. I learned later that he was being indicted for bribery and they were hot on his tail.

I'd sure like to meet that police schmuck today with my age, experience and military background. It would be a very different playing field. Then, I was a teenager with a growing attitude about the police and government.

The Maggot's visits coincided with times when Frank Bompensiero's police tail lost him during his trial. Apparently, the Maggot was looking around for anyone who could help him.

The minute they lost Frank or he left town, the Maggot would show up. I did not know who was pressing the buttons on Magdalena, but it was continuous. Not that Frank's location mattered anyway. Over the years, police history involving any major conviction of Frank Bompensiero seemed to be inept or crooked. When I told them to go and ask my father, they ignored me.

Christ, they didn't realize that Frank was the furthest thing from my mind. Besides, we never saw Frank unless he wanted something. Most of the time I believed Frank lived outside of San Diego. But, my continual harassment really shook me up, especially when they threatened the safety and well-being of my father and mother.

When that failed to get their desired response, they'd threaten me with incarceration. As Magdalena looked at me with beady eyes and shouted, "Look, punk, your family, including your uncle, won't find you after we put you away, punk."

Their threats to arrest me for crimes I had never heard of, or accusing me of thefts, robberies or crimes that I wasn't involved with, terrified me. They wanted to shake my tree and did a good job. In time, I became a nervous wreck. I was told to keep everything said in our meetings to me and, if I blabbed to my parents, they would not be there the next time I went home.

"What do you mean?" I asked. My silly question resulted in a silly answer.

"They will just disappear."

Okay, I was naïve, stupid and troubled by their hard-fisted methods, but I did not know what to do. Finally, following one last session with them, I went home in a frazzle and during dinner, I could not eat. Mom and Dad figured something was happening at school.

Dad persisted and wanted to know "what in hell is the matter?

"Goddamn it Joe, what is bothering you. Tell me!" Dad was picking on me, and I could not hold back and burst out in tears.

"I'm in trouble with the police because of your stupid brother. The cops have been after me for weeks, taking me out of school and threatening me."

Dad's eyes grew dark and his face flushed. For a change, he looked visibly shaken. He realized the police were castigating me for his brother's troubles. I knew that his Sicilian skepticism of police, law and perceived lack of fairness reinforced his position. Now he was pissed

The Niputi ...the Nephew

because he finally realized that they were coming after his son.

After dinner, Dad called C.H. Augustine, his attorney. The next morning, we drove to his office. Dad asked me to relay the whole story to Mr. Augustine who said he would create my deposition, a formal statement and had his secretary record my statement. Next, he called the District Attorney. He discussed my testimonial statement and said that the SDHS principal had validated my comments about being pulled out of class on several occasions by the two detectives.

Augustine's side of the conversation was blunt. He wanted the BS stopped immediately. Any delay would generate a lawsuit against the two detectives and the police department. Augustine ended his conversation on a somber note. He was clear: Without DA assurances, his next call would be to the press and police department harassment would be the key point of discussion before filing suit against the cops, the department and SDHS. We were not privy to the other side of the conversation, but Mr. Augustine assured my dad, that it was over. He turned out to be right.

I was never bothered again and I even started to enjoy school. This relief from persecution also opened the door to the fifties for me. I learned to enjoy the other side of teenage life which included having fun with a new couple of pals and meeting many girls.

✹ ✹ ✹

From 1956 on, it was drive-in movies and car-serviced food stops with carhops on skates. Popular drive-ins like Oscar's on Pacific Highway and Zanzibar at the corner of Midway and Rosecrans and Lawton's on Market and on University Avenue were our hot spots. I think it was late

1956 that I met John Mangiapane. We had a lot in common. He was a fellow Sicilian fisherman and he introduced me to his pal Rene Galindo. We all became life-long friends. We all enjoyed dating and hanging out. They were both older than I by almost two years but we were friends. Both young men had graduated high school and John was attending an engine mechanics course to become a chief engineer on a tuna boat. Rene decided to join the Coast Guard. Both men are significant in my discussion because they were there when Frank Bompensiero's notoriety became front-page news.

John and I still maintain our almost sixty-year relationship and talk as old friends often do. Though 78-years young and tough as nails, John spent his life as a professional tuna fisherman. Today, he still kicks and sews fishing nets to eke-out green to buy his loving wife and companion, Elvira, wine and flowers. Additionally, he spends his time resolving the world's political problems--all of them.

Rene had seen the fishing life aboard the "Bernard Pedro--John's father's boat—and wanted no part of it. Besides, the thrill of the sea washed away after years aboard a San Diego based Coast Guard cutter. Rene was an Aztec warrior and an athlete who at almost six feet tall and huskily built was stoic, subtle, and a pussy cat at heart. Raised by his grandmother, Rene was a gentle soul and a pleasant person to be around.

He and I would drop in unannounced at John's house on Sunday afternoon knowing Mangiapane's was open for dinner. There, papa Joe and Patrina Mangiapane sat on either end of a huge table set for ten plus-diners. Sons, Frank, Bennie, John, Tony and Joey Jr. sat one side. Any others including Rene and I were seated on the other side and would enjoy a full Sunday feast of pasta, salad, meatballs and fresh fish. Ten pounds of pasta was the norm.

The Niputi ...the Nephew

After dinner, the sons, like a mechanized infantry platoon, took to their stations and cleaned up everything for mom as they had done all their lives.

With his handsome looks, coal black hair, steely eyes and copper-toned skin, our Aztec warrior excelled as a high school foot ball player. Of all of his qualities, he was an honorable friend and unfortunately got caught up in the web of collateral damage caused by bureaucratic bungling. I never knew about his internal strife until later in life. Then, it was too late.

Mom and Dad treated my friends as sons and part of our family. Just as with the Mangiapane household, there was always vacant chairs at our dinner table for John and Rene. We were running companions–chasing girls and fun in that order.

Rene had career intentions of becoming a San Diego policeman. He grew up in the Barrio near National City, spoke Spanish and knew the streets better than any cop. He also wanted to keep the streets clean of drugs and crime. That was his career path. You never heard of Rene getting into a fight because he always steered clear of any trouble.

Following his completion of duty as a Coast Guardsman, he took his honorable discharge for serving his country and opted to join the San Diego Police Department. He applied for, was accepted and began his training as all seemed to be in order. He excelled in the athleticism requirements and bookwork. However, when personal references were requested, he provided the only sound references he could think of: John Mangiapane and his wife Patrina and Sammy Bonpensiero and Mandy—all parent figures to Rene.

The police investigative interviews with John's parents passed. However, when it came to Sammy Bonpensiero, the officers had another agenda. They pressed Rene for his personal associations with me and my family. As we will learn, Frank Bompensiero was on the police radar and they needed a source of information. Everyone in the police department knew the Bompensiero's were involved with the Mafia. Even if they weren't, in the eyes of the police, they were still up to their ears in operating unsavory bars, nightclubs and other operations around town.

In the interview, Dad answered the investigative officer's questions regarding Rene and left it at that. He told me they asked simple questions. "Do you know Rene Galindo? How Long? How often do you see him? Do you find him to be honest and trustworthy? Do you know of any criminal activities ever committed by Rene Galindo?"

But the police investigators took a different tack with Rene and decided to press his buttons. They asked him "what-if" questions relating to the arrest of Sammy Bompensiero. The police attempts failed miserably as Rene didn't respond favorably to the first question asked of him following their interviews with the Mangiapane's and Bonpensiero's. "Cadet Galindo," the inspector began. "If asked to arrest Sammy Bonpensiero would you comply?"

"Of course," Rene responded. "If there was just cause for his arrest, I'd uphold the law."

Rene later recounted to John what happened next. Rene was asked the same question not once but three times. Rene's response was always the same. After being badgered for an answer palatable to the officers, he got the gist of what they were after. Rene asked to be removed from the list as a contender for police academy. And, as the quiet and honorable friend he was, in his own way told the SDPD to shove their job.

The Niputi ...the Nephew

Rene left his beloved San Diego, departed for Los Angeles and became an L.A. Sheriff Deputy. Years later, he told John that his friends were just beyond the L.A. county border and his career was in L.A.

After a solid career in resolving gang warfare crime, robbery, narcotics, etc. Rene became an on-the-job cancer patient until he succumbed at age fifty.

Rene Gallindo was a wonderful friend who left a loving wife, daughter and son. Unfortunately, I never got a chance to say my apologies for the price he paid as a faithful friend. Like so many others, Rene became collateral damage to the Bompensiero legacy.

Again, guilt through association raised its head as I attempted to date many young beauties. One, I vividly remember was Laurice Saliba. I was about sixteen years old when I met this dark-haired beauty walking down the halls of San Diego High's Grey Castle and we hit it off.

After several encounters, she made it a point to introduce her parents to me so we could date. However, when I followed-up by asking her father for his permission to see Laurice, he asked me to find someone else. His reason was clear. Although I seemed like a nice kid, he did not want his daughter going out with a known Mafia family member's son. Laurice knew I wasn't a part of my uncle's gang. But, I was not one to stay around where I was not wanted. She quickly found a new beau. A couple of years ago, we ran into each other at our fiftieth high school reunion. We smiled and hugged as we recalled those long-ago days when we embraced as teenagers. It happened many other times with other girls and I filed those experiences in the mental archives—under bad memories.

When I matriculated at State College in September, 1957, I joined the USAF Reserve Officer Training Corp. (ROTC). Later, during the Air Force and FBI historical review of me as a perspective AF officer candidate, I was concerned about making the cut. You couldn't have a police record of any kind. That meant traffic tickets as well as arrests.

Although I had never been arrested, I remembered my harassment and rousting by the SDPD and their threats. I also recalled a number of traffic tickets I received for loud glass-pack mufflers on my customized Chevy—about eighteen as I recall. I mentioned my concern to Dad at dinner one night and he said, "I'll see what I can do. But don't worry about it." That was it.

About a month later, I was in the ROTC study hall, performing some operations research for the Professor of Air Science on a special study for his graduate degree. Our field sergeant was there and I inquired into the status of the FBI background check. The NCO on duty said, "We didn't find any open records in your local police, state or federal files. You are clean."

"I thought I recalled a ticket or two along the way" I said.

"Nope. As far as the Air Force, FBI and San Diego Police Department are concerned. You are clean."

I was silently flabbergasted, but pleased because I had yet to fill out my contract application.

Now to fill in the blanks with a clear conscience.

When I got home that night, I had a smile on my face as I told Mom and Dad what the Air Force investigation revealed. Dad interrupted with, "What did they find?"

"They found nothing, Dad. No records, nada."

He replied, "That's good. Well, whaddya know?"

"But Dad, I thought I had a bunch of tickets in the San Diego police department records section."

"Maybe they don't keep them after you become eighteen? Who knows? I am not a cop. Sometimes good things happen and you do not want to know how. I don't have a clue what happened. I recall my brother having 48 bindles of heroin in the police department and it disappeared. Who knows what goes on?

Bastante! (enough).

"Remember son, this is not a perfect world. If people were honest and didn't lie, we wouldn't need police, politicians, or priests. And no one would cheat on their wives."

My answer then and now is still the same. Yes! I only have to reflect on things I learned along the past fifty years about politics, presidents and kings. It is all the same. All things are muted in gray. There is nothing black or white in man's world. If you think so, wait a bit and watch it change like the law before your eyes. I don't wonder if something is right or wrong anymore. The underlying moral aspect of an issue is by nature, a moving target. To me, this means whomever has an opinion in vogue at the time and backed by power will win out. As the old cliché implies: It is all about whose ox is being gored" and that's the way the world turns.

I didn't know at the time how any of what he said made sense, but he was serious, no doubt. "Get on with your life said Dad. Don't be concerned about things you can't change or control. Besides, it will always cost more than a case of booze.

"Life is never as perfect or as righteous as those without a blemish seem to think. Remember, the Bible said, 'He who is without sin, cast the first stone.'"

Dad liked that one. "All mankind would fail the test. Deep down, everyone has something to hide, especially when you're trying to protect those you care about. You do whatever it takes."

I thought about his comments in light of those people indicted or convicted with Frank Bompensiero, Charles E. Berry, San Diego's California State Board of Equalization (SBE) division chief, and non-government employee Al Bennett, business broker. Though indicted (but not extradited to face trial), William Bonelli, director of the California State Board of Equalization ran off to Mexico where he lived and died. He never faced a U.S. court. One might wonder about the others in California's political gambit. Of course there were others up the food chain on the take, but . . . they worked for you and the State of California. That was all that was ever said about that issue. We never spoke of it again. And there went the fifties flying by.

CHAPTER 18

FRANK'S JOINTS
...JUST ASK HIM

By conscious omission, some people allow others to assume they're something that they're not. Frank Bompensiero was one of those who would use any opportunity to further his own desires. When specifically asked a question in a crowd of people, he would pounce on the situation and/or inflate himself and his accomplishments. This was his nature. It insulated him and made up for his shortcomings. This also enhanced his loud mouth, persona and career achievements, of which there were few to none. He also expected the media to enhance his notoriety. His brother was not left out. When asked about Sammy's success in business, Frank would say, "What, are you kidding? I'm always helping my brother. We're a family." I sat in the background listening to the mouth that roared while shills for the police and FBI also listened and planned. Their goal was to push Frank's money supply cart off the road. They did not succeed. Frank never had a money supply cart tied to Dad's ventures.

❋ ❋ ❋

Frank had an uncanny ability to make people believe that he knew what he was doing, most of which was a charade, an act supported by a loud voice, a glaring stare and convincing facial gestures.

One only has to think for a moment of how expertise comes about. It might come to a child naturally as a gift from God, but that wasn't Frank's way. One might have worked as an apprentice and perfected a talent, or gone to school to gain knowledge and thus acquired a certain ability. However, none of these attributes applied to Frank, especially when the word "work" was involved. He never liked work and he didn't excel at any of the field-hand jobs he actually worked in.

However, he went the field-hand route for Jack Dragna because, after killing a man in Milwaukee at age seventeen, he was hunted by both the law and a criminal element. Thus, Frank's options were slim to none. For all the bull slung around about his learning a trade, there wasn't much to learn from his only teacher, Jack Dragna.

If history serves, when troublemaker Bugsy Siegel blew into L.A. like a tornado, he took no prisoners, and Dragna lost his pride and some turf to a Jewish white guy who had the bigger stones of the two men. Siegel had enough *chutzpah* and gravitas to choke a horse. He, like Frank, could only reflect disgust and disdain about anyone who questioned his ability. The difference was that Mr. Siegel was a smart hombre and used his head as he learned from smarter, more knowledgeable men. That couldn't be said for Ignacio Adragna.

Frank never worked in a field where he became someone you'd call professional, like a bartender you'd hire to provide a service at a party. That would be work and Frank didn't like work. He learned all of that as a footman, bar bouncer and doorman. Those were not the positions he wanted out of life. Sure, some paid him to bury someone, but that was different and he was crude and rough at that. Frank was only astute enough to do what he was told. He was more like his mentor, Jack Dragna, who no doubt had a very similar background.

Conversationally, Frank was fine when you were listening and he was telling a story about what he and someone else accomplished—after berating and beating some character silly. On rare occasions, he'd listen, but he was only doing it to learn something that was important to him.

He was not ignorant, but realized men's weaknesses and fears and decided that he would play their fears to the hilt. As long as people accepted his machinations and held him in esteem, Frank was winning.

It was only when he was confronted with creative thinking or the need to solve a problem by the likes of Frank De Simone or Johnny Roselli (his personal nemeses) that he became enraged. He was out of his bullshit element and had to face reality. He couldn't compete with these men and on their level. That frosted his nuts and made him the man he was, dissatisfied with his lot in life. Accordingly, he leveraged himself to the likes of Jimmy the Weasel Fratianno, another who, like himself, was a mouth that roared akin to Joe Pesci's character, Nicky Santoro, a feisty nut job character in the movie "Casino." Ironically, Santoro was supposedly based on a real-life thug known as Anthony "the Ant" Spilotro, whom Frank Bompensiero would team up with later in life. Both were known to have participated in the unsolved murder case of Tamara Rand in San Diego.

On the ladder of notoriety, Frank was the only crime face in town. Even the Adamo and Matranga brothers had more name-dropping connections, but they didn't have Frank's bullheadedness to put his head down and charge, always obeying the familia capo even if he didn't like it. But he'd let him know it, as well. Besides, Frank was also made a *Consigliare* (counselor/advisor) and was supposedly held in high esteem by family members and they weren't. The elders listened to Frank...so did the FBI. But, that comes later.

This attitude left the familia uneasy and wary. They knew Frank to the core. They would point him in the direction and he would kill. But, Frank was a worry. They had to wonder, *What if he went off his rocker, like Joe Adamo crazy, and tried to kill everyone around?*

✳ ✳ ✳

Frank was prone to petty crimes as a youth. That was the easy way and maybe the only way he knew, be it theft, drugs, or the like. But every criminal at one time or another could say that. We, as members of the human race, have to accept and recognize that a percentage of people are inclined to be thieves, robbers, rapists and murderers. By the percentages, that made sense. Frank's ego was fed only when people started to talk about his activities—committing crimes and staying out of jail. When the public didn't have any respect for his efforts, it ate at him.

Later in his life, after he was released from San Quentin, there was a certain cadre of groupies, who, if you will, uplifted his spirits and did the homage thing for him. On a bi-weekly basis, they met for lunch at Johnny Tarantino's Restaurant in Point Loma. Frank would in effect hold court there. He'd have his favorite lunch of fresh crab drizzled in olive oil with fresh lemons and minced parsley garnish on top and a sprinkle of sea salt and pepper. And, *voila*, he became king.

With his small entourage, he would tell tall tales of the old days in the mob to a contingent of wannabe's who sat in awe of the aging walrus. They wanted to hear Frank tell them his stories. To them, he was credible. They wanted to

The Niputi ...the Nephew

be able to swear that Frank Bompensiero was connected as part of the notorious Mafia and wanted to play cozy with them.

How did they know? Did Frank tell them? Absolutely not! I may have had opinions about Frank and his big mouth, but I'd bet that he would never openly discuss any of his connections or affiliations with anyone. That was not Frank. He just allowed people to assume or he'd rant about whom he knew.

People, I learned, in general were like that. Be they Jack Armstrong of the FBI, some officers at First National Bank, or senior officers in the military. They all wanted to rub up against Frank's weird ideal of celebrity or secrets he knew. Frank played that to the hilt, but to my knowledge no one ever asked him the direct question, nor would he ever admit it had he been asked. To him, it would be like a stranger walking up to him and asking the following question and expecting an answer: "Is it true that your mother puts out?" It just wasn't going to happen. Although, looking back at it now, thirty-five years later, such seems silly. It wasn't then.

The liquor business changed dramatically after the sixties as the world turned. The old-school thoughts and moral pressures started to disintegrate. City and state bureaucracies loosened their laws, protocols and procedures.

Conversely, the state's laws seemed to reflect the need by the public for more skin. When I was a kid, we tried to sneak into the burlesque shows and get to see some ladies taking it off. There was a theater on "F" Street called the "Hollywood Theater," which was the hottie show for San Diego burlesque. However, when I returned after four years in Europe, the whole scene of blue-nose pasties on boobies was gone. San Diego for one had been liberated. Take it off—all off— was in. The nudie renaissance occurred.

What about the vice squad, ABC enforcers and religious outcries? I came back to bare breasts, bump and grind and then, within a few months, it was muff city. Full-naked dancing was "in vogue, and in good taste," according to the revised laws and regulations.

The moral code of the California populace had changed and the same guys who took a little to look the other way a few years earlier were now sitting at the front tables with their tongues wagging and enjoying the show.

The liquor business was a demanding drain on the body and one's family life. Most of the owners I knew were much older and were tired. Those who didn't get in and out but tried to beat the system were over the hill or dead.

Although many believed Frank was a knowledgeable individual, most actual busines people didn't. They took his antics with a grain of salt but kept their mouths shut. A.J. Kahn and his sons were one such Jewish business family. I point out Jewish because as a rule in my company Frank spoke as a bigoted person who seldom had any couth regarding another person's religion or heritage unless they had power and could do him harm. Because of his comments to me on a number of occasions, I always wondered how he ever got into business with the Kahn family in the Algiers. An associate of the Kahns, Nathanial Rosenberg, was also Jewish and in a later chapter, you will learn about Frank's contriving with Jimmy Fratianno on an extortion agenda for Nate in 1969.

Throughout the years preceding Frank Bompensiero's incarceration, minimally 1922 through 1955, he became an experienced criminal with all the word entails. You name the crime and most likely Frank did it. However, procecutorial indictments were few and far between. He freewheeled and had his hand in any action he could find.

When he got out of prison in early 1960, he was pulled into another Hollywood scam. This was also with his friend and buddy Jimmy Fratianno and Frank found himself up to his rear in doing another Mafia-related business deed. Supposedly, some in the Italian community took umbrage over the hit show "The Untouchables." The Desilu production operated by Desi Arnaz labeled the Italians as gangsters and thugs in the shoot-em-up, bang-bang TV series.

According to Jimmy Fratianno in "The Last Mafioso," after he became a government witness sometime in 1978, he blabbed as how he was directed to take action and put a hit on Desi Arnaz. This word came from Johnny Roselli, Sam Giancana's boy. Roselli supposedly told Fratianno that Frank Bompensiero had been given the contract and that Fratianno should work with Frank. The hit, of course, was never carried out.

However, during one of my dinner conversations with Ziu Chiich he brought up Jimmy and him talking about doing the contract on Desi Arnaz. He said, "I didn't like the idea to whack him and told Jimmy. I liked some of the work that Desi did with Lucille Ball. But business is business, Niputi. So, we had to wait and see if we got the 'Do it' order. Lucky for Desi, nothing ever came of it."

CHAPTER 19

WEST COAST BOYZ

The men who came to dinner that night in 1948 were just Dragna team players who subsequently grew in the organization. They rose in terms of stature and notoriety individually and might have had an impact on crime specifically, but not in the modern era. For example, the Black Panthers of the sixties--political terrorists or Latino gangs of L.A. who allegedly control the streets. Dragna's guys basically stuck to old hustles. Some of them were called before the 1950 U.S. Senate committee investigating organized crime in America, headed up by Senator Estes Kefauver of Tennessee. By that time, I was an adult and not much escaped me. When I questioned mobster-related editorials in the paper or saw things on the TV, I asked my father. He gave me his brief opinion. He knew that if he didn't, I'd search long and hard before I'd shut the door on the story.

✷ ✷ ✷

Frank De Simone was originally from Colorado, and a lawyer by trade. I wondered why such an intelligent man could be enticed into joining the Dragna family. In my juvenile years, many things like that were mysterious. Later in life I learned that no matter their intellect, men would do anything for self-aggrandizement, greed, or power. It was especially perplexing to me when I discovered in talking with De Simone that his father and siblings were all professionals in education or medicine.

The Niputi ...the Nephew

Through years of observation, I learned that the majority of those who chose a criminal career path unfortunately lacked the capacity to think rationally. Okay, a few were well-read and a few might have been brilliant. I can't recall their names, but they were most likely anomalies.

As *Ziu Chich* told me while I visited him in San Quentin: "Niputi, ninety percent of the stooges in here are fools who stole fifty dollars from a gas station while using a gun. Armed robbery will get them years in this hotel."

Prior to the industrial revolution and the great immigration, most of those who became criminals had never gone to school, if only for a few years, because of simple economics. They liked to eat and they found work. Most were poor readers or couldn't read at all and, like Frank, didn't have money, clothes, cars or broads, so they took the quickest route to satisfy their base desires. They shoved their way through the populace with fear and intimidation backed by an equalizer—a pipe wrench or the like. At the other extreme were the Bernie Madoffs of the world who, though intellectual, fell to greed and depravity. His actions wreaked more havoc on people that most hard-core criminals ever did.

Frank De Simone was an anomaly as well—a thinker and, some might say, a Renaissance man, well-educated yet mentally flawed. He sought education and power to balance his own physical and emotional weaknesses. His family also carried a stain.

His father's nephew, Tom De Simone, was a known enforcer for New York's Lucchese Family. That information impressed Jack Dragna, who periodically tried to keep the East Coast families happy so they'd stay out of his meager Los Angeles business holdings. Dragna desperately wanted De Simone to become a member of his family. To do that, De

Simone would have to prove he had the balls. That meant doing the dirty deed—killing someone.

Smart as he was, De Simone failed at becoming a killer. Even with the help of the "Bud Abbott and Lou Costello" twins—Frank Bompensiero and Jimmy Fratianno —Frank De Simone couldn't get it up and couldn't get it done. I wasn't surprised to hear that he couldn't take anyone down. *Ziu Chich* said in passing, when we discussed his former boss, "De Simone was a *mala minichiatha* (sick prick). Jimmy "The Weasel," the mouth that roared, however, never mentioned De Simone's weakness in his tell-all book, *The Last Mafioso*.

Noted crime author Allan May, who has written many tales of the American Mafia, cited De Simone as part of a team that failed to kill Mickey Cohen, protector of Benjamin "Bugsy" Siegel—Mr. Las Vegas. Numerous reporters picked up the story and ran with it as if it were gospel. How did they know? Did Frank, Jimmy and De Simone call a press conference? Not likely! Yeah, I know people talk, but that wouldn't cut it for the likes of the Dragna family. However: it begs the question, what were Mr. May's sources for this claim? Mickey Cohen?

From the late '40s to the mid-1950s, De Simone represented many of Jack's boys, including Jimmy Fratianno for extortion and Frank Bompensiero on bribery charges. Both of De Simone's efforts failed as Jimmy schlepped behind the walls of Folsom Prison and Frank spent five years north of Alcatraz in San Quentin.

Win or lose in court, De Simone was Jack Dragna's organizational attorney and for that Dragna paid handsomely for the privilege of having him around. Dragna, a crude but successfully shrewd capo, noted an air of refinement in De Simone. He was smooth and an intellectual who could explain things to Dragna when his normal circle of associates couldn't.

Dragna also noted that De Simone had an underlying need for the glitz and glamour of Hollywood and Vegas. Jack introduced him to "Handsome Johnny" Roselli. Roselli was the well-known insider of the Sam Giancana top-ranked *Mafia Familia*, and under Sam's protective mantel Jack found it beneficial to bond with both men.

De Simone was therefore encouraged to bond with Roselli.

Roselli was the mob's man in Hollywood and Las Vegas and skimmed as much as he could from a variety of Vegas spots where the East Coast families had loaned money to casinos for operating capital. Roselli made sure that he got his cut, as well as a share for "Da Chicago Boyz." That kept everybody happy.

Roselli was well-known by those in Hollywood movie production circles as well. He became the source between the dark side of capital investment when movie funding was required. In time, his social acceptance prompted him into a couple of high-roller gambling schemes that bilked notables like Harry Karl, shoe magnet and husband of Debbie Reynolds, and other stars for millions of dollars. In time, Roselli served several years in prison for his illicit activities.

For years, the federal government frowned on gambling outside of Las Vegas. Then somehow, over the years, Indian tribes of the Old West were emancipated. Those who could would build and operate gambling casinos. One might ask, where did the tribes obtain the money to finance their casinos? The government? I don't think so. Maybe Bank of America? That would be a stretch.

I'll bet a search of federal banking rules and regulations won't divulge protocols for cash loans from banks to

Las Vegas gambling casinos or to finance the gambling operations on Reservations. Some people even asked, "How did the casino consortiums get legal (clean) investment capital? Possibly a union loan.

They are historically private loans authorized by the union hierarchies to increase profits for the pension funds of themselves and their members. They can, I believe, lend to whomever they wish, just as you can. But, it has to be disclosed so the auditors have a paper trail for the IRS. As long as it is legitimate and recordable on the union's books with attested-to sound collateral—the building and a signed loan—it is most likely available through the lending institution.

But, someone always asks, "Who controls the unions?" I'd say simply honest, hard-working men and women in the trenches who care about doing the right thing by American labor. They have the power united to throw out any bum leaders they want. And, if that becomes a problem, then the Justice Department might lend them a hand, if it doesn't get too politically controlled.

Hell, unions are the backbone of our country. They saved men, women and children from slaving away twelve hours a day in sweat shops. Their workers saved the Red, White and Blue. Unions in the post-Roosevelt era were affiliated with the American Federation of Labor-Congress of Industrial Organizations—AFL-CIO, the United Auto Workers—UAW, and the Teamsters among others. Most Democratic presidents, including Franklin Roosevelt, courted the unions because their members were the blue-collar substance of America's industrialization. They were our economic power base and numbered in the millions. They carried a big stick at the voting booth, which in time became part of the seedier side of American political life.

In the past, Las Vegas operated as the skim cash capital of the world and generated millions in "black money dollars" that fed the family. That was until successful businessmen—industry giants/multimillionaires, like Howard Hughes, et al, MGM Grand, and others— came to town and built some huge casinos and changed the landscape of Las Vegas forever.

Before this happened, however, most untaxed cash "black money" must have fallen off the back of trucks to make loans, help control employee unions, and to provide steadfast enforcement. You can guess who that was . . . and it wasn't the federal government. However, as an investigator for the USAF Inspector General, I can attest to a curious mission in 1984 involving black money.

We were directed to visit and evaluate the U.S. government's Satellite Control Facility operation, which sat in a stone white multi-story building in Sunnyvale, California.

Even with top-secret security clearances and crypto-plus adds, we were denied access to many offices of the facility. Each floor belonged to a separate entity of the government, Air Force, Army, Defense Department and CIA. Although all apparently seemed in order, we could not verify/validate any information because we were not allowed entry to the individual sites. It was like auditing an account without a bona fide record of expenses. Our random check of reams of computer-generated documents revealed hundreds of millions of dollars coming from unknown sources and going to a variety of sources that were not tied to any federal budget source codes.

Shaken by the revelation, our team of seven officers gathered and verified our data and validated it with the unit's commander, who disavowed any knowledge of the findings.

Subsequent information about our query for direction was received from the USAF Inspector General—a three-star general. We were told to document the findings and return to base. The "black money" tracking was never spoken about again. What does that tell you? Ask yourself, where does the untraceable or black money come from and where does it go? Is there a "black world" within the bowels of the bureaucratic government as some speculate. Nah, it's squeaky clean. That is why we have Inspector Generals in almost all government departments.

※ ※ ※

Untraceable money is the basis for involvement by *familia* members in many major cities of the country as in West Coast operations. De Simone was encouraged to climb toward the top of the food chain in the Dragna operation due to power and money, black money no doubt. It was untraceable, non-taxable and allowed you to buy whatever you wanted. Eventually De Simone accepted Jack's invitation to become a member of the family. Whether he had to perform some modified ritual is open to question. One as astute as De Simone knew there was always a way to create a protocol to get around anything. He was a thinking lawyer!

De Simone and Roselli's stature in the organization ate at Frank Bompensiero. Everything he did with or for these two men failed. Frank was trapped in the sewer of the underworld, swimming in the vitriol of his unfulfilled desires. Ultimately that affected his attitude and loyalty.

Frank's apparent hatred for De Simone was surpassed only by fear as he watched him climb the organization's ladder unabated. Eventually De Simone won the total trust of Jack Dragna, his sons and other Mafia clan brothers.

For over thirty years, Bompensiero devoted his life to Jack Dragna. For Frank, Dragna was more than a savior and mentor; their bond was as strong as blood. The Mafia was everything to Frank—his meal ticket and his family.

I can imagine how devastated Frank was when less than eight years after that 1948 dinner at my parents' house, Jack Dragna died of a heart attack and Frank De Simone succeeded Jack as new head of the L.A. family.

The other dinner guest, Girolomo "Momo" Adamo, achieved a modicum of success and notoriety, but his inglorious ego coupled with a nasty temper and testy wife sealed his fate with almost humorous finality. Originally a member of the Kansas City organization, Adamo arrived in Los Angeles in the early 1930s. After meeting with Dragna, Adamo rose quickly and was second only to Jack in the organization.

By comparison, Frank Bompensiero arrived in L.A. early in 1922. Though he hoofed it for Jack for years, Frank never progressed beyond a soldier. Occasionally they called him *caporégime* (head soldier), but that was little more than window dressing for the aging mobster and speaks volumes about Bompensiero's lack of ability to adapt, and his value as a leader to Dragna. Frank mentally grew very little over the years.

Leadership is tough and competitive. As a two-star Air Force general said to me when I received the flag of command of a 750-man squadron at Tinker AFB, Oklahoma, "Colonel, be proud of your achievement. Few are meant to lead, most can only follow."

As times changed, the Mafia needed to develop a new type of business acumen. That's why Jack sent Momo south to San Diego, to tighten up the purse strings. Momo purchased a "white guy image" business, the Gay Paree bar on Fourth Avenue. He also started tapping into known resources of available assets— money lending, music service, wire service and extortion, to name a few.

One of Momo's first targets was Tony Mirabile, an enigmatic Sicilian who played the gentlemen businessman. After making thousands of dollars in "black money," non-taxable cash, Mirabile moved his nightclub operation from Mexico to San Diego, where the Italian community offered him a more rewarding home, and where he could take advantage of those needing seed money for their business enterprises.

Momo reached out to Mirabile, got close to him and introduced him to Jack Dragna. He also assisted Mirabile in moving some (laundered) cash into the pockets of needy Italian bar owners for notes payable to Mirabile in return. This was a great money exchange, because the juke boxes again regenerated cash. This raised Momo's stock with Jack.

Mirabile appreciated Dragna's power on the political and bureaucratic scene. He also liked Jack's avant-garde lifestyle. The two men shared fancy food, black money and attractive women. Mirabile forked over big bucks for Jack's approval so he could claim Mafia influence and power. Prior to that, he had none!

Poor dumb Frank had no choice but to help Momo Adamo become familiar with the San Diego operation and help him enforce Dragna's ground rules. Besides, Momo was a decent sort as Mafia criminals go. Frank liked him and his wife, Marie, and partied with them.

Years later, as an adult, I had occasion to meet Momo. He seemed like a reasonable guy, except when it came to his wife, Marie, a flashy clothes hog who acted like a chippie and a flirt. This didn't sit well with Momo. The two lovebirds acted like vultures during breeding season. They were constantly at odds.

It's not very exciting to write that 1959 was a bad year for Momo and Marie. Their ongoing battles led to a particularly intense argument during which Momo grabbed a .32-caliber pistol, a lady's gun, and shot her. Thinking he'd killed her, Momo turned the gun on himself and pulled the trigger. As the fates are fickle at times, Momo died.

That's what happened, but as cited by crime author Ed Reid, a "police informant" says that Frank De Simone raped Marie in the presence of her shocked husband, Momo, and this was done to show Momo who was boss.

Adamo was allegedly shamed. Although he failed in his attempt to kill his wife, he succeeded in committing suicide. My opinion was that it never happened. Knowing De Simone, I'd say he didn't have the balls and, second, Momo Adamo would have physically taken some action. The public is eager for trash talk and "make-believe notoriety." People want to be shocked, and besides it sells books. As those who spoke Sicilian and knew those in the Mafia would say, "*Iddi sapiri nienti! Bastante!*" They know nothing! Enough said.

✱ ✱ ✱

Meeting Frank Bompensiero as a child in 1948 left an indelible impression on me. I still retch at the thought of him and the bad taste stuck in the corner of my memory. I never liked him, but I couldn't just blank him out; as soon as I thought he was gone from my life for good, he'd show up again.

CHAPTER 20
HOLLYWOOD WISHES

In 1954, Joe DiMaggio married Marilyn Monroe, and Gamal Abdul Nasser became the leader of Egypt. The U.S. Supreme Court ruled segregation was illegal. Lockheed Aircraft unveiled the F-104 Starfighter and "On The Waterfront" was voted best picture of the year. That same year, Dad called from "The Spot" and invited me to take a ride to Hollywood with him and Uncle Frank. He was going to see some movie star about a business proposition. To this hot-to-trot fifteen-year-old, it sounded exciting. It would be. It would also add fodder to another side of life's reality.

✻ ✻ ✻

Sometimes, Uncle Frank didn't like to travel alone if he didn't have to. Frank didn't trust most people, especially the man he was going see. On occasion, and for moral support, he invited his brother along. I listened as Frank said to Dad in Sicilian that he had to see Johnny Roselli.

Frank said, "Some actor's got a problem and needs help, so they called me in. It was probably too tough a job for Johnny. Either that or he didn't want to get his hands dirty, the cocksucker! But as the Hollywood and Vegas point man, we have to run all business through him."

Sitting in the backseat of Frank's green Caddy, I learned that *Ziu Chich* felt it would be financially worth his while. However, he had to stop off and talk to Johnny and get the address before going to the actor's office. We drove into Hollywood and pulled up in front of an office building. Frank asked us to wait in the car. When he came out, he was fuming. He got into the driver's seat and slammed the door, yelling, "That son of a bitch Roselli, the dirty cocksucker! He's trying to cut in on the deal. He's already talked to Brasselle."

"Brasselle?" asked Dad.

"Yeah, Keefe Brasselle, the guy who did the *Eddie Cantor Story* last year. You know."

"Yeah, yeah," Dad replied.

I recalled seeing the movie too.

Frank continued, "Supposedly, some studio guys, producers or whatever, have been leaning on Brasselle and he needs some help, and I was called in. If I know Roselli, he wants to smooth-talk the guy because he knows the players involved. Sammy, this Roselli is a real asshole with his fancy duds and his relationship with Sam Giancana. Big fuckin' deal! That SOB will try and play both ends against the middle. That's the kind of prick he is. Knowing him as I do, I'll end up with the shit-end of the stick."

Dad didn't respond. Frank pulled in behind Roselli's Cadillac convertible and we followed him to Keefe Brasselle's office. When we arrived, Roselli led the way as if he knew his way around. We entered the foyer of the office and a beautiful secretary sat waiting for no one in particular. Roselli said, "Please advise Mr. Brasselle that Roselli and associates are here to see him."

"Please sit while you're waiting." We all took chairs and I sat next to Dad. Frank took a lone chair on the other side of the room. He was still huffing. A moment later, the main office door swung open and out walked Keefe Brasselle, just like in the movies, black hair and big, welcoming smile. He addressed Roselli directly.

"Hi, John. Please come in."

We all got up and followed Johnny into the office as Brasselle walked around and settled behind his huge desk.

"Please relax, look around, be comfortable. Care for any refreshments? Maybe a soda for the teenager?"

With the secretary following behind, she responded to whatever her boss suggested. Dad gave me a smile and I accepted the offer. I was the only guest to do so. Keefe said he would have his special, which turned out to be a puke-green colored malt drink. It left a mark on his upper lip with his first sip.

After the prelims he said, "I'm sure glad to have you gentlemen here. Mr. Roselli tells me that you, Frank, are somewhat of a problem-solver. I sure can use one."

Frank smiled and huffed, "Roselli is right about that, Keefe. He and I run in the same circles and have similar acquaintances. I've been associated with him for years."

At Frank's remark, Roselli quickly interjected, "Keefe, Frank hails from San Diego. He brought his brother Sam and Sam's son Joey along for the ride because they're great fans and wanted to meet you."

With that, Brasselle turned his wholesome grin on, got up, drink in hand, and walked around the office showing us his "I love me" wall, which of course included photos of him with various politicians, studio dignitaries and beautiful young women.

Admittedly, I was a starstruck teenager, but Brasselle's bragging, coupled with Roselli's pandering, rang phony. *What bullshit*, I thought. *Roselli was just a mouth with ears.* That was just the first lesson I'd learn that day.

Roselli said, "Keefe, with your permission, I'll summarize your situation to Frank to save time and if you've got any added comment, please jump in."

"By all means, Johnny," Brasselle said.

Johnny quickly recapped some events that he said affected Keefe's current plans for promotion and future movies. "His long-term plans have him linked to a studio-level executive production with CBS. However, there are some unnamed people of the establishment that are standing in the way and are in a position to do Mr. Brasselle harm in terms of his future." I watched Brasselle nod in agreement several times as Roselli spoke.

Suddenly, Frank broke into the conversation. "Johnny, I think I've got the lay of the land. So, what would you like me to do Mr. Brass...elle?" Frank stretched the pronunciation of Keefe's name in a strange way. Then, after removing the huge Bering Immensa cigar from his mouth, he said, "How soon do you want to remedy the situation? Mr. Brass...elle. Do you want these guys temporarily removed or permanently fixed?"

There was a slight pause as Frank waited for an answer. Brasselle's face scrunched up like he'd just bitten into a lemon. Roselli saw it and winced.

Everyone in the room, except Frank, acted in varying degrees of discomfort. Frank, however, seemed unconscious to the obvious. He had delivered his message and was done. From the look on his face, he just needed an answer.

It was Brasselle who finally broke the pregnant pause. "Johnny, I think that Mr. Bompensiero might have misconstrued our intentions. Possibly, you were not clear in your preliminary discussions, although I felt as if you were right on target."

"Johnny was right on target to me too, Mr. Brasselle," Frank said.

"That's possible, Keefe," Johnny said, color disappearing from his face. "Frank probably misunderstood."

"Bullshit! You were clear enough!" huffed Frank. "In my business, the fix is either temporary or permanent. I can do both and Roselli knows that. So, let's cut with all the Mr. Nice Guy monkey business and pretend crap. We all know why I'm here."

I watched as Brasselle's hand slid stealth-like beneath his desk. Then he said, "Well, assuming there has not been any misunderstanding, John, I think we can conclude that I will most likely divert my problem-solving into another direction. You know, one has to be fluid with planning. But, I appreciate your time and trouble, Frank. Thank you for coming. Then he turned to Dad and me and said, "Sam, Joe, it's always a pleasure to meet one's fans."

As if requested by a mind communicator, his secretary entered the room.

"Mr. Brasselle, your one-thirty is here."

"Thank you, Mary," Brasselle said, standing. He came around the edge of his desk and offered his hand. "Our guests were just leaving. If you gentlemen will excuse me, I have another meeting."

We departed Brasselle's office and saw that, indeed, another well-dressed man and woman were standing in the foyer. As soon as we left the building, Johnny tapped Frank on the shoulder.

"You really fucked that up, Frank. What, are you crazy? Mr. Brasselle is a gentleman and you shocked the shit out of him. 'Temporary or permanent fix.' You talk to everyone just like you're addressing some schmuck in Dragna's goon squad."

Frank turned ugly with rage. "Go fuck yourself, Roselli. I knew you were going to screw this one up for me. You know if it wasn't for you-know-who you'd be looking at the sky, cocksucker."

Frank concluded by putting his thumb and fingernail to his front teeth and flinging it out at Roselli, signifying the deepest disrespect a Sicilian can pay to another—he wished him death. Frank turned and headed for the car. Once inside, he let go with a barrage of cursing Roselli.

"That dirty S.O.B. I ought to clip that fucker. That phony bastard." He started the car and peeled away from the curb. On the ride back to San Diego, Frank went on and on for about a half hour as I recall. I fell asleep with Frank still bitching.

"I knew that prick Roselli was going to fuck me out of this deal. Now you know why I don't like the sonofabitch and don't trust him at all. That prick!" Dad said nothing.

Dad and I never discussed the trip again, except maybe to laugh at his brother. On occasion when Dad was faced with a problem, I would toss out a *Ziu Chich's* problem-solving solution for Dad, "Hey Dad, regarding this problem, do you want a temporary or permanent fix?"

He'd smile, laugh and shake his head. "What in the hell are you gonna do? He's my brother and sometimes he's a little *Meshugana* (crazy)."

As an interesting side note, I learned later in 1968, while Dad and I were getting ready to open the Star & Garter, about a novel making the talk-show circuit and it was loaded with big-name reviews. The author's thinly-veiled "tell all" painted a picture of the underlying crassness of Hollywood, including a high-powered network executive who had busted the author's chops. The novelist covered the whole menagerie of phonies, fags and wannabes who do it all for a screen test. The book was *The Cannibals*. The author was Keefe Brasselle. I read *The Cannibals* and enjoyed the venue and my early-life recollections of meeting Brasselle and Johnny Roselli.

As a transient comment, subsequent research revealed a clip from a Wikipedia comment on Keefe Brasseelle "Hollywood star": "Brasselle had a close friendship with CBS executive James Aubrey. Brasselle started his own production company and Aubrey granted Brasselle's company three television series without any previous script, pitch or pilots. The insider-chicanery resulted in a lawsuit against Aubrey and Brasselle launched by CBS shareholders. There were rumors that Aubrey had no choice in the matter due to threats from the Mafia, with which Brasselle was known to be connected."

Well, I'll be darned, somehow I was part of a Mafia discussion as a young lad and didn't even know it.

CHAPTER 21

VEGAS DREAMS

In May of 1960, several things happened in the world that made a lot of people nervous. Cuba and the USSR exchanged ambassadors; the USS Triton circled the globe in eighty-four days, mostly under water; Israel's Mossad captured Adolph Eichmann; Sputnik IV was launched by the Russians; and, on Monday, May 16, Frank Bompensiero was released from San Quentin prison. Dad met him as he walked those last few freedom paces out the side gate.

✳ ✳ ✳

Dad involved himself in the Thriftco operation as explained in Part III, so Frank would have a place of employment upon his parole. Dad's intentions were to provide Frank a place to go, get on his feet and get on with life. Oh yeah, and to relieve me of my seeing-eye dog marathon taking Frank around the city. As I recall, it was in September or October when Dad called one morning around nine-thirty. This was quite unusual.

"Hey Joe, you want to take a ride to Vegas? I have to meet someone and I'd like the company. We can spend the night and have a great dinner and maybe see a show. We'll come back tomorrow."

"What's up, Dad. Got something going on?"

"I'll tell you when I see you. It's fairly important." That was all I needed to know.

We still lived in the big house in Point Loma when I received Dad's call, and I had invited my good buddy Patrick to spend the night.

"Sure, Dad. But Pat Montgomery spent the night and he's still here."

"What the hell! Bring him along. He's family. We'll have fun."

"Okay. When do you want to leave?"

"As soon as you get down to the Corsair. We'll take off from here in my Cad. It's more comfortable."

Pat was already awake and dressed. I handed him a cup of coffee.

"Hey hombre, Dad wants us to go with him to Vegas. We'll have a ball."

Like me, Pat had been up to his ears in midterm exams. We both figured a break would fit right in. Pat was all grins and eager to go.

We drove around the Naval Training Center and across Harbor Drive, finally cutting east to Front Street. I turned onto Broadway and found a parking spot in front of the Corsair. Dad was parked just up the street and we walked over to his gleaming white Caddy. Moments later, he cranked up his Cad and we were headed for Vegas.

As we drove up Highway 395 toward Bakersfield and the desert, Pat and I talked about school or just enjoyed the scenery. Dad asked Pat if his father was out of Quentin. Pat's father was doing time in San Quentin Penitentiary for an altercation in a bar that resulted in a death and manslaughter conviction. Frank knew Pat's dad in Quentin.

"No Papa Sam. He's still got some time before parole."

We arrived in Vegas and, instead of heading to one of the better casinos, Dad drove to a small gambling joint, "a poor man's casino," down off the strip in the old part of town. Supposedly, the mob owned it. Neither Pat nor I knew why in the hell we were stopping at a creepy joint. It certainly was strange. Later, Dad said Frank wanted him to look at the joint as a possible investment. A former client of his supposedly owned it and wanted Frank to get a piece in payment of an old debt he owed Frank.

Dad introduced us to the manager, then Pat and I gambled a little while Dad walked around, observing the back bar and the action. Dad was subsequently offered a comp'd (no charge) room and could stay for several days. Dad asked if we wanted to stay for the night. Our expression gave him his answer.

We left, and Dad, who was driving, suggested the Flamingo. He dropped us off there and told me to get us some rooms. He drove off to meet someone. I had about a hundred bucks on me and somehow made five or six passes, doubling the bet line as I won. Three passes in a row and I felt hot. I won about two thousand dollars with subsequent numbers and finally decided that's it. I'd won about two grand and passed the dice. I felt the stares from the players as I picked up my chips, tipped the houseman and left.

Later we found out Dad was meeting Uncle Frank.

While waiting for Dad, I purchased a handmade, two-hundred-dollar knitted sweater for Mom and a silver money clip for Dad. I also paid for several more days in the hotel and allowed for expenses. That evening, Frank had a dinner meeting with Dad. Pat and I went to see a show and dinner, courtesy of Vegas.

Dad never liked to gamble except on horse races. He played some cards, poker and an Italian card game called Briscola, but wasn't into casino gaming. After one day, Dad was ready to get back home. He was uncomfortable with

Frank's friends and didn't want to dine with them again. So I bought him a ticket on the next plane out while Pat and I stayed a few days longer, then came home and went back to school.

We had a good time on Vegas money. As for the piece of Frank's action, it never materialized. Nothing happened with the dumpy casino. We never spoke of it again. However, we learned in later years how it all fit. We just didn't know it at the time. Frank later shared a tale with Jimmy Fratianno about a Detroit caper that went sour and how Johnny Roselli, his nemesis, was at the center of a problem resolution.

Supposedly, Frank was going to receive a cash payoff or revolving payoff from a casino in Las Vegas vis-a-vis compensation for a hit Frank performed. He did a YAIGYO (you ask, I give, you owe) thing by clipping some guy for a Detroit mobster. Frank laughed as he bragged about giving the guy a story about having to clip some guy and asked for help because of his blood pressure or some other ruse. The obliging fool helped Frank by digging the grave. But he didn't know he was digging his own grave. When the grave was dug and the guy asked Frank if the hole was deep enough, Frank shot him in the head several times. Unfortunately, Frank had to cover him up. Then when Frank visited his contract employer, he reneged on the cash. Times were tough, and the guy said he could be paid over time from a joint he owned a piece of in Vegas.

It must have been that dump we went to see. At the time I wondered, why would Frank ask Dad to look at the operation. Frank was the all-knowledgeable bar man, remember? This tidbit was further proof of Frank's lack of understanding of the liquor business, The Gold Rail and his primary responsibility for tubing the Algiers. We also learned that the joint Frank asked dad to look at was a shill. The actual place his debtor had a piece of was in the Flamingo. Then all the pieces in the subterfuge fit.

When we got home, I asked Dad if *Ziu Chich* ever got resolution to his problem. He laughed and said, "Frank went to see the Vegas connection and it turned out to be his arch enemy, Roselli, and he told him he would look into the matter."

Subsequently, Frank was still pissed and didn't know whom he could trust. Some months later, while Frank was in Vegas again and ran into a couple of Da Boyz, he learned that Roselli now had a piece of a gift shop in the Flamingo Hotel. Apparently, Roselli apparently made a deal to pick up a piece of their gift shop via some Detroit mobster who had a piece of the shop. Frank knew that Roselli was doing him again. In time, I learned from Dad that Frank said he saw Roselli again after the Vegas venture went sour. Roselli finally told Frank, "I looked into the problem and unfortunately the man couldn't cover the action." Frank again felt screwed by his nemesis Roselli, that fucking Roselli . . ." In time, Frank was sure, Roselli would get his!

Frank never was thrilled knowing Roselli was a buddy of DeSimone and also in the rack with Jack Dragna, but he couldn't do anything about it.

Frank thought Roselli was stuck up because he knew most of the Hollywood crowd, including Sinatra, and walked Hollywood Boulevard like he owned it. According to Frank, Roselli had his nose in the air because all the Jew producers knew he was connected with the East Coast families and couldn't be touched. Frank thought about burying him, but even for killer Frank, that was a no-no.

Roselli was the East Coast operations moneyman in Hollywood and Vegas. But what pissed Frank off was the Keefe Brasselle affair, where Roselli brushed him off like ass wipe. Frank never forgot that sign of disrespect. Unfortunately, Roselli and the new Los Angeles boss De Simone were buddies, and that meant Frank was screwed in the organization. He had nowhere to go except down.

Ten years before this action, Roselli was to be deported because he had never obtained U.S. citizenship. This bit of information must have fallen through the bureaucratic cracks. However, Italy refused to accept Roselli and he stayed in the USA. How you may ask did that occur? Supposedly, Roselli helped the CIA in a foiled plot to kill Castro. Oh yeah! They got the whole story at the local investigative journalist bar headquarters on Broadway.

Yes, America, you can be proud of your U.S. Immigration Service. Eventually, Roselli was convicted of being in the country illegally. Hurray for American justice. Hell, Roselli had already been drafted, served in the Army, done a three-year prison term on a ten-year beef, and nobody knew. The army, the FBI and the bureau who knew everything: Just ask Bobby Kennedy. Even Frank Sinatra, who sponsored Roselli into the Friar's Club, Hollywood's high celebrity in spot. No one knew Roselli wasn't a citizen. Give me a break. He was ordered deported by the INS, but remained in the USA. What the F...? Over! Does something smell fishy to you? Where were our wunderkind ace investigating police, FBI and IRS department gurus? Upholding the rights of honest citizens, I'll bet!

In 1970, just before Dad passed away, Frank became involved with a former associate he knew from Chicago and his *Lo familia* travels. He called him Tony Spilotro, a.k.a. Tony Stuart, who became the man in Vegas to maintain the Midwestern Boyz skim (multiple Vegas Hotels), and act as enforcer when needed. Spilotro also invested his own $70K in a Circus-Circus partnership under the name Tony Stuart, which netted him $700K when it sold in 1974.

With proceeds, he started a loan shark operation with *Ziu Chiich* Bompensiero. Spilotro had connections with Alan Glick, a friend who at one time needed financial help and obtained a loan from millionaire San Diego real estate developer Tamara Rand. Spilotro solicited help from none other than a compatriot in San Diego, Frank Bompensiero. Spilotro wanted to help his buddy Glick and to cash in. Though Tamara Rand was just trying to get her debt paid from Glick, she was already marked for a padded coffin. She was found shot in the head in her home. And when Uncle Frank was questioned by the police, he of course said, "I know nothing." And as usual, the police could prove nothing to indict anyone and so the Boyz walked away, clean, clean, clean.

Later in 1976, the year before Frank took the long journey to oblivion, Roselli was found sunning himself down in Florida. Unfortunately, someone arranged to have him strangled, shot and his legs cut off so they could cram his remains into a fifty-gallon drum. He ended up like a butchered and rendered calf, and someone pushed the drum floating off into the swamp. There in the heat, he decomposed faster than fresh Osso Bucco (veal bone with a hole) in a bath of sulfuric acid.

Who knows what happened? Frank really hated Roselli enough to get it done. But your guess is as good as mine. It could have been the Detroit boys, someone in Vegas, even possibly the CIA. Who knows, but everyone with a beef who wants to get even, or ahead, normally does.

✸ ✸ ✸

On a softer note, some might think that my talking about Frank in the negative was the way he was all the time. Not true. On occasion you run into someone who recognizes my surname and tells you a tale. It isn't long before you know that what you are hearing is the truth. It is, of course . . . all about the people.

That recently happened to me. Caryl, my wife, and I were recently invited to spend an evening at the Aquillas home in Las Vegas to watch a broadcast fight. They had been Caryl's friends for decades. Caryl and Linda sat sipping wine while chef Tony cooked up a storm and we shared stories of the old days prior to watching the Manny Pacquiao loss to James Bradley in the farcical debacle at the MGM Grand. The judges were either bought off or ? Go figure! The bookies must have taken it in the shorts or insured their positions.

In conversation, Tony asked how I kept busy in Vegas. I responded, "I'm writing a memoir about living under the shadow of my uncle, Frank Bompensiero."

"Hell of a guy," said Tony. "He helped me back when."

"Fill me in," I said. It would be nice to add a good deed to Frank's infamous past. Tony poured a Pomegranate-vodka with a splash of soda, took a sip and began.

"Back in the early seventies," said Tony, "I was tending bar at the Fireside Restaurant in Encino. Two brothers owned the dinner house and featured a reasonably priced menu with fresh fish and good steaks. My wife, Linda, and Caryl worked the restaurant as waitresses. As the main bartender, I pushed solid drinks to keep the customers on board and happy. That coupled with a melodic piano bar pumping out velvety smooth New York hits, like Sinatra's "Let's Fly Away", "Feelings" and "Cabaret," and we could really hold a crowd."

The Niputi ...the Nephew

The ice in Tony's glass clinked as he took a swig. "However, when things slowed down, and they always did, the California ponies started up and with the Santa Anita, Hollywood Park and Del Mar racing seasons coming on, I had the yen to shift gears to my first love, bookmaking. Originally from the East, I enjoyed gambling, numbers and other methods of increasing my daily bread.

"When business slowed, the brothers knew I'd be looking for a break from the routine and allowed me time off to make some scratch. I loved to beat all comers on the odds of the game. On one occasion, and over a three-week period, Hal Carlos, a local car dealer, made a few bets of a grand each. I covered them and when I stopped by to see him to collect, he wanted to go for a couple other bets and get even. As you would know, that never gets you even, but digs the hole deeper. With a total of five thousand bucks owing, I had expenses and my vigorous-percentage profits covering the bets were being threatened on both sides.

"When I became persona non grata at Hal's place of business and he wouldn't answer my calls, I got fed up with the gaping hole in my bankroll. Hell, it impacted my ability to generate and cover more bets. Besides, I was getting some heat. I called a friend by the name of Marty Allen. Marty was a straight shooter who knew Hal and had covered some of his action before. When I complained a bit about the current state of affairs, Marty said he thought he might be able to help. But Hal could be tough at times, so Marty would need a smooth talker with muscle and balls. 'Hal will buckle,' Marty said. 'I think we can get your money, Tony. But, it might cost a bit.'"

Tony got up and fixed another drink. When he settled back in his chair he smiled and told me the rest of the story.

Apparently, Tony—no slouch when it came to green—was agreeable because Hal's failure to pay was digging into his stash. Tony says Marty and Frank caught Hal off guard with a ruse of some kind, like buying a car, or whatever. Then each grabbed an arm and almost wrenched them off. Hal wailed in pain and about crapped his shorts. Between Marty suggesting he not welsh on gambling debts and Frank promising a lonely life for an armless man with no tongue and arms, Carlos decided to pay what he could. At the time, he had a thousand on him. Tony was subsequently given the grand and pleased to see some return.

After the dust settled, Tony indicated that was the only money he ever saw. Hal Carlos was worried and no one could blame him, considering that Frank was known as a digger of ditches in Los Angeles. Hal supposedly ran to the cops about the strong-arm business. Of course, he didn't mention any names. Doing that would be signing his death warrant. Frank promised to place him in a deep sleep in the desert before the sun rose if he ever mentioned who made his arms sore.

That was Tony's experience with Uncle Frank, and it was not surprising to me. Like Dad said, "Frank never walked away when someone would refill his always-empty pocket." That wasn't in his nature, especially if someone owed him. As has been mentioned, when Jack Dragna taught Frank about, "You Ask, I Give and You Owe," Frank never forgot. Favor to Tony or not, Frank most likely went back in time for the remainder and took it out in cash or maybe a car. He was not a forgiving negotiator.

CHAPTER 22

ROWDY DAY AT DEL MAR

It was 1957. While I was heading out of San Diego on El Camino Real, The Kings Highway, toward California's premier racetrack, the radio flashed that internationally a couple of guys named Nikita Khrushchev and Charlie De Gaulle became leaders of their respective countries. President Eisenhower ordered Marines into Lebanon, and the U.S. Supreme Court told Arkansas to integrate its schools. Racial equality was slow in coming to America as Martin Luther King called out for tolerance and peace, unaware that his future "I Have a Dream speech" would have a significant impact on American race relations. And me, I headed to Del Mar to play seat usher to throngs of racegoers and enjoy a day in the sun, or so I thought.

✹ ✹ ✹

Taken in by the natural beauty of the surrounding area, I ignored the radio's blare and felt mesmerized by the azure blue waters of the Pacific Ocean lying west of Highway 101. The road nestled between two higher rises in the surrounding land mass and the beautiful track, which had opened in 1937, was just a few feet higher than the adjoining ocean. It surely validated the racetrack theme song and slogan: *Where the surf meets the turf at old Del Mar.*

Hollywood celebrities Pat O'Brien and Bing Crosby, et al, owned the track and enjoyed the thoroughbred and occasional quarterhorse races, along with a multitude of aficionados, which included my parents.

Mom and Dad were two fans who had box seats for the season, and they visited Santa Anita and Hollywood Park as the races moved up the coast. I was heading into my junior year at San Diego State College and searched for local summer employment when my dad came to the rescue. He happened to know a track bartender that knew a guy, who knew a guy who owed him a favor. Before you knew it, I was decked out in the Del Mar employees' Spanish green pants and sun-gold shirt.

As a seat attendant in the clubhouse, I not only made several dollars an hour plus tips, but I met some very nice people and enjoyed watching the races. After a few days of orientation with another seasoned attendant, I felt comfortable with the position. Soon after I started full time, Mom told me they would be coming to the track. I looked forward to Mom and Dad's visit and arranged to swap my regular station for one near them. I knew it would be a great day since all three of us shared a love for the track and horses.

Unfortunately, before the first race I got a message that they couldn't show because Dad had an employee problem. Another cocktail waitress or bartender didn't show for their shift and it really screwed the pooch.

Uncle Frank would be coming instead. He was bringing his friend Jimmy "The Weasel" Fratianno. I was told they would use Dad's seats. As I recall, thunder struck twice that day as three things stood out in my mind. I met Billy *Dui Scarpi Cafoni* (Two Shoes Lout), saw my uncle at his worst, and was enthralled by the beauty and courage of a famous songstress, Lena Horne.

I knew my uncle Frank Bompensiero as a pompous and villainous thug who normally meant every word he uttered. The press continually reported that Frank was a Mafioso henchman, thug and murderer, although never arrested for those crimes. After hearing and reading those repeated allegations over the years, I always wondered why no law existed that punished those in journalistic circles who couldn't prove what they claimed. I definitely believe in freedom of speech, but not freedom of creating the news, since as an arm of the people's influence, they have a responsibility to report facts rather than allegations or suspicions.

However, my thirty-year-long association with Frank validated that he was what was claimed, and a real bad dude. And that came from his mouth on many occasions. I viewed Frank as a Don Rickles look-alike with a vile mouth. Frank, though, was more coarse and much ruder than Rickles' comedic talent.

Frank and his hoodlum sidekick Fratianno arrived before the first race. They were loose and mouthy from too much to drink. I escorted them to the box seats. Soon after they were seated, Frank scanned the area and yelled down to someone walking the grandstand pits, "Hey Shoes, get your ass up here!"

It was a beautiful and light-breezy summer day as Billy, a.k.a. *Shoes*, was idly strolling along the low fence out in the pit. There he and other also-ran handicappers talked, gawked and told lies to each other about who had the best picks of the day.

Shoes heard his name, looked up, recognized Frank and started trotting toward the clubhouse. Although Shoes appeared to be a nice fellow, our first meeting was a put-off. Frank introduced me to Shoes and added, "Shoes, you and my Niputi have something in common. You walk the pits and dream of picking a winner; he walks the aisles and cleans the seats of the high rollers wishing he could be one. Ha."

I turned away embarrassed, thinking that Frank was at his belligerent best and implanted the event in my memory.

By the time Bing Crosby's crooning of the track's song, *Old Del Mar*, concluded the park was full of people and we had a nice turnout of Hollywood celebrities. One of special note was Lena Horne, the beautiful and nationally acclaimed songstress. She, another female associate and several businessmen were entrenched in a celebrity box just in front of and to the left of Mom and Dad's box.

By the mid-fifties, Lena was concentrating her career in nightclubs after having been somewhat blacklisted during the McCarthy years as left-leaning. However, there was no doubt that she was big-time. Her presence caused a lot of attention as her admirers and fans ooh'd and aah'd her arrival. As she strolled in dressed to the nines, wearing her giant Ipana Toothpaste smile and adorned in a flamboyant canary-yellow dress, her surrounding fans cheered. She was definitely a knockout. She topped off her apparel with a broad-billed yellow chiffon parasol hat trimmed in white. She was the favorite of the day, that is, except to Frank Bompensiero and his pal Jimmy, who missed her entrance.

The boys were taking a break and stopped by the bar to celebrate the "sure thing" bet provided by Shoes. They were loud and laughed about their soon-to-win bundle. As they returned to the box, a passing waitress came by and they ordered two more double scotch and waters.

"I don't want my drinks running dry," bellowed Frank as he gave her a five-dollar tip. The waitress no sooner left than two empty glasses were sitting on the stoop, and the men were guzzling their second.

The Niputi ...the Nephew

I was standing in the rear of the box as the first race ended, with Frank losing his "sure thing" bet. His lousy Two Shoes tip ran second and Frank was really pissed. He hadn't bet "across the board" to spread the odds and lost his big-time wager. Conversely, Lena Horne screeched loudly in her unmistakable husky lilt, "Ladies and gentlemen, I picked the winnah. Hoo! Hah!"

Those patrons sitting around her box did not mind her outcry and clapped for the win. They were not surprised by her antics because she was having a fun day. Her pick happened to be a long shot that shoved Frank and Jimmy into the losers' position. Frank didn't like it and didn't appreciate losing. He felt sorry for himself. Frank heard Horne's excitement and bellowed loudly, "Who in the fuck does that nigger bitch think she is?"

A dead hush came over the area and Ms. Horne's box in particular, but no one in the group responded. However, a hundred eyes turned toward Frank with disgust at his vulgarity and racist remarks. Someone in the Horne box also turned and looked back while Lena, the polished professional, didn't even bother to give notice to her attacker.

I must have turned red as several men with Ms. Horne rose, no doubt with retribution in their hearts. She turned toward them and most likely said something like, *Ignore that lout's bigotry. He's nothing but a fool.* Whatever she actually said, they listened. They looked sternly at Frank and sat back down.

Frank, never the meek one, especially with several drinks in him, pushed harder. "If you cocksuckers or your big-mouth lady friend has a problem, come on up and I'll give you what for! Capesh?"

A wide-shouldered, six-foot-four, two-hundred-fifty pound linebacker type in his thirties rose again. Lena

Horne grabbed his shoulder, most likely saying, *Let's not be the ones who make a spectacle of ourselves.*

I leaned forward and spoke into Frank's ear. "*Ziu Cheech*, that is Lena Horne, the singer. You are drawing attention to yourself and my supervisor is heading this way."

"Fuck your supervisor, Niputi. I don't give a shit who he is nor any other pricks with her are. You go tell him for me, if he has a problem then get his ass over here and I'll kick him in the *colognes*."

"Unc, he's got two uniformed police with him. Besides, I don't want to lose my job, *Ziu*."

"Big fucking deal. That's all you do is stand around like a *Strunza (turd)* all day, kissing people's ass."

"I don't see it that way, *Ziu*. This job helps me get through college and Dad got it for me. Maybe you ought to tell him how you feel because you're the one that may cause him to lose his seats."

Frank sneered at my reply. He could never take a retort and mulled it over behind his pig eyes as he saw two armed security guards heading toward my supervisor. He turned to Jimmy and said, "Come on, Jimmy. Let's get the fuck out of this joint. I'll buy you another drink."

"That'll be the day," Jimmy replied. They rose and walked of, carrying their almost-empty second drinks.

As soon as they departed, my supervisor came over to tell me that when something like that happens, I must immediately request security assistance so people of that ilk can be removed from the premises. I nodded in agreement. However, I didn't want to tell him the nut case was my uncle. I was embarrassed enough.

Not surprisingly, Frank didn't even say goodbye when he left. After my shift I went home and during dinner I told Mom and Dad what happened. My Dad shook his head and said, "My brother is crazy. He and Jimmy will always be in trouble."

He then looked at me and said, "I'm sorry. I'll take care of it." I thought to myself, *Poor Dad would never mention the incident to his brother. Besides, what the hell would he say.*

I subsequently learned that Frank's penchant for insulting people with his big mouth at the racetrack was not limited to Del Mar, nor to women or blacks. This time his racetrack run-in was with a person of more celebrity than Lena Horne. It was J. Edgar Hoover, director of the FBI. Jimmy Fratianno was the source of this tidbit in his book *The Last Mafiosa*. However, I confirmed the incident with Frank years later while speaking with him and Dad at the Star & Garter in 1969.

Apparently, Jimmy was with his sidekick Frank at a track in 1948 when the notorious West Coast Mafioso taunted the esteemed lawman to his face. Fratianno pointed out that J. Edgar Hoover was sitting in a box in front of the two men and Frank said, "Ah, that J. Edgar is a punk. He's a fucking degenerate queer."

Supposedly, when J. Edgar heard his name, he turned along with several others in his party and Frank stuck out his chest and said, "Yeah, you heard me, you degenerate."

Later, Frank ran into Edgar in the men's room and the FBI director was astonishingly meek. He reportedly said, "Frank, that's not the way to talk about me, especially when I have people with me."

"Frank's comments," said Fratianno, made him believe that Bompensiero had absolutely little or no fear of J. Edgar Hoover.

Subsequently, in a 1969 conversation in the Star & Garter Go-Go lounge with Dad and Frank present, I asked

Frank directly, "I heard that you had a run-in with J. Edgar Hoover back in 1948 with Jimmy the Weasel. Someone said you called Hoover a queer?"

"No," retorted Frank. "I told that prick he was the government's only queen that I knew. Then, I called him a friggin queer."

My father, hearing Frank's remarks about the incident, added, "It was common knowledge among Frank's friends and associates that Hoover was a queer." Frank then indicated that the organization used the information against J. Edgar just like Hoover used Hollywood's whoring information against Jack Kennedy's clan to keep them in line. "They were the government's mostly crooked bastards, anyway," Frank barked.

It is interesting to note that eighteen years after Hoover died, the FBI—our staunch defenders of law and order—grabbed Frank Buttino, who had been a special agent of the FBI for twenty years. They placed him on leave without pay, removed his security clearance and fired him. This action was taken because he was a homosexual.

The FBI refused to consider his exemplary record and fired him, citing "exploitable sexual conduct." The GLT-Gay and Lesbian Times of San Diego was the source for this information. The above is ironic in that Hoover and his lifelong sidekick Clyde Tolson were alleged to be lovers and were even buried side by side. However, no movies or documentation existed validating that the two men had hot blazing sex together. Frank would say, "They didn't ask the right people."

※ ※ ※

As a fitting end to this vignette, I learned that the stellar American vocalist and great lady Lena Horne passed away quietly in May 2010 at the glorious age of 92. Her memory and great music were my motivation for including Frank's encounter within her in this story. I felt her fans would like hearing about her class and poise.

NIPUTI PHOTO ALBUM

Joe & Mandy Zottolo
"It all started with a Wedding"
(Nov 14, 1937)

See Chapter 3 "Woptown"

The Niputi ...the Nephew

Zottolo Family
(Circa 1924)
Left to right: Dominic, Joe*, Mary, Vito, Frank
*Author's birth father Joe and brothers Dominic and Frank drowned while fishing

See Chapter 3 "Woptown"

Family Bonpensiero
Pvt. USA Sam & Mandy Bonpensiero with Joe
(Circa 1943)

The Niputi ...the Nephew

Time Magazine
(May 1977)
Surprise Announcement
See Chapter 1 "Time Magazine Obituary"

M. V. Giuseppina
(Circa 1944)
See Chapter 3 *"Woptown"*

The Niputi ...the Nephew

Frank Bompensiero
(Circa 1927)
"In the Chips"

Pvt. Frank "Da cigar" Bompensiero
(Circa 1943)

The Niputi ...the Nephew

Frank Bompensiero Family
Mary Ann, Frank & Thelma
(Circa 1942)

Trinacria
Traveling in separate directions
Frank Bompensiero, "Niputi" Joe, and Sam (Turi) Bonpensiero
(26 Jan 1962)
See Chapter 28 "The Camera Lies"

The Niputi ...the Nephew

Wladziu Valentino Liberace
"Mr. Showman"

(Photo Circa 1952)

See Chapter 11 "Manhattan Misstep"

Keefe Brasselle
Actor, Dancer, Singer, Director
(Circa 1954)

See Chapter 20 "Hollywood Wishes"

The Niputi ...the Nephew

Lena Horne
Songstress, Actress, Fine Lady

(Circa 1960)

See Chapter 22 "Rowdy Day at Del Mar"

One of Da Boyz
Aladena James Fratianno "Da Weasel"
Any score, Any time, Anywhere
(Circa 1978)

See Chapters 19 thru 34

More Heavy Boyz
Frank De Simone and Filippo Saco
aka Handsome John Roselli

(Circa 1959)

The Niputi ...the Nephew

1951 Custom Chevy
Birthday Gift (Sweet Sixteen)
Hot Rod Magazine- 12/56 Issue
(Dec. 1956)

Algiers Restaurant

(Circa 1952)

Kahn/Bompensiero Business venture
See Chapter 14 "Corsair Imbroglio"

The Niputi ...the Nephew

*Grand Opening Algiers Restaurant
(Circa 1952)*

Bottom L-up Irvine & Mrs. Kahn, Mother Kahn, Yale & Mrs. Kahn, Leo Patella, Joe "Niputi" & Marie Adamo. Center (L-R) Sam Bonpensiero, Thelma Bompensiero, Spaghetti Joe, Frank Bompensiero, Mandy Bompenisero & Mickey and Ms. Goldfarb Right Side up: Grandmother Maria Bompensiero, Tina, Grace & Joe Corrao, Mary Ann Bompensiero, "One eyed" Frank Dragna and Ms. Patella (Leo's Sister)
See Chapter 14 "Corsair Imbroglio"

Angela Gooding (Kiva)
Queen of the Fan Dance
Hollywood Theater Dancer
(Circa 1995)

Photo provided by Ms. Gooding
See Chapter 25 "Date Night...Scent of a Woman"

Pals at The Spot
Leo Patella & Sammy Bonpensiero
(Circa 1952)
See Chapter 15 "Travels with Leo"

Bompensiero House
2125 Locust, San Diego, CA
(Circa 1957)
See Chapter 16 "House Above the Bay"

Two Goofy Guys

Joe Bonpensiero & Larry Matranga
(Circa 1958)

Tina's Memorable Wedding

*Sam Bonpensiero & Tina Corrao Matranga
(5 August 1961)*

The Niputi ...the Nephew

Joint Family Photo
Sitting: *Lt. Joe Bonpensiero, Anna Maria Bompensiero, Frank Bompensiero*
Standing (Left to Right): *Larry & Tina Corrao Matranga, Thelma Puccio, Patrina D'Acquisto, Sammy Bonpensiero, Grace Corrao, Mandy Bonpensiero, Josephine & Norbert Kirkpatrick.*
(January 1962)

College Graduation Party
L-R Stnd: Frank Marino, Unidentified AF Sgt. Frank Bompensiero,
Patrick Montgomery,
Sammy Bonpensiero, Bartender, Alfred Garcia, Uncle Joe Asaro, Unidentified AF Sgt., Abe Stone
Kneeling: Lt. Bonpensiero ("Niputi")
(January 1962)

The Niputi ...the Nephew

Patrick's II

Built-Owned-Operated
Larry, Tina and Mario Matranga
Gas Lamp, San Diego, CA
(Circa 2011)

Matranga Family
Mario, Kathy, Tina, Larry
Mom-Josephine Matranga, Joe and Grace Corrao Carini, Cindy, Chris
Brianna, Nick, David & Joshua
(Circa 1990)

The Niputi ...the Nephew

Sam "Turi" Bonpensiero
Good Friend, Fine Husband & Great Father
RIP
(April 20, 1970)

Amanda "Mandy" Bonpensiero
Wonderful Mom, My Friend, Best Wife,
RIP
(April 20, 1983)

One Flower Gone
Samantha J. Bonpensiero
(June 9, 1965)

See Chapter 29 "England Getaway"

PART IV
IN THE MIX

CHAPTER 23

FRANK BLOWS IT
....BIG TIME

Frank was bound to screw up, and 1955 was his year. He did so many things without thinking of the consequences that it was bound to happen. In his crime-filled lifetime, he had gotten away with murder—literally. Outside of a brief stint for bootlegging, he never had to pay for the crimes he committed as a mobster, never made restitution for his thieving and robbing, and never was caught for the killing machine he had become for Jack Dragna—just ask the cops. Frank was proud of never having to do time for his "achievements" in the world of crime. There was that minor flap over Prohibition in the Thirties, but no big deal—eighteen months or so was a vacation. But that was petty work. Frank always had aspirations. As with any ambition, there was the element of risk. For Frank, that risk would come clothed in the robes of government bureaucrats with a taste for bribes.

✳ ✳ ✳

Frank met and developed a beneficial relationship with William J. Bonelli, known in crime circles as "Slick Willy Bonelli." Bonelli was a California bureaucrat who was viewed by those not doing business with him on the side as "an honorable man," a man with "upstanding integrity." With his Juris Doctorate in Law, Bonelli reached the pillars of California political society. He was known as a "well-connected politician," and even did a stint as an Assemblyman. In time, and with skillful maneuvering, he would become a greedy, conniving official who gave the honest, hard-working government employees a bad name. Bonelli was also a thief, and on the receiving end of an audacious bribery scheme.

Bonelli saw the lucrative market of vice and corruption that was rampant from Washington, D.C., to the state Capitol in Sacramento. He wanted his share and he wanted it in cash. Frank Bompensiero was introduced to Bonelli via Charles E. Berry, a State Board of Equalization member in San Diego. Frank, always in the market for a safe place to make an easy buck, struck a deal with Bonelli and moved the money through Berry. With Bonelli's sanction, Frank became the go-to man. He was the direct conduit for hard-to-get liquor licenses and funneled bribes to Bonelli. After a time, an "uninformed buyer" who had applied for a liquor license I.A.W. (In Accordance With) licensing procedures, was caught up in the normal bureaucratic delays generated by typical red tape and paperwork so common in government. He complained about the time delays, which could affect his timely purchase of a bar/café license due to the license procurement. This "uninformed buyer" was advised that there was a speedier way to obtain a license. He was referred to Frank Bompensiero, who had contacts that could expedite license approval. He approached Frank, but the singular deal went south and the man didn't pay in cash as previously agreed upon. He gave Frank a personal check.

Frank, in need of his spendable cut, got greedy. He endorsed the man's check with his signature and deposited it in his own bank account. That ensured that the check was easily traceable by any first-year bank clerk back to the endorser, namely Frank Bompensiero. This proved that Frank was complicit in the bribe of a public official and was easily proved to a court and jury.

Years later, Frank would say to me, "Niputi, can you believe I would have walked if I hadn't endorsed the check." So much for his conscience.

The jury convicted Frank of six counts of bribery with seven years for each count. San Diego Superior Court Judge "Hanging John" Hewicker took all of Frank's possessions to pay fines, court costs and the usual. Frank owned two lots in Point Loma and a portion of the Gold Rail's license. That was the first thing to go, and a car and anything of record where Frank's name showed up. All was confiscated. The judge then meted out a prison sentence of six counts of bribery, with seven years for each count. A total of forty-two-years in prison. It started off in Chino State Prison and ended up in Marin County's San Quentin maximum security penitentiary north of San Francisco.

At my father's request, I went north to visit my Uncle Frank at San Quentin and to give him a message. I flew up for a stay of indeterminate duration. Dad also asked me to go to San Jose and meet a friend of Uncle Frank's. The man's name was Salvatore Marino—old-school and connected. I knew Dad respected him or he wouldn't have sent me there. Marino was the CEO of the California Cheese Company and his son Angelo was the company president, who handled the day-to-day operations and was politically connected in and around the S.F. Bay area. According to Dad, he would be an ally to help obtain Frank's parole.

When I arrived at the San Jose airport, I was met by a fellow in his early twenties named Joseph Piazza. He drove to his home and introduced me to his mother, then out to visit his elder brother, a local almond farmer. They were a decent family.

I learned later that the Marinos were mentoring Piazza. I didn't know if that meant for the cheese factory or whatever. We were close in age and had much in common.

Over a two-year period, Piazza and I became friends and shared quite a bit of things, including women. Along the way, Piazza shared his ambitions with me. Joe's parents were Sicilian and he was quite interested in Uncle Frank and admittedly in Frank's *Cosa Nostra*. It was obvious Joe wanted membership in the Mafia.

He said he would help any way he could. I knew what he meant. "Look, Joe, I'm strictly on the periphery of what you speak and that is by choice. My Dad is not affiliated with *Ziu Chichu's bus-i-ness*." However, I told him I would introduce him to my uncle Frank after he was released, but I would not be of use in supporting his baptismal objectives. I didn't go there.

I was warmly received and taken in as a member of the Marino family. And, as was custom, I referred to Salvatore Marino as "*Ziu*" (uncle). I spent several days in the company with *Ziu Marino's* younger son Joey and Piazza. Joey Marino was about thirty— and afflicted with a serious disease, diabetes.

Joey gave us a complete tour of the cheese factory, then next day he took us to the American River and we spent the day water skiing. Finally, we toured the San Francisco sights as well.

Ziu Marino seemed to have a respectful attitude toward my father. Marino also had a reverential view of my Uncle Frank that I did not share. I knew Frank differently. I had come to believe that any homage paid to Frank by businesspeople outside of his Dragna family affiliations was probably more out of fear of him than respect. However, Marino was from a Midwest city—a different family, and was respected. He was one of the few connected businesspeople who made money the old-fashioned way. Regardless of how he viewed my Uncle Frank, I respected Marino. He was a man who had accomplished much since he arrived from Sicily as an immigrant.

A few days later, *Ziu Marino* called me into his office. He gave me a simple message to pass to Frank. Essentially paraphrased, it was: "Have strength. I have made arrangements. Your brother will meet a lawyer friend soon." Before Joe Piazza took me to the San Jose Airport for my departure, Joe stopped at the Marino home. There, Mr. Marino wished me farewell and passed me an envelope. "Joe, please give this to your father with my good wishes."

"I will, and thank you for a warm welcome and hospitality in your fine city."

My visit to San Francisco and with the Marinos would simply be a matter of formality, for when I returned home to San Diego and gave Dad Mr. Marino's note, he handed it to me and said, "Please read it." Basically the note provided a man's name and phone number. I told Dad and he grinned and said fine." I'll take the note" he said.

Unbeknownst to me, it was a gilded invitation/introduction that Dad had been waiting for. He subsequently called the man and made a luncheon appointment with him.

It would only be a few months before Dad asked me if I would join him for a trip to San Francisco. He had to meet an acquaintance of *Ziu Marino's*, an attorney, for lunch.

We headed to San Francisco and met attorney Joseph Alioto at the Fiore D'Italia, a great restaurant where lunch was wonderful, but painful, and cost Dad several hundred dollars for the three of us. We were not provided a menu upon sitting. At Fiore, you ordered whatever you wanted, according to Alioto.

Unfamiliar with their no-menu ordering, Dad and I hesitated and suggested to Mr. Alioto that since he picked the restaurant, he could pick the food. Alioto seemed pleased and proceeded to order. I recalled that we had antipasto of tomatoes and anchovy. A dinner salad and a small *primipiate* of linguini with clams and cream. Delicious. Later, I saw the bill. Tomatoes were three dollars each. Coffee was four-fifty, and this was in the fifties!

During lunch, Dad and Alioto spoke in circles about the San Francisco climes, fishing and the old country. Eventually Dad said, "Joey, do you need to go to the restroom before we leave." I knew he meant, "Leave us alone." As soon as I rose and said excuse me, Dad began speaking in dialect to Alioto, who smiled.

When I returned five minutes later, Alioto was gone and Dad said, "Oh, Mr. Alioto had to leave for another appointment. He said goodbye and it was a pleasure to meet you." Dad rose and started to walk out, and I recalled the small black bag he had brought with him and placed under the table.

"Dad, what about the bag?

"*Lo Sinistru!*"—It's gone!"

There was no doubt the bag contained a Sicilian goodwill gesture of *pane*—bread, the green kind. *Sure it did.*

A few years later, in December of 1959, after another trip to visit Uncle Frank, Joey Piazza and I discussed taking a vacation south of the border. I address this trip as a side note since it speaks to the depth and breadth of Frank Bompensiero's relationships south of the border. We spent a month in the southern climes of Mexico City, Guadalajara and Acapulco.

With the exception of my parents knowing where we were going, no one else knew. However, as we disembarked in Mexico City's airport, the terminal loudspeaker announced that the Americano passenger known as Joseph Bonpensiero—me— had a phone call at the customer service center. Piazza and I looked at each other and wondered: *What in the hell? Who died?* At the service counter I introduced myself and showed an ID, and a finely dressed gentleman walked up as the counter attendant spoke my name. The man introduced himself as Jacobo Guss, a local businessman who wanted to meet Frank Bompensiero's nephew.

I was alarmed and somewhat apprehensive as he shook my hand and I introduced him to Piazza. He made it known that he was at our disposal for our trip and if he could do anything for us, he would consider it an honor. I said, "Thank you, but for now we want to get to our hotel and rest after the flight."

"Of course, of course," he replied. "Let me retrieve your bags and I'll take you to the Presidente Hotel. That is where you are staying, correct? It's a fine choice." We took him up on his offer. Let me say that our two-week stay in Mexico City was wonderful.

We were introduced to many available nightspots by Mr. Guss and had dinner one evening with his wife and children at their villa. Then, off to Guadalajara and New Year's Eve in Acapulco. Wow, what a trip. I guess Jacob Guss knew Frank well and, through his hospitality to us, paid Frank Bompensiero some respect.

When Frank obtained an early release from prison, much to the surprise of family and local law enforcement,

I remembered the luncheon with Alioto where Dad accomplished two things; set the wheels turning for his brother's release and taught me that even the impossible can be had for a price.

Dad had done what he could to influence people who could influence parole boards. Was this illegal? No. It's just the way the world turns. It's a form of negotiation to achieve one's objectives, and all who read this know that is true. The attorney Joseph Alioto could have been one of those whose words were influential. I wouldn't know for sure.

However, years later, I read that Mr. Alioto denied under oath ever knowing anyone with the "Bompensiero" surname. As I recall, we didn't use any alias names while dining at *Fiore d' Italia* with Mr. Alioto. I also learned, while the two discussed business during lunch, that there were other nameless people in Sacramento who spoke a one-word language that I was familiar with, "showmethegreen." On this trip, I also saw Dad do something he had never done before or I ever witnessed again. He carried a small black valise.

Looking back now, I realize that my Dad did whatever was necessary to get his brother out of prison, including see people and pay, pay and pay. No family members, including my mother, ever knew the truth. According to Judith Moore's account in *A Bad, Bad, Boy*, Frank's daughter Mary Ann thought my father was hoarding a stash of her father's cash. Her father spent money like water and never had any substantial stash or businesses. Our business operations or dealings had nothing to do with her father except for Dad accepting Frank's knowledgeable elder brother's influence and verbal generosity in knowing the playing field of the liquor business.

However, if you take Frank's two cents worth of advice in the Manhattan Room regarding our piano player, he buried Dad. All of Frank's efforts had to do with helping Dad and Uncle Joe Corrao get into the Algiers and obtain a liquor license at The Spot. But when the dust settled, all realized that Frank was hustling and couldn't manage his ass. All of Frank's involvement "helping" cost us more money than his daughter ever saw in her life.

What of the Marino family and my friend Joey Piazza?

Salvatore Marino and his son Angelo built his cheese company into a multimillion-dollar operation and gained national acclaim for their *Precious* brand of Ricotta and Mozzarella cheese specialties, named after Angelo's wife, Precious. Angelo took over the entire business after his father passed.

The Marinos were white-collar businessmen who had a legitimate business enterprise and, as we learned, had close ties with the San Francisco Mayor Joseph Alioto. Angelo was a solid businessman and a respected member of "La Familia" as well. Additionally their family was closely aligned with San Francisco crime family boss Jimmy Lanza, and also an acquaintance of Frank Bompensiero.

Though the press and FBI speculated that Sal had been a longtime member of the Midwest *La Familia* crime syndicate, his personal cheese business operation was his own and not connected with any nefarious organization. The nature of a legitimate cheese/food supply business and the imagined criminal element of "La Familia" didn't collide until one day in 1977.

An old-country (Sicilian) employee named Orlando Catelli, who had been with the company for over 25 years and lived in a trailer on the factory grounds, asked for a favor. He wanted Angelo to hire his son Peter, who was in need of a job. For whatever reason, Angelo decided against hiring the young man.

In retaliation, Peter tried to extort $100,000 from the Marinos. If Angelo didn't pay, Peter was going to spread the word that the company was Mafia-owned and operated. Angelo reacted with irrational rage. He, Joe Piazza and his son Salvatore (named after his grandfather), now a member of the familia, called in Orlando and Peter. He told the boy's father, Orlando, what his son sought via extortion. When confronted, Orlando was embarrassed and apologetic, but Angelo was not in a mood for apologies. He would decide what was and wasn't fair. He ordered Orlando to kill his own son. Orlando refused, and so both men were shot, dumped in the trunk of Orlando's car, driven to San Francisco and parked on a street where the bodies were left to rot. However, one mistake was made. No one checked to be sure both men were dead.

Peter Catelli was killed, but his father, although thought to be dead, survived. After the two were left in the trunk of the car for several hours, a passerby heard Orlando's cries for help. The senior Catelli subsequently testified against Angelo, Salvatore, Joe Piazza and Tom Napolitano, another soldier associate. The accomplices served three years for their participation. Although Angelo Marino used his bad health to avoid going to trial for three years, he was convicted in October of 1980 of second-degree murder and attempted murder. However, the conviction was overturned on appeal and Angelo was released. Angelo didn't escape the Grim Reaper, however, as he died in 1983 of congestive heart failure attributed to diabetes. His son served a substantial sentence and was released on parole.

I imagined my Uncle Frank—had he been alive at the time— saying something like, "Can you believe it? They did the job on their own property and didn't bury the bodies?" *Que Pazzo!* (They were crazy.)

CHAPTER 24

THRIFTCO
...AND THE TOP DOG

It was 1959 and Sammy felt as if a ton of weight was lifted from his back. He knew his brother was going to be paroled soon. From their discussions, he knew he'd have to find Frank a job. After five years behind bars, Frank had no property, no money and no future. The courts took everything not nailed down, and his parole officer would keep him on a short leash. His former life of freedom was history. As Frank would say, "I can't take a piss without the bastards checking my fly." Writing in A Bad, Bad Boy, Mary Ann, Frank's daughter, assumed that his friends in the "organization" would take care of her and him financially. Such thinking was naïve and showed her ignorance of her father's business, as he liked to call it. Since Frank went to prison for his own mistakes, not for any familial criminal affiliation, no one owed him anything. To them, he had been stupid and foolish to endorse a check and, worse yet, he was greedy. He never offered his pals a cut. It seems there is a code of honor, even among thieves: We want ours too!

✸ ✸ ✸

While operating his bars, The Spot, Kelly's and the Corsair, Dad was enticed into a new business opportunity, and because I was twenty years old I was Dad's sounding board on business issues.

The Niputi ...the Nephew

The new venture was called "THRIFTCO." Dad's eyes lit up when he mentioned it. It was a follow-on and similar to a business that was founded by Sol Price—California's "Price Club."

THRIFTCO was going to open just off of Rosecrans and Midway in the Point Loma area, and Piggily-Wiggly, one of the largest retail grocery operators in San Diego, could provide a foundation platform for the store's operation.

Like the Price Club, it would have clothier vendors and everyone else would have a piece and parcel of the operation. Dad opted for the liquor store and the food operation, meaning a hot dog stand. Knowing he had a hidden agenda, I said nothing. I knew it had a lot to do with getting his brother re-established.

Frank was going to be an "ex-capo"—that meant on his own, broke, with no way to make a living. It was a thriving economy, business was good, and Dad's bars were making money, so he started to accumulate an emergency fund for Frank. Regardless of who (or what) Frank was, he was still Dad's brother and he loved him. Dad always felt like Frank had his back. I would be the first to disagree. So, whether he took money from any excess business proceeds or from his own pocket, Dad paid legal fees and appeals and the "other" costs of getting his brother out on parole. And as I continue to say, it cost a bundle. For example, Frank's daughter Mary Ann was a grown woman, married several times and with children. But Frank also asked Dad to help his daughter out financially when he could. Mary Ann never lived at destitution's door. Rather, she still wanted to live her pre-marital lifestyle and didn't care who paid for it. And yes, it was expensive. She had always relied on her father to bail her out of financial difficulties while seeming to be unacquainted with the reality of his own dire financial straits. Frugality was a word not in her meager vocabulary.

For the record, the brothers (Sam and Frank) were never in business together! Frank's mentor, Jack Dragna, died while my uncle was in prison and was replaced by Frank De Simone as head of the L.A. family. Frank couldn't associate with the liquor industry and he didn't know anything else. Like prison, parole would be a bitch and life on the outside would only be a reminder of better past times. I learned that none of this bothered Frank. He was oblivious to his financial condition and his status. He acted like he would do what he damned well pleased. Perhaps because he knew his brother would bail him out.

Within a couple of months, he was back to his former self, big cigar, big mouth and braggadocio persona. His former austere life behind bars was a flash in the past. Frank was back!

While Frank was in prison, Dad kept his eye open for any venture that would generate some income for his brother. Supposedly, Frank lost his interests in Maestro Music, unless he never owned a piece of that either. Since Alcohol Beverage Control, the state's liquor license department, would never again let Frank back into the liquor business, he was screwed. Sure, he had a sideline business, extortion and putting guys to sleep, but he wasn't good at much else. From Prohibition days through his indictment for liquor license bribery, liquor was really all he knew.

He couldn't even extort money from William J. Bonelli, the State Board of Equalization director, who issued state liquor licenses. Bonelli was a practicing white-collar bureaucratic racketeer and was up to his eyeballs in criminal behavior for receiving cash for licenses. That Bonelli was on the take was not even a consideration. He knew too much and could pull down many friends in Sacramento and in the governor's mansion. As I recall Frank saying many times when speaking about Bonelli, "That prick will never see the inside of a courtroom, Joey. Everyone is on the take." And he was right.

While Dad was operating The Spot and Kelly's on Third and Broadway, and the Corsair on lower Broadway in the late fifties, a new business opportunity came up in discussion one day. He was having coffee with a pal of his who operated Dick Tyrell's Jewelers, down a couple of doors from the Corsair. The pal's name was Nate Rosenberg. Nate and Dad had become good friends over the years. Nate knew that Dad was concerned about what Frank could do to earn a buck after he was released. Dad later told me about the conversation.

Nate asked, "Is he well-fixed, Sammy?"

"Hell, no! He's broke. Christ, Nate, he's got nothing and less than he did when he arrived from Sicily at seventeen. The courts took everything. It's worse than that. He has shit for opportunity. Now the cops will be on him and roust him just to find out who he talks to and what he knows. You know, he never said a fucking word about anything while he was in the slammer. You can bet some prick of a parole officer will be so far up Frank's ass that he'll have to pry him out to take a shit."

Nate laughed at his friend's use of his "Sammy-speak." Sammy never minced words.

"It's going to be a real problem, Nate. The cops love to see a pain in their ass like Frank on his knees. You know the bastard blue suits who were on the take before will be coming around to see if he has any more scratch, the cocksuckers! Frank is fucked! He can't play the big cheese anymore. They have him by the balls. If he does anything to screw up, they'll send him back inside and throw away the key."

Nate nodded in agreement.

"His total sentence was seven counts with a max of six years each, that's forty-two years, all total he's been in almost seven. He's going to have to play straight or they'll nail him and send him back for the rest of his sentence. He'll die there."

Nate thought a minute. "I may have an idea you could pursue. You might be able to get him a place to work and make a buck yourself. One of my Hebe brothers is going to try to replicate one of Sol Price's store concepts. It's in the final stages right now. It's going to be down on Midway near the Cotton Patch."

Dad was skeptical. "What kind of joint is it going to be? You know he can't be connected with a liquor license."

"No problem," said Nate. "This is sort of a warehouse store with groceries, jewelry, clothes, a liquor store and food counter, and toys and shit for the crowd. The cornerstone for running the departments is Piggly Wiggly Markets, the nation's first self-service grocery store. The San Diego franchise owner is a pal of mine. We play poker and socialize together. I'll call him. He's investing a couple of big ones and would like to open a dozen stores like this one if it pans out. I've been offered the jewelry franchise. Do you want in, Sammy?"

"Hell yes, if the liquor franchise is open, I could take that and give Frank the food operation. He wouldn't give a shit and he can be the manager. He could come and go as he pleases."

"I'll check it out, Sammy, and get back with you."

"Make it quick, Nate, I won't have a lot of time to get him a clean job and I've already told his parole officer that he'll have a place to work."

"I'll let you know later today."

And so it was. Nate introduced Dad to the top man in the organization and they got along famously. Dad's affable way and his varied business acumen were appreciated, along with his expertise in the liquor business. He was given the approval to obtain the off-sale liquor license and permits for the food operation. Although he never had operated a liquor store, it turned out to be a snap for him.

He contacted his liquor distributors and McKesson-Robbins, one of the largest, who sent over a marketing representative to provide some design and layout advice. The basics were all Dad needed. He understood the operation and purchased merchandise stands, a register and a small safe for the back storage room. Pricing for the operation was a snap, and since I had taken a semester off from college and was almost twenty-one years old, Dad put me in charge. That way I could help keep an eye on the place and knew what was going on.

Off-sale liquor licenses were available and mostly fair trade, so you were locked into established pricing. As far as pricing was concerned, he used the standardized distributors' price points and discounted them to support the store. The food operation was just as easy since Dad already had a hot dog stand at the Corsair bar. After Nate's introduction and a meeting with other vendors, Dad became a major shareholder and member of the board at THRIFTCO.

Dad opted for the liquor store and the food operation concessions, meaning a hot dog stand with minimum equipment, but with a little flair. The place was designed as a classy little outdoor eating area housed within the massive warehouse setting. It was all show with a yellow faux umbrella over the dog stand and a soda machine. It had a three-foot white fence surrounding the eating area, a few banana plants and four small round tables and a trash can. It looked great! It also had a sign above the stand, "Frank's Dogs."

Dad had operated a successful hot dog stand at the Corsair downtown. When THRIFTCO was successful, so were we. Unfortunately, THRIFTCO was destined to be a one-trick pony. It would not survive.

We were living in Point Loma in the big house, not far from THRIFTCO, and I was attending SDSU where I was finishing my degree and commission in the Air Force. When not in class, I worked the liquor counter or the clothing store at THRIFTCO and assisted my cousin Tina, who was operating the hot dog stand. She had it down to a science and put out a good dog with all the trimmings. When it was slow, I moved over to the men's department and assisted selling menswear. Besides, that department had a very attractive brunette working there and I decided to make a run for her. Suffice to say we became friendly and went out several times.

In San Diego, Frank moved in with his daughter and played at being grandpa while trying to adapt to freedom. The day finally came for him to report to his parole officer and to view his new place of employment.

We had been operating the liquor department and hot dog stand for a couple of months. Most of the new business kinks were gone and the stage was set for Frank's visit. I could not wait for him to see what we had done. I was proud of how hard my father had busted his hump for his brother.

Frank's parole officer had already been down, looked over the hours of operation, and approved the employment site. A couple of days later, I had an unannounced visit from a couple of plainclothes detectives. They came down to visit Frank and automatically came to the liquor department. When they approached and asked for him, I told them he wasn't there and wouldn't be working in the liquor department. He'd be operating the hot dog stand. They said they had heard that Frank would be working at THRIFTCO and stopped by to say hello.

"Well, you've come to the wrong place," I said. "He won't be working here due to his parole restrictions—no liquor license-related jobs. We've already had his parole officer down and he approved of his workstation. He'll be operating that hot dog stand over there." I pointed to the fenced-in food center where Frank's Dogs stand stood in the middle of a pseudo garden with tall plants, an umbrella and tables and chairs. "As you can see, it's set up for him."

They looked around. The one called "Bill" smiled and said, "The fence can remind Frank of his last residence-- you know, being penned in." They both chuckled. "A nice touch," said Bill. "Was that your idea?"

I ignored him. *What a prick!* I debated telling him we put up the picket garden fence to control traffic flow. I thought better of it. The less I had to do with them the better.

"Just tell Frank that Bill and Tom from Vice stopped by."

Bill handed me a business card and I never saw them again.

When Dad finally brought Frank in a couple of days later to see the operation, people looking for a bedraggled and downtrodden ex-convict would have been disappointed. As usual, Frank strolled in looking like the fashion designer at *Cosmopolitan Magazine* had dressed him, right down to his brown alligator shoes. He wore a dark brown suit, silk tie, and white-on-white dress shirt monogrammed with his initials, and he sported the ever-present cigar. Much thinner after his term in prison, he looked good. He cast an eye around the huge warehouse store.

"You've done well, Turi. You've done well."

After a quick tour of the store, he and Dad stopped at the dog stand which, because of the time of day, had a lunch crowd lined up. So, just being Frank, he played to onlookers by removing his jacket and donning his apron, with "Top Dog" stenciled across the chest. He even served a couple of hot dogs while chuckling, "With this job, I can laugh all the way to the bank."

However, that was not to be the case. Frank returned to his dog stand maybe a dozen times over the next few months. Because of the lower than anticipated traffic count, Piggly Wiggly decided to pull out and THRIFTCO closed its doors. And it was "adios" to Frank's dogs.

Frank was nowhere to be seen for a few weeks. He disappeared, marching to his own drummer. Dad was worried about him. He didn't even show when Dad had to close out the liquor store and hot dog stand. It was typical Frank behavior, doing what he did best, being the absent one until he saw a score or was forced into doing something. Watching or running the enterprise that his younger brother bought to give him carefree employment didn't interest Frank.

Then, one night, surprise! Where he was nobody knew, but Frank called Dad and said he was ready to come out of the shadows and get out on the town.

I knew this because at dinner that night, Dad turned to me while Mom filled and served our plates and said, "Joe, I need some help."

"Anything, Dad, just ask."

"Well, my brother called me today."

I interrupted and said, "Well, are we lucky or what. It's been over two months since he's been around. Did he get arrested or is he in trouble?"

Mom was surprisingly kind. She said, "Joe, he probably feels cooped up with Mary Ann and the kids and just needs to get out. I understand that Mary Ann is between husbands."

Dad interjected, "I guess he talked to his probation officer and explained about THRIFTCO not making it. Anyway, he's got the approval to go out at night to see his old friends who might be able to get him a job. But, I need someone I can rely on to go out with him. *Capesh?*"

"*Yeah Dad.* What do you want me to do? Be his driver or chauffeur? I can only do that a couple of times a week. I'm hitting the books heavy right now."

Dad stared at his plate. He looked haggard and drawn. "No, son. I don't mean like just dropping him off. He wants to be taken out to dinner and get involved with the night life."

"Cheezus, Dad! I'd rather take you out. You're the one who needs a break. I hate *Ziu Chichu's* bigmouth bragging. Besides, I'm not a nightclubber. I'm in school. Graduation's coming up. I have to hit the books. I can't be committed to *Ziu Chichu* so he can show off around town."

"Joey, you won't have to be with him all the time, just when he needs to get out. I would do it but, I'm locked into operating the bars, paying the bills and—you know."

"I know, Pop." I thought about what I was getting involved in. Taking Frank around the town was a very personal thing.

Dad was a workhorse who routinely worked fifteen to twenty-hour days seven days a week. Even when he was off on Saturday and Sunday, he still went to the bars to check out all the registers at ten a.m., then six p.m. and finally closing at two a.m. That was his four-joint operation, and when he was not ordering booze or banking for all the places, he'd be visiting his mother or trying to help his brother.

How could I say no? I couldn't. Frank and I went out almost every night during the first month. Frank felt there were a lot of bar and restaurant owners in San Diego who owed him, and if they didn't owe him money they owed him respect in terms of homage. He was Frank Bompensiero and that meant something to his over-inflated ego.

I studied his behavior during this period and thought of him as one sick son of a gun. He talked about how he felt alone. He bragged about the old days and what he had been, and what he still thought he was. His desire for recognition was above all things. He wanted people around him to look up to him, but no one sought him out.

He thrived when some maître d' would come by our table and recognize him. Frank would invite him to sit while he played the big shot. Frank thrived on a need for respect and consideration of the locals. It was a huge ego thing and he saw himself as invincible. No one could break him.

Frank couldn't peddle influence as he once did. He no longer had the fix on a liquor license where he controlled the outcome. Many times, he would say that he still could influence the outcome of things. Eventually, he resigned himself to reality.

He usually felt that business people owed *him*—not his Dragna family. He was angry that no came to see him in San Quentin. No one paid him honor of any sort. And no one took care of his daughter, Mary Ann, and her family. He believed she couldn't make it without him and, with the husbands she chose, he was probably right. Without

The Niputi ...the Nephew

Frank's contribution of food and money, even though she was married, she had a difficult time. How do I know, you ask? Because I knew her husbands, from Dutch Roberts, a good-looking young man and soldier who served his country honorably and was injured in Korea, to Jimmy Garafalo, who couldn't support Mary Ann's lifestyle—even to paying the rent.

However, Jimmy had a roving eye and was there to hit on my cousin Tina when Mary Ann wasn't around. What nerve! There were many times after Frank was in jail that Mary Ann called on "Uncle Sammy" when she needed money. As we were moving into the Point Loma house, she called repeatedly and drove my father crazy. "We can't make our mortgage payment and may lose Dad's Braeburn Street house. You've got to help us." I personally addressed the issue with *Ziu Chich* when I visited him in San Quentin and found him noncommittal. It was obvious that he was uncomfortable and didn't want to tell his daughter the truth about what he owned, didn't own and what he could expect from his brother, like paying his continuing attorney's expenses to get Frank paroled, as well as greasing the palms of bureaucrats to open doors and get things done.

We hit all the best restaurants in San Diego, so Frank could show his face and get comp'd just for visiting. I took him around from restaurant to restaurant so he could test the waters, and it cost two to three hundred per night. He didn't want to appear as if he was broke. He wanted to see who brought a bill to his table, and I realized that he was keeping tally so when he supposedly got back on his feet, he could square up. He made sure that I always left a handsome tip upon departure to the waiter and the maître d' and it wasn't just ten or fifteen percent. You have to remember this was in the late fifties and he was encouraging me to drop a fifty-dollar bill after enjoying a hundred-dollar dinner. It was over the line as far as I was concerned. But Frank's take was always the same, "I want to show 'em I still can, the bastards."

While I felt that ten percent was quite acceptable, twenty to thirty percent was strictly bravado, and egotistical on Frank's part, and he always rounded up and not by the change remaining. As far as I was concerned, we were tipping Dad's money. Frank, however, was ostentatious in his liberal tipping way, whether he was at Del Mar, Lubach's, or Tarantino's. Wherever we were, at the seafood houses in La Jolla or Point Loma, La Costa or Rancho Bernardo, he had this need for recognition, even though the recipients knew quickly he was full of hot air and had no money.

After I backed off my seeing-eye-dog routine, he made it a point to go to Tarantino's, where he could play the "Bishop" and obtain homage from those seeking to rub against criminal status, like groupies from the old days. I watched him. His ego swelled as he relayed stories of his activities and how he outwitted the police. Most got a thrill out of hanging with a notorious Mafiosa Capo. Most of them didn't know the man outside of his entertainment circle and saw something in him that I never did.

Frank never picked up a tab during these sessions. He simply expected it. The only time he did was when I arranged the one and only date for him. He wanted to impress some young girl, but it didn't work out well, as you will learn.

However, if he had a wad of big bills, he was all bravado. "I'll get the bill," he'd say, and with all the flair of pulling out a roll that would choke a horse, he fiddled through hundreds and fifty's, riffle out a few and say, "Keep the change, you earned it." He must have learned that early in life watching Jack Dragna operate.

"Show 'em you got it, Joey. Show 'em you got it. Frankie's back and there's no change," he'd say, night after night.

And I of course responded in similar fashion. "You got it, *Ziu*. Show 'em you got it."

CHAPTER 25

DATE NIGHT
...SCENT OF A WOMAN

Frank Bompensiero was lonely. His wife, Thelma, had died of cancer in 1955 soon after he was incarcerated in Chino Prison. As he viewed the encroachment of old age alone, he missed the relationship they shared. Now he was not looking for a wife but a void to fill and a good time. His libido hadn't waned during his years in prison—if anything, he thought about women a lot. I caught him many times scanning the skirts in a room. He craved female companionship—a romp in the hay, maybe a blowjob—whatever. Unfortunately for me, I had to reintroduce him to his former nightlife after a month of playing seeing-eye-dog on a nightly basis for meals costing $$$ and paid for by his brother. I endured all the veneer of pretense I could stand. I had enough. Then unknowingly, Frank let me off the hook by making a personal affront to me by eyeing a girl I'd been dating for years. Then he expressed his horny thoughts to me. She and I hatched a scheme to get even. Oh, baby!

✷ ✷ ✷

After transferring from Chino prison, Frank's physical frustrations were satisfied the day he scurried from the gates of San Quentin prison, about five years later.

Dad said, "I have a couple of surprises for my brother when he gets out. I arranged for his personal clothes; you know suit, shirt, shoes, silk tie to make him feel better. Then I put them in a classy room in an upscale hotel with an open terrace and a roman bath. He will have total privacy except for the San Francisco Restaurant that is catering a special crab and lobster lunch for him. Then, I'll bring a bottle of JB scotch for him to sip on while he's waited on by two pro's. They'll take care of his needs."

It was bound to happen. After THRIFTCO failed, Frank's legitimate business closed and Dad was worried about Frank's attitude. He asked me to take him out to visit his old haunts. Dad saw it as a chance for Frank to feel like the man he had been before prison. At Dad's behest and with his funding, I did just that. It became an every-night activity for over a month. It wasn't long before Frank let me know that he was looking for some action.

At the time, I had been dating a young girl named Gracie Gooding. Although it was an-on-and-off again relationship, we were good friends and had been as far back as high school. Because of our schedules, me in college and her building her hair-dressing business, we didn't have much time for dating. She was a busy beautician and I was scrambling to finish my classes in preparation for graduation and pilot training. There was my other job—keeping Frank busy with social outings and out of trouble. My free time was at a premium. It wasn't long before Frank made it plain that he wanted me to "hook" him up with "some broads." I managed to dodge that bullet. But one night after midterm exams were over, I was celebrating with a night on the town with Gracie. She had helped me prep and cram for several tough class exams.

We were at Yale Kahn's Chuck Wagon on Midway Drive. It had one of the best nightclubs around and they always brought in top-named entertainers. Gracie and I both enjoyed good music. That night, as I recall, Louie Prima and Keely Smith were the headliners.

Auburn-haired Gracie, always a stunner, turned heads as we headed into the club. It was a packed night and we could tell it was SRO. We joined the rest of the queue waiting for the next show. Frank happened to come out of the lounge for a restroom break and almost bumped into us. He saw Gracie and immediately made a big deal about us joining him at his table. Actually, Frank was seated at the owner's table with A.J. Kahn and his son Yale. I looked at Gracie and she gave me a smiling look of approval. We communicated effectively.

Previously Gracie and I spoke of my dreaded evenings with Frank on the town. She knew it would be awkward not to go along with Frank's invitation. Frank positioned himself next to Gracie, ordered us a drink, and fawned all over her for the entire time we were there. I didn't appreciate his lecherous ogling of my date. We stayed for one set, thanked him and the Kahns, and bid all good night.

The next day, Frank called and asked me if I would consider giving him Gracie's phone number. I almost fell on the floor. He was about fifty-five at the time and was trying to hit on my twenty-year-old girlfriend. I was pissed and went for the jugular.

"Look, Unc. I had been dating Gracie on and off for a couple of years. She had met Mom and Dad and we had been out together several times. They like and respect her. Besides, she's about eight years younger than your daughter, Mary Ann."

"Yeah, I know. Most are twenty-something, Niputi. Big fucking deal. See what you can do. Call her!"

"Seriously, I doubt she would be interested. Besides, you're older than her father—and he's a Marine colonel."

"Yeah, yeah. I know all the reasons why not..."

"Okay, *Ziu.*" *I said.* "I'll call." Then, I thought, *What the hell, I'll play to the old bastard's ego.*

"You know Unc, she's got some beautiful friends who'd love to go out with a mature gentlemen like yourself." Frank didn't pick up on my subtlety.

"Yeah, fine. I want someone classy. Ya know, none of those trampy-looking sluts. Capish?"

"Sure, Unc, no dogs. I'll see what I can do."

"Just so you know, Joey, at my age they all are going to be younger. But who gives a shit? They all go down the same way. Right?"

I was no prude, but listening to him disgusted me. I figured I'd call Gracie and level with her about what he wanted. I hoped she would say, "Tell Frank to screw off." As it turned out, Gracie had a better plan.

"Joe, you've got to be kidding me, right?"

"I wish I were. He's serious."

"So you want me to line Frank up with one of my friends?"

"Well in truth, he wanted to go out with you. *But just to tease her because we never were intimate,* I said to him that you had a devilishly weird perversion you liked. And he responded, 'I'm not into any of that weird shit, nephew. Count her out.' This is what I wanted in the first place."

Gracie's response was something off-color that was supposed to put me in my place. Then she said, "You know, mister, Angela might be interested in dating an older man."

I about choked. "Angela" a.k.a. "Kiva," was Gracie's sister. She livened up the Gooding household and worked as a top-notch burlesque queen. This was much to the chagrin of her Marine Corps colonel father, an older brother and, to a lesser degree, her younger more liberal sister Gracie.

Gracie and I chewed on that a little and finally she came up with a plan that didn't involve her sister. I was glad, because I wasn't sure if Uncle Frank would get the joke. I didn't want to put Gracie's sister at risk, and Angela came up with her friend Eva.

"I hope he won't think Eva's going to swoon all over His Nibs."

"Eva, huh? Franco and Eva. That has a ring to it, almost romantic. But, as far as I'm concerned what he or they do is their business, not mine, yours or ours."

"Okay by me," Gracie said.

I found Frank at the Grant Hotel barbershop. He was thrilled with the news. Frank told me to pick him up at Mary Ann's and that we'd be heading downtown to Charlie Pepitone's. His father was an old friend of Frank's and allegedly connected.

"What's up with the stop at Charlie's?"

"Charlie has this brand new, fire-engine red Cadillac convertible. He's going to lend it to me tonight. I'm not going out tonight without the best ride."

We picked up the Cad and I told Charlie I would drive it as if it were my own.

"You'd better drive it as if it were your father's car." He wasn't kidding.

Before we picked up the girls, Frank asked me how much cash I had.

"I've got about five bills."

"Let me have it, Niputi. I'll pay tonight." That was typical of Frank. It didn't surprise me. I was too excited about the surprise Gracie and I had cooked up for Uncle Frank. I only hoped it didn't include her sister.

We picked up the girls at Gracie's house. To say Frank was pleased would be an understatement. Eva was a knockout and if Frank had a tail, he would have excitedly wagged it. She looked like a fashion magazine model. About five-foot-seven, and wore spiked heels. They added several inches. She was a gorgeous blonde and Gracie styled her hair into a beehive that added a few more inches. Eva towered over Frank and her striking beauty turned heads.

Eva was dressed in a cleavage-revealing, tight-fitting blue silk dress that matched her eyes. She didn't have a blemish that we could see, but with all the makeup available who really knew? Still, Gracie had outdone herself with Eva. *This was going to be a fun evening.*

The girls loved the plush leather seats of the Caddy. I drove to Lubach's, an upscale dinner house across from the finger piers on the waterfront near the Civic Center. We enjoyed a leisurely three-hour dinner while Frank played all his cards. He was in his glory with the stunning Eva on his arm.

After dinner, Frank picked up the tab with much fanfare. Then he said, "Let's take a ride over to Yale's." I knew he meant the Chuck Wagon. There was a nice quartet playing when we arrived and Eva and Frank made their grand appearance as she sashayed and he strutted up the stairs to the club.

Gracie and I couldn't stop laughing. However, Frank turned and asked what was so funny, and I had to tell him that Gracie told me the funniest joke I ever heard. And we cracked up again. Of course, he wanted to hear it, but Gracie said, "It's just too embarrassing, Frank."

"You can call me Frankie, sweetheart." I started to laugh again and I thought Gracie was going to pee her panties.

After a few drinks and a couple of dances, it turned out to be a fun evening and finally Gracie said, "I've got a couple of early appointments and have to get some rest. Can you take me home, Joey?"

Gracie never called me Joey, so I knew she was just mimicking Unc's "call me Frankie" comment. Of course, I started to laugh again and she joined in.

"I've gotta get Gracie home, Unc. She needs her beauty sleep or turns into a real coyote in the morning. I've seen her, honest!"

"You are such a liar, mister. That will cost you," Gracie interjected.

Eva asked if I'd put the top down on the convertible. The stars were out and it was a clear night. In truth, it was the perfect night to drive with the top down.

I drove Gracie home and, as I walked around and opened her door, I noticed Frank trying to kiss Eva on her chest. She moved away and rose in her seat and stretched.

"Look, Mr. Frank, I've had a lovely time. Let's not ruin it with a lapdog physical bit. I did not sign on for a grab-and-grope evening. But, I had a wonderful time. Besides I'm not in the mood."

Frank looked like he had just been kicked in the gut.

"What? You kidding me?"

Eva said, "Frankie, you're just not my type. We've had a nice evening and let's leave it at that because I've had them all and to tell you straight—I'm not."

"Not what?"

"Straight, Frank. Straight. I like soft and squishy, lovely smelling girls." With that, she got out of the car.

"Are you a fucking dyke— A Les-been?"

"No, Frank, I'm not a "Les-been" and the word is lesbian. I am bi-sexual when it comes to the younger crowd. As I said, I'm just not in the mood for the physical tonight. And thank you again for a lovely evening. Bye, love."

She hugged Gracie, kissed me on the cheek, and headed for her own car.

I about doubled over laughing as I walked Gracie to her door. We were both laughing so hard we had tears running down our cheeks. We could hear Frank cussing and grumbling across the street.

When I got back in the car, Frank leered at me and spoke.

"Did you know?"

"Know what?"

"About that *Lebanese* bitch?"

"Lebanese? I thought she was Italian."

"No, I mean les-been."

"You mean lesbian, Unc?"

"Whatever! Jesus Christ, I don't go out with perverts or lizards that change their fucking stripes"

"You mean colors, *Ziu*?"

"Yeah, what the fuck."

"Gee, Unc. Goddamn it. I didn't know! I'll have to ask Gracie what the hell was up with that."

We left it at that. I had a funny at Frank's expense.

In case you're wondering what happened to Gracie's sister Angela, she became quite successful and turned her act into a Las Vegas club headliner. David Cary, PhD, chose Angela (Queen of the Fan Dance) to grace the cover of his treatise on "*A Bit of Burlesque.*"

Angela was fun, but didn't run in Gracie's circles. She had her own friends who ran the burlesque circuit. Her friends were male and female, straight and not so straight. The fifties were tough on many who broke social norms or who had unique hormones.

✳ ✳ ✳

Not all parents were willing to let me date their daughters. I was turned away from several young ladies' doors. I almost became skittish waiting for a burly dad's rebuke, "Not with my daughter." I was aware of the possibility and kept a low profile.

Once after I went to pick up a girl who wasn't ready to go out, I sat in their living room while her Dad and Mom were watching TV. On that night, the news came on and mentioned Frank Bompensiero and some crime crap affiliation. The man turned toward me with an odd questioning look on his face.

"Are you any relation to that hoodlum that was just on TV?"

I said, "He's my father's brother." His face lost all expression and began to turn white. When he found his voice, he told me to leave and forget his daughter.

✳ ✳ ✳

Despite that occasion when I set Uncle Frank up with a "date," he still trusted me and insisted on my company when he went out. But our constant nightclubbing was taking a toll on me. It was a grueling couple of months and I told my mother I couldn't keep it up.

"This nightlife is killing me, Mom. Every stinking night for over thirty days it has been the same thing. Pick Frank up, head to a dinner house, cocktails with Frank, and listen to him bullshit every restaurant owner in town. It is either the Kahn's joints, the Grant Grill, The Lighthouse, Tarantino's, or Lubach's, you know the drill, and it's getting to me."

I told her how all of the owners were so polite. "Hello, Mr. Bompensiero. Welcome to our restaurant, Mr. Bompensiero. Thank you so much for joining us for dinner. How have you been, sir? Can I kiss your ass, Mr. Bompensiero? What crap!"

"I hear you, honey," she said. "But that's between you and your father. You've got to talk to him and get it resolved. I'll do what I can do, but you know how he is with his brother."

"Yeah, I know, Mom. I don't want you to have to fight this battle for me. I'll handle it."

It would be another few weeks of entertaining Uncle Frank before I could ditch my babysitting job. There was one more outing that stuck in my mind. Even I had a break point and this turned out to be the last time I played Frank's chauffeur.

We went to a place just off the beach, south of the Del Mar Racetrack. Although Frank liked to talk as if we had been there, this was our first time as the owner greeted Frank with a welcome sir.

"Enough with the *sir* talk," Frank, replied. "I'm no jailer. But thanks anyway. I am fine and doing well. Those mumzer bastards couldn't make me break a drop of sweat. You didn't think they could break The Bomp, did you?"

"Oh no, Mr. B. That would never happen."

"You got that right, Abe. Many tried to disrespect me and we know what happened to them, don't we?... They disappeared!" Then he snickered.

Just watching him spew his mantra was disgusting. What a fucking implied threat. Were they all crazy or did he have all these people hoodwinked?

"Well, it's sure good to see you," the proprietor said again. "You've been missed, but you look real healthy. You look real good."

"Just call me *Frank*! I let most of my f-r-i-e-n-d-s." He said this, slowly stretching out the word. And, I do consider you a friend, right, Abe?"

"You got that right—Frank."

Just about that time, Ralph the maître d' came up. The owner turned and said, "Ralph, make sure you take excellent care of Mr. B. He's a dear friend and I'll be taking care of this, Ralph."

Turning to Frank, "It's a pleasure to have you here, Frank. This one is on me."

"Why thank you, Abe. My nephew and I appreciate it. Oh, excuse me, this is my nephew Joe. He's soon to be an Air Force officer. He's graduating from San Diego State College soon."

Frank reveled in his ability to squeeze and intimidate people to get what he wanted. Fear was his only motivator.

Dinner with Frank was an embarrassment. Why, then, did I do it? The obvious always stands in the way. He was my father's brother. They were Sicilian and had a blood bond that went back way before my time on the earth.

I had been raised in that same custom, with added education from my intelligent mother and a semi-liberal father. I was not about to say, "Fuck-it." And walk away from two of the best parents anyone could have.

Yes, with Frank's mouth always open, it was pure drudgery listening to his stories of manipulation and his successes evading the law for over forty years. It's not that some of the stories (one's I hadn't heard before) weren't interesting. But listening night after night became a drag and I didn't know when it was going to stop.

After my classes at SDSC, I'd head home to get in what studying I could before having to pick Frank up. Around five o'clock I shaved, showered and dressed for the evening's adventure. Then, if Dad wasn't home, I headed to one of our bars to see him. Normally, I'd catch him at one of them around six-thirty since he changed shifts at six p.m.

I filled him in on the latest and told him where his brother wanted to go. Dad gave me cash for the evening. Then it was a drive over to pick up Frank at his daughter's, or the last place I dropped him off. He'd be waiting outside by the door and always looked dapper, like he was going out for a big night on the town.

The first month came and went and I was getting worn out. Plus, eating like we were every night, I had gained weight and was up for a final flight physical. I had no life other than with Frank, and there I was acting like Frank's driver or his steering boy, keeping him clear of any trouble and getting him out in the public eye.

I had to do something. I was just finishing up the last few classes and would soon be graduating, and here I was doing a favor for Dad and playing nursemaid to an ex-con who had just done five years in San Quentin. Besides, I didn't like him anyway. The local and state police and the FBI were all over us and we were able to spot them nightly. Hell, we were both under surveillance.

Did I feel like some kind of idiot? You bet. The FBI had already cleared me for confidential and secret clearances and I signed a government contract to accept my commission. And here I was playing driver to a known hit man. Great way to start a career. *I'd have to have a heart-to-heart with dad and soon.* As far as I was concerned, what to do with his brother was his problem.

Although Frank often boasted about the people he made disappear, it was often a shallow boast. In my estimation, the law was never successful in getting him for blackmail, extortion, witness and jury tampering, and assault, let alone murder.

Frank wasn't that smart. But neither was the law. He found pure joy in citing his exploits, but never around the female side of the family and not where anyone with any connection to law enforcement could hear. Later, his inability to understand the technology of the times really must have driven him crazy, and that was just about the time they squeezed him and made him a turncoat.

The reason for Frank's steadfast ways could always be found in the heritage of the *Omerta Code* (death code), which he and his associates held with the conviction of a religious zealot.

In *The Smell of Sicily, the Garden of the Mediterranean* by Will S. Monroe, PhD, the author says and I totally agree: "The most favorable statement of the herd (Mafia) is neither a sect or an association. It has neither regulations nor statutes. Its members are neither thief nor rascal and in the rascals' own estimation—a Mafiosa is simply a bold and valiant man who will not tolerate any insult whatsoever. The term then is the consciousness of one's individuality, the exaggerated conceit of one's strength, which is regarded as the sole arbitrator of every dispute, of every conflict and intolerance of anyone else's superiority or worse yet, anybody else's power."

This, I tell you, was Frank Bompensiero—to the core.

CHAPTER 26
RETRIBUTION RAIDERS

It was late in the year 1961. Frank had been released from prison in the summer of 1960 and business had been good. We were living in Del Cerro and Dad was operating his three bars, The Spot, Kelly's and The Corsair. After his release from prison, Frank Bompensiero toyed with the THRIFTCO operation until it closed, and then moved on his own to find a job that made sense to him. He was either out of town or lying low. Dad had not seen him in months and his sisters hadn't either. I was just finishing up my final semester at SDSC and I would graduate in January 1962. Life was good and things were smoothly running. That wouldn't last long.

✳ ✳ ✳

Mom kept busy running the house while Dad and I did our thing. He was out of the house by nine-thirty, heading for town and the bars. If Mom or I ever wanted to contact him after 12 o'clock noon, we knew where he'd be.

That thought alone brings back the memories and a smile crosses my face thinking about it. He had his special hangout across from Horton Plaza. Dad loved horses and the Old West, so he'd be hiding out in a western movie.

His routine was like clockwork. He'd check in at each bar, tally the night's receipts, cross-check the bottles used and refill/reorder as necessary. Then he'd be off to the bank and make his deposits. After a quick coffee at the Turf Café a few doors down from Kelly's on Third Avenue, he'd head to one of two movie theaters across from Horton Plaza. He would be at the one where Gary Cooper, Joel McCrea, or Roy Rogers played.

He also liked the ideals of the American West. He loved justice and fairness and honesty. Dad's sense of justice was met by watching it play out on a movie theater's big screen where the local sheriff/lawman, generally outgunned and outmanned, would gather together a ragtag posse and ride off to catch the cattle rustler, bank robber, or killer.

While Dad found avenues to gain support at the political level to gain influence to help his brother obtain favor for parole, I know he took advantage of that avenue, at the local level, with Italianesque quid pro quo favors for traffic ticket disappearances, etc. Abuse of the law in the pure sense of the word—there was never a doubt he still believed in the men in blue protecting the citizenry.

There were times, however, when Dad even found that hard to accept. There were some in "plainclothes and blue uniforms" who discreetly played their power game to better themselves. I was aware of some of those as well. On many occasions, I had no problem carrying several cases of liquor out the back alley door and placing them in the trunk of a private car. I saw no one and met no one. Leo Patella's three monkeys (hear, say, see no evil) were my guide while around the business.

Dad played the game as shrewdly as he could. However, he never forgot his experience with Coronado's Chief Jordan and the Manhattan Room. He learned a hard lesson about those with the Forza (power) hole card.

You'd lose every time trying to fight City Hall. You were overmatched before the fight began—no contest, game over. Throughout my years, I have seen it carried out all around the world, in all walks of life, including the military and governments and in every country visited. It seems to be the nature of the beast—man.

Despite Dad's refusal to enter into the life and go down the road his brother chose with the Mafia, he still maintained old-school principles of honor and respect for the common man because he was still in essence a simple fisherman trying to survive. He also knew that most men in political jobs and on the police force were honest people.

However, there were those among them who took a little here, a favor there, or a degenerate priest who used the sanctity of the church or his above-reproach position while he looked for a young one. There were always going to be black sheep who played their own game. Such was life.

But in December 1960, Dad unfortunately learned that sometimes the sheriff goes after the wrong man for whatever reason. In this case, and for the second time, "guilt through association" would guide the local lawmen. They would create a plan to raid Dad's bars—all of them—in hopes of shutting down Frank's money supply.

Perhaps they were working in legion with the FBI, which had been trying to put muscle on Frank to turn and rat out his Mafia brothers. Or perhaps it was simply a ploy to force Frank's hand. Maybe they were looking for a shootout at the O.K. Corral. Maybe they were just bullies looking for a punching bag. Whatever the motivation, they put their plan to action, starting with Dad's Third Street bars, The Spot and Kelly's—a partnership with Alfred Garcia, an old fishing friend. Right before the end of 1960, they made their move.

I stayed late at school doing some last-minute research in the library. I missed dinner. When I got home, Mom met me in the kitchen. "How's tricks, stranger?"

I gave her a kiss on the cheek. "I'm good, but hungry."

"Aren't you always?" We both laughed.

"I've got a plate for you and it's probably warm since I put it in the oven. I knew you'd be coming home sometime. Dad and I had dinner about six and he only stayed an hour and was gone."

I started to chow down and Mom hung around. Finally she said, "Joey, something's gnawing at your Dad. I'm worried."

"You want me to talk to him later?"

"I'd feel better. You know how he keeps everything to himself." Mom smiled and nodded.

After dinner, I headed to the den and switched on the TV. It was not long before I was sawing logs on the couch. The sound of the garage door opening woke me. It was only one a.m., and too early for Dad to be home. Dad didn't usually get home until after three a.m.. I rose and went to the toilet near the kitchen just in time to see Dad almost stumbling as he entered the kitchen from the garage. I flicked on the light switch.

"Hi, Dad, what's up? You're home early."

He opened the fridge door and grabbed a jug of water, chugging down several swigs. When he turned toward me, I noticed his eyes were bloodshot. I knew something was wrong.

"It finally happened. The bastards came after our joints tonight."

Mom, hearing us talking, came into the kitchen.

"How are you, love?" she said softly. There was worry on her face. "You look so tired."

"Yeah," he said. "And I've got a helluva headache."

"Dad? What's going on?"

"I'll make it simple," he said, as a jaw muscle twitched. "I was almost arrested tonight at the Spot. I had to bail Blackie out of jail."

"My God, Turi," Mom's voice cracked. "What happened?"

"It was like the Old West. The posse stormed into The Spot, Kelly's, the Corsair —a planned raid."

"Sounds more like a hit!" I spat.

Dad continued, "I was in the office at The Spot making a bank for tomorrow. All of a sudden, the Western song blaring on the jukebox stopped playing. I figured someone pulled the plug by accident. I opened the office window and looked down as the lights came on. There were two uniformed cops, one inside, and the other at the door. All I could hear was some loud voices and sailors bitching." He took another swig of water, more to calm his nerves than to quench his thirst. He waited a moment before continuing.

"I headed down the stairs and made my way through the crowd. I recognized a vice cop coming in behind the uniforms. The same guy who's been in and out of the joint for years—he always seemed like a sleaze. I never liked him. But he never found anything to complain about and he left us alone. Tonight, though, he walked up next to a sailor who was resting his head on the bar. The kid looked like he was asleep. Then, the cop flashes his badge at Blackie."

"Why in hell didn't you refuse selling booze to this sailor? He's obviously drunk!"

"I shut him down almost a half hour ago," Blackie says. "He's just been sitting there."

"Then the cop says, 'Yeah, yeah! So, why are there four more drinks in front of him? Are you just hustling him? You running a dirty bar?"

Blackie shot back, "The hell you say. Never have, never will. The boss will vouch to that." Blackie nodded to me. "Then the vice dick gets nasty."

"Don't swear at me," he says, "or you're going downtown." Then he turned and shouted into the crowd milling around. 'Where's the owner?' "

I stepped up behind him and said, "I'm right here. Why are you arresting my bartender?"

"Maybe you'd like to be arrested, too. Then you both can go behind bars. I hear it runs in the family, Sam?" Dad shook his head.

"Can you believe he says that to me, the dirty bastard, especially with my brother just released from prison."

It didn't take a brain surgeon to see what the cops were doing. Had it been on a chessboard, it would have been a smart move to "checkmate." They obviously had been watching Frank play the model parolee—cruising around town, going from his hot dog stand at THRIFTCO, with his nephew as chauffeur, hitting the high-priced restaurants, acting like he owned them.

I imagined the cop's conversation went something like this: "So, how is it that 'The Cigar' has no income, yet he's eating at some of the best places in town? Places we can't even afford to leave a tip? Then, this morning, while shaving, it comes to me. Big-mouth Frank loses his house and the only bar he has a piece of with that scumbag Dragna, goes up to the big house, spends five years Then he comes out and has his own chauffeur, Sam's son. Bingo! That's the link. Sam's son."

The cops sitting around in the situation room having coffee and doughnuts look from one to the other. Then another guy says, "Yeah. It's not about Frank, it's about Sammy. Frank is the owner of all the boats in the fleet. Sammy only skippers them for his brother. That makes Sammy the shill. And that, gentlemen, is how we get to Frank. We take away his money supply."

The Niputi ...the Nephew

I imagined him to be the nefarious thinking cop looking around at his teammates and smiling.

"We just haven't applied the proper leverage," I imagined a cop saying. "Now we can. Here's what we do. We re-check all the money operations where those bastards operate. Bring in the county health department boys and state ABC guys involved and collectively nail them for food and health reasons, like spilling drinks, spreading germs, spitting on the floor—whatever. Then between Health and ABC we'll pull their license and shut them down.

"When we're done, Frank will be begging on the streets like a hobo. We can hand him to the FBI on a platter and he'll be squealing, telling all about his crony crooks and the Mafia."

I didn't recount my theory to Dad and Mom. It would only upset Mom. Dad, I assumed, would turn a deaf ear to anything involving his brother.

Dad continued. "So, this vice cop says to me, "Sammy, you appear to be knowingly violating the law. You've got ABC and health violations. You've got drunken sailors asleep on your bar. Those are multiple violations, Sammy, and ABC's probably gonna pull your license.' "

Just then, the phone rang and Blackie our bartender answered. 'Sammy, it is the Corsair. Larry T. needs to speak to you."

"Sammy," says Larry, "vice cops, ABC and the Health Department boys all showed up ten minutes ago. One of them saw a drink spilled on the floor and the health guy ruled it a violation. He pulled our 'A' card."

"I told Larry to give them what they wanted and not to get arrested. Just get rid of the crowd, shut the doors, and put the cash in the safe. I think they hit what they thought was all of my places tonight. I'll come by and see you in the morning about eleven at the coffee shop."

"Okay, Sam, you're the boss." The phone call ended.

"I then told Blackie I'd bail him out in about an hour. I cleared up the joint and closed up."

"Dad, how'd you find out the other bars were hit?"

"I asked Mollie, a waitress, to walk over to Kelly's and check out the street's joints. Molly said they hit Kelly's, but not any other bar owners, only ours. The Matranga's joint, the Hula Hut and Green's were operating as usual."

Dad looked drawn and old, unsure of himself. I was worried he was going to keel over. He was pissed. All of Dad's bars had been hit. It was a planned event to put him out of business. Though Don Augustine, Dad's attorney, tried to resolve the standing issues with the Alcohol Beverage Control, County Health Department and the police, the wheels of progress were indeed rusty when it came to any Bonpensiero issues. All liquor on the bar premises had to be returned to distributors or sold to other bar owners. Our "A" card health permits were in a drawer somewhere in the Health Department. Sam Bonpensiero, by "guilt through association," had been screwed by the system. Oh, and all the equipment and bar fixtures, they went like used shoes and trash—for chump change.

For any normal joint Health, Safety or ABC violation, you could be back in operation with a suspension, fine, or something reasonable. At most, you would be closed for thirty days. However, after nailing four places with multiple violations from several agencies, and the law standing in the way, it would be nearly impossible to financially survive. When coupled with all the red tape generated to slow the normal dullard-like bureaucratic pace, Dad's sullied reputation would prevent him from ever getting back in the liquor business, or at least he thought so.

The Niputi ...the Nephew

Years later, Dad confided in me that he had to sell any and all to survive. Fortunately, he had previously sold the big house above the bay for a very handsome profit, which included ten acres in Kearny Mesa, a 28-unit apartment complex, and enough cash to buy a smaller house in Del Cerro. However, with continual attorney bills, outstanding business vendors to pay back and a dwindling rental environment in the apartment house, negative cash flow got the best of him.

In less than two years, after I left home, he sold the Kearny Mesa land for quick cash and "Joseph Manor," our apartment complex. Mom went to work at a local dress shop and Dad became manager of a friend's bar.

What about Frank and the law and the grand scheme to force him to rat out his Mafia cronies to the FBI? Frank continued doing what he had normally done; he ate well, talked to his friends, and made phone calls, and since he was not on parole anymore, he made some trips. And again, Frank went about his business and slithered under a rock unscathed.

While the law enforcement agencies believed they had Dad all but bankrupt, he fooled them with his own scheme, which no one including me knew about. That is until we sat across from each other in England. It was 1965 and we savored a seldom-had measure of VSOP Courvoisier cognac.

CHAPTER 27
COCKFIGHT AT PUCCIO'S

It was late in the year, November 1961, and my cousin Josephine Puccio became engaged to Norbert Kirkpatrick. A celebratory engagement party was held at Thelma Puccio's—her mom's home in Mission Hills. That was the day the gods decided to let the tough dog off the leash and offered me up as the likely meat for him to chew on. I believe family squabbles happen in everyone's house, as sure as night follows day. The only difference in the Sicilian culture is that they are not supposed to happen between old and young relatives. The younger individuals, by custom with its implied threat, would not, could not, and dare not contradict an elder relative. If a dispute arises, the younger—male or female— would shut their mouth and walk away like a scolded dog or bitch. Normally, it would take no more than a stern look or hand gesture to make it happen. More importantly, any disagreements were to be held in private and never aired in public. Somewhere along the way to my 21st birthday, I forgot that rule.

✸ ✸ ✸

Uncle Frank had been out of prison for almost a year. I had completed my seeing-eye-dog routine of squiring him around and was finishing my final semester in college and preparing to enter into the Air Force as a commissioned officer, soon after graduation.

Frank had not been openly doing much with his Mafia family and he felt deserted. In addition, he thought his blood relatives avoided him, but that was not the case. They just didn't know how to react to him. He always wore a false front and thought that was okay, but it was really at the heart of his psychological problems.

Tonight, he was late and worried about finding a parking place. A couple of young punks were out in front of Thelma's clean, three-bedroom, 1930s vintage bungalow. They sat talking and smoking. Unfortunately, there wasn't any parking for Frank.

Frank was driving a Chevy Corvair, a step down from what he used to drive and "a piece of shit toy car" in his own words. He was fuming by the time he found a parking place and angry at everyone and everything for as many reasons.

It must have galled him to see his brother Turi's car, a new white Cadillac hardtop with fancy red leather upholstery, parked close to the front door and just behind my aqua-colored Pontiac hardtop. Frank finally found a space around the corner and dreaded the hundred-foot walk. He hadn't been in a good mood that day. He slammed the car door and had to raise his arthritic knee higher than usual to climb up to an elevated curb. He looked around and thought, Yeah, *everybody's got a spot but Frankie.*

He fumed as he walked up the front steps. In Frank's mind, his position as the eldest in the family meant that he should be respected. At the least, he should have been left a parking space at his sister's home.

Frank had not been in a good mood for a long while. Little things pissed him off. Things in the organization were way off. Money was in short supply and his position precarious, especially with that ballbuster, De Simone, playing like God. Frank knew he was being screwed. He didn't have any *Soldata* (soldiers) under him and he was being verbally pounced on by every asshole in his, the former *Dragna familia*.

Frank had complained loudly to his brother that there was little respect in his business, and it showed with the new people they brought in. They were all pussies with big mouths and *Nudu Colognes* —no balls. He lamented to himself, *What kind of bullshit had risen in the last ten years, five of which I spent in the joint sitting on my ass. Managgia* (frustration).

Maybe Frank needed some blood family time around those who ooh'd and aah'd when he showed up. Knowing him, he'd attend just to prove Thelma's status for her friends and the rest of the family. He couldn't turn her down. Her eldest daughter's engagement was a big occasion for her. Her husband had died years before and as the family elder, Frank had responsibilities.

Though he didn't know the Kirkpatrick kid, he thought of him as just another young *Americano* with an Irish name. A white guy. None of the young fellows he'd met since he got out of San Quentin reminded him of men. Frank didn't mind the stage he was on, but not the forum and the bullshit where the women ooh'd and aah'd and the men looked away when he caught their eye. *And, rightly so,* he mused. He was Frank Bompensiero and should be respected and feared. His time in prison had not drained his power or his lust for life. And around them, he was boss. Frank still resented his time in prison and those who hadn't visited.

He then put on a big grin as he walked into his sister Thelma's modest home. He knew her friends must have asked, "Will your brother Frank be there, Thelma?"

The Niputi …the Nephew

"Of course. Please come and meet him."

"Hello, everybody. Frankie's here, now the party can start." There must have been 30 men and women sitting around in a circle from the living room into the dinning room. The younger generation had taken over the kitchen to gab and drink among themselves.

He went over and kissed his mother, then smiled at his brother Sam, Mandy and the crowd. He also kissed his sister, but paid no non-family member any real attention until Thelma rose and said to all, "This is my brother Frank." He immediately rose from his seat and turned and smiled. Hell, he didn't care who these people were. He was just there to please his sister. Someone told a Sicilian joke in dialect and most in the crowed who understood laughed.

Frank's opening words fell unceremoniously into the din when he realized he wasn't the center of attention as he thought he would or should be. Things were loud and boisterous in the kitchen where the younger set was happily raising hell. Frank noticed Thelma wagging a finger at him, trying to get his attention. He leaned over and Thelma whispered something about her younger daughter's behavior with her boyfriend, John "Babo" Crivello.

"We're going to have trouble, Frank. I'm worried sick about Mary Ann. Babo has been feeding my daughter Mary Ann a lot of liquor. Can you say something?"

"What? He's feeding your daughter booze in your house? Has he no respect? I'll take care of his crap! Don't worry, sister. I'll take care of everything."

Frank entered the kitchen doorway and with a grin on his face scanned the room.

"All of you are having a good time? Maybe you are having too much of a good time? You don't want to drink too much because it can get you into trouble."

Then Frank saw me sitting off to the right near the door, sipping on a plain tonic and lime. And he said, "Right, Niputi?"

"Yeah, right-on, *Ziu!*" Then I said, "How are you doing *Ziu Chich?* I didn't know you were coming."

"I just arrived and good thing too. When the cat is away the mice will play, heh?"

I wondered what the hell he meant with that old cliché?

But something in his features caught my eye and I wondered why he continued to stare at me. Suddenly, I felt like he was angry at me for something.

"What are you talking about, Ziu?"

"Don't give me that bullshit. I saw you sitting in there while Babo was feeding your cousin Mary Ann alcohol. She's underage. You and Norbert could care less, just talking and laughing when you should be concentrating on Mary Ann with her punk boyfriend trying to get her plastered. What the hell's wrong with you, Niputi? She's your cousin and you don't care enough to be responsible! I thought you'd be more honorable."

I still didn't get what he was grousing about. But he was embarrassing me in front of family and others in the room.

"No, Ziu. I do know she's underage, but her older sister is sitting next to her and her mother has been here all day while the young ones have been boozing it up. But, you are wrong about one thing, Ziu. I am not my cousin's keeper. They are in their own house with their mother. And by the way, her mother gave Mary Ann her first drink. If she wants to drink, that's none of my business. Besides, what better place for them to be drinking? Right in front of her mother and not on the street in the back of a car. Her activities in this situation are none of my business."

The Niputi ...the Nephew

Frank stepped closer to me. But those around us heard him very well.

"Well, I am making it my business, Niputi!" There was no mistaking the menace in his voice. "Let's take this outside." His voice carried into the other room and you could hear the noise calm down to just audible voices. They heard Frank's menacing growl.

With his last comment, I got up and moved outside. I could feel the hair on the back of my neck standing on edge as Frank's potential threat fell from his lips. *What the fuck is he going to do now, bitch as usual or spank me? It would be nice for Dad to come out and see his brother in action for a change.*

The groom to be, Norbert, and several others, including Babo, followed. They must have figured I was going to get shoved around and wanted to be in on the fun. Word spread quickly that Frank had called out his brother Sam's son. As soon as he heard that, Dad scurried from his chair and went out the front door with Mom in tow. One look told him what he needed to know. Frank reached for and grabbed my shoulder. And though Sam started toward us, he was already too late.

I was ready and watched for the old bastard as he grabbed at my lapel. What Dad missed was Frank's earlier ravings at me. But he got to hear the best and the response crunch.

"Listen here, Niputi!" yelled Frank. "When I speak, you'll fucking listen."

In retrospect, I had just about all I could stand of my uncle. Over the last few months I had squired him around and paid for the privilege with the hard-earned money Dad earned. I had been embarrassed by his crude and pompous actions in public and had endured his crass fawning over my girl. Maybe the years of "guilt by association" and all the degradation it meant had taken its toll. I didn't know, nor did I care. The fact that I hadn't been drinking because I was driving only gave me a sugar high.

Frank attempted to put his fucking paw on my shoulder, this in front of my aunt's family, relatives and a host of strangers looking on. As he sounded off so all could hear, I responded, "Take your fucking hand off my shoulder, Frank." After faking toward my left, I swung upward and shoved my fist into the side of his face and heard the sound of a crunch as I said, "Take that, you miserable prick."

Frank jerked his hand back like he had just been zapped by static electricity. At the same time, he swung his right fist at me.

Instinctively, I let fly with a left cross and another right that nailed him on right cheek and eye. Frank flew back as I countered with a shot to his midsection that almost made him puke. He went to the ground grunting. Suddenly, I went crazy. I was on him with a barrage of punches with all the fury that twenty years could unleash.

The next thing I knew, someone was pulling me off Frank. It was my Dad.

"Joe Joe, get off. Stop! Stop it! He's your uncle."

"No, he's your brother. I don't have an uncle." Dad helped his brother rise and steady himself. Frank was wobbly and began to sway back and forth in a daze.

I hunched down in fighter position and cajoled Frank. "You want a little more, you convict prick? You're no tough guy. You're just an asshole with a big mouth! I've listened to your shit for years. Fuck you, and yours, Frank for all the crap you have done to our family. It's over! Stay the fuck away from me!"

I relished looking at Frank, who was bleeding profusely all over his white on white shirt from cuts on his cheek and nose. A goose egg was growing under his right eye.

"Joe! *Finitu* (stop). Bastante (enough)," Dad shouted.

"Dad, stay the hell out of this. It's between me and this asshole, not me and you." About that time Mom came across the grass toward me."

"Hey, Frank. You were saved by a lady."

"Dad, you have a choice tonight: It's me or your piece of shit. He may be your brother, but he sure as hell is not my uncle. He has caused you, me and my mother a lot of grief over the years and it's probably not over yet. I could finish him off right now and we'd all be better off!"

Then I looked at Frank. "Not that I care what you think, Frank. But, for the record, with everyone here listening, I didn't get your niece drunk. Her own fiancée did that with permission of your sister Thelma. And as always, Frank, you picked on the wrong guy."

"Frati," Frank said to his brother, "Your *Figghiu* (son) has some stones. I'll give him that!"

"You'll give me nothing, you prick! Shut your fucking pie hole, Frank, or do you want some more?"

Dad leaned over to me. "Son, let's talk."

He put his arm around my shoulder and led me away as Frank turned and headed back toward the kitchen, dusting off the grass from his disheveled suit.

Dad looked around and leaned close to me and said quietly, "Joe, you are my son and I love you. Between you and me, you made me proud tonight."

I must have looked at him in shock. It wasn't what I expected him to say. I hugged him. Mom came over and gave me a hug. Then she said, "How are my men? Good, I hope."

"We are better than we've ever been, Mom."

Then I said to them both, "I've got to get out of here. Pay my respects to the family, which for me excludes Frank. He's never been family.

"Mom, Dad will fill you in. I'll see you later at home, Mom. I love you both."

I slowly walked toward my car as another chapter closed in my life. For some reason, I flashed back, thinking of an old friend and a man whom I respected that Frank Bompensiero injured one day long ago in the office at Kelly's. Had Frank Marino wanted, he could have broken Frank like a twig. But at the time, Marino didn't know that. Perhaps Marino was more concerned for fear of his wife and daughters than his own self.

An interesting side note happened over thirty years later via a phone call. While living in Granbury, Texas, I heard that Norbert Kirkpatrick was approaching eighty years old and residing in Austin, just down the way a bit. I called Norbert and I enjoyed discussing the old times and the night I took down "The Cigar" *Ziu Chich*. It was a hoot!

✳ ✳ ✳

And then, like nothing had ever occurred, the future was now and graduation was upon me. Five in my class elected to graduate in January 1962 rather than do the commencement bit in June with our college class. Mom and Dad planned a celebration party for my classmates and me. Big China Chan and several other guys from my ROTC graduating cadet class were commissioned as well. We invited a limited number of guests, but one person was specifically not invited and I went out of my way to tell Mom and Dad that I didn't want to see him at my party: Frank Bompensiero.

You guessed it. Frank showed up, no doubt invited by my father. That was the only time in my life that my father ignored my request. I initially took a personal affront to what he did and let him know it. From that point on, I knew I had to tighten the reins anytime I wanted to be sure that Frank would not be involved. The reason was simple; my father could not refuse his brother on any issue involving family. Dad's allegiance to his brother above all else was clear to me now, and more than any other time in my life. I would never forget it. Dad knew I was pissed and came over while I stood alone.

"Son, can we talk?"

"Sure, Dad, you can always count on me." Though I wondered if that is a two-way street.

"Please understand, I know how you feel, but believe me. I had to have him here today. He had to witness our family success and see how proud your Mom and I are of you. You, my son, are a college graduate and a commissioned Air Force officer. No one in our family has ever accomplished so much and you did it alone."

"Not true, Dad. I had you and Mom all the way and I love you both."

Nothing more needed to be said. Dad insisted that the photographer he hired take some pictures of the group and one photo (see photo insert) where I concluded that the camera lens lied, seemingly reflecting the threesome in a jovial scene. Frank eventually found himself out of place and finally departed. I only saw him one more time.

CHAPTER 28
THE CAMERA LIES

Before you read this chapter, please take a look at a picture of three men—in the photo section of this book. They are the Bompensieros, and the main characters in this story. Unfortunately, the picture was staged. Dad asked me to take a photo with him and then next thing I knew Frank joined us. It was January 1962; I am in my Air Force uniform in the center of the photo. I am the most distraught member of the trio. I imagine that Dad, to my left, was the happiest as he was able to satisfy his familia need to have his elder brother present (whom I did not invite) and didn't want around. This chapter will hopefully provide some insight into their cultural differences, which contributed to ongoing family discord. Other immigrants had similar if not more demanding challenges. They strove to be winners in a foreign society and carved out a good life for themselves and family, unlike Frank Bompensiero.

✳ ✳ ✳

The Bompensieros, as you know, were of European stock and emigrated from Sicily to the USA. But unlike common Anglo names like Smith or Jones, Bompensiero was Sicilian and was sneered and shunned as being associated with the criminal element of society . . . the infamous Mafia. They weren't all bad, were they? What about the other Bonpensiero, Buompensiero, families, etc. who were also maligned by society?

Their heritage was from brothers whose names were changed/misspelled as immigrants when they came to America. Some were fishermen, administrators, teachers, etc. They never got a break. Niputi speaks of their attitudes, dreams and desires as well as the antagonist of the story, Frank Bompensiero.

He faced life's challenges by seeking out the dark side and taking the easy way out. Unfortunately, he and his brother were inseparably linked by one brother's association with the dreaded Mafia and a criminal history that spanned his lifetime. Though tied together by family name, they were dysfunctional, with the two pulling in opposite directions. In many cases, they were related to each other by circumstances beyond their control.

In this 1962 photo of a San Diego State College graduation celebration for Joseph Bompensiero, all appears jovial, but beneath the smiling faces lays discord. Pictured left to right: Frank Bompensiero, notorious former Little Italy resident, center is Joseph Bompensiero, recently commissioned USAF officer, and to his left, his father, Sammy Bompensiero, Frank's brother. The camera catches them in an off moment in what appears to be a convivial scene. It's a lie. Over my expressed objections, my father invited his brother to the party. Accordingly, I fumed at Dad's action but should have expected as much, considering his years of absolute loyalty to his brother.

Such was the pattern of Sammy's fraternal and family loyalty. It was an old world tenet that he lived by, and to break with it meant to renounce his family. That he could not do.

I never tried to gloss over my father's shortcomings. He had them like every other man I've known. But I won't dwell on those. In the scheme of life, he did many more good things than bad, and it would be a waste of time to try to compare. I not only respected my father but also knew him to have an introspective pride. He was never ashamed of where he came from, or what he could and could not do. In his eyes, he had been a reasonably good man, husband, father and provider. What more could you ask? He was a success.

Yes, he was a simple man and some might consider him a *cafoni* (peasant) because he was not worldly and could not read or write. However, when his shoe leather hit the pavement, he busted his hump to survive and succeed at every task given or sought.

No matter that he was born in Milwaukee, Wisconsin. He was an immigrant just like anyone else who was born in Sicily. When you are taken at three months old and grow up with two non-English-speaking Sicilian parents, you learn your native tongue, customs, and mores'. Without schools to attend in Sicily, you learn a trade from your father and he teaches you how to be a man. You learn self-control, how to defend yourself against those bigger and stronger, and you learn to control the fear that comes from within, especially when Mother Nature savages your vessel during a Mediterranean winter storm. You will always be confident because you are Sicilian and you are a survivor.

I've tried to provide the uninitiated with a researched background of the *Mafia and the Mafiusu*, the concept, and the people within it, as it thrived in Sicily, its home. And not, if you will, as it continually appeared in movies, magazines and novels about hoods, knaves and the celebrity Dons who supposedly made up the continually foundering organizations also known as the FBI-sponsored "*Cosa Nostra*"—our cause or our thing.

The Niputi ...the Nephew

For those who wonder, the word *Mafia* was never used in our home. I think I mentioned it once as a boy and was castigated. Later, as a young man, the word became more of a joke from my non-Italian friends who referred to me as Mafia, Dago Joe or Spaghetti Head, WOP One, et al. I find it strange that the media, papers, and TV used those terms. Yet none of the writers knew or cared what it all meant, or from where it derived, but neither did the people it represented. Nobody said the Sicilians were all smart. Then again, some, though smart, make themselves say stupid things.

It's also interesting that its etymology is neither Sicilian nor Italian. But as I explain later, something more akin to Arabic . . . But it is strange that it represents an early Sicilian henchmen organization created by the hoodlum element of a broken society to gain a foothold (extorting) landowners, businessmen, the church and the Sicilian police in the 1800s.

Those of this ilk, according to some scholars, considered themselves to be thugs, brigands or hoodlums, but with a title or name. They were prideful and brave in their minds and compared what they did akin to England's Robin Hood, stealing from the rich but keeping it themselves. Hollywood's Old West bad guys—Jessie James, The Daltons, Billy the Kid, and the like, were of the same ilk, but most of it is created muck, not reality.

I believe that crime is and was news. Often you could attach an element of intrigue into the story as the news media often did to create fear and sell newspapers when that was in vogue. Again, not only the Old West comes to mind but also the dark heroes of the twenties. The local press pundits made the ruffians and criminals into heroes.

When I was a twenty-year-old living in Del Cerro, a Mission Valley suburb near SDSU, Frank Bompensiero introduced me to many men. Two of them were prominent in the annals of crime. Joe Bonanno (Joe Bananas) and his son Bill. They were invited by Frank to spend several days in our home. Then he pulled Dad aside and probably said, "You don't mind do you, Turi." The prick never would ask my mother, because she would have said, "Hell No."

Several years earlier in San Jose, I personally met and knew Salvatore Marino and his son Angleo and his grandson Sal. He was named after his grandfather. I also met Joey Marino, Angelo's brother. They in turn introduced me to Joey Piazza.

Through the years, Frank introduced me to the rest of his tribe, as in Jimmy the Weasel Fratianno, Johnny Roselli, the Dragna sons and the Matrangas and others. Frank was connected, no doubt, and he could pull strings, even some dirty political ones. But all can rest assured that Frank Bompensiero was not a nice man.

None of the above was much different than in far-off Sicily, where the politics, security, religious affiliations had been a nightmare to the people who lived there. In our Old West, we had native Indians who were bothersome, so we kicked their ass, rounded them up and pushed them off their lands, then threw them in a Florida swamp/pardon me, jail. Excuse my wit— I meant reservation. Then, some years later we freed them and taught them to make money the old-fashioned way. Our government authorized them gambling licenses to use on their land so they could make money. Unfortunately, for the blacks they didn't own any land or if they did we would've taken it away from them.

Some of the vignettes and words you read in this tale are hard to believe. Others might be embarrassing and a few are just shocking, However, I didn't have to stretch the truth to eke out excitement from Frank's brazen crassness.

He provided it himself. I heard him and watched him intimidate physically stronger, more powerful men. I also listened and observed him react to a divisive retort with a more boastful and devilishly sinister promise.

As his bravado grew, the evil spewed out and his facial veins would expand, and the venom of his words would strike fear into the hearts and minds of those he intimidated. He would always revert to what he knew and it wasn't pause, bow your head and walk away. That was not Frank.

There are memories, though. Several of us will sit around on occasion and discuss those times in the past. Guilt through association, as I recall, had a bitter taste, and living in Frank Bompensiero's shadow afforded me a close-up and personal view of the nasty side of life. Being a faithful and attentive brother injured my father, although he would never admit it. Frank embarrassed and disrespected my mother, but she grinned and bore it. Some of the old family photos capture those feelings. With the exception of his daughter Mary Ann, who was never around, his actions always touched the children in a negative way. Most of us who grew up around our grandmother's house, which he seldom visited, were afraid of him. As in the boogieman. While at Nanna Maria's, family children spoke in hushed tones when *Ziu Chiich* was around for fear we would have to kiss his ring. Fortunately, that wasn't often. His fawning mother, Nanna Maria, and his sisters allowed it! No, that's wrong. They encouraged it, as if he were a bishop, cardinal, or pope. Then he would toss a coin or coins in the air and laugh as the kids scrambled for the money. My mother wouldn't allow that sort of obsequious submission for me. Dad never said a word. Adults outside the family also cowered for fear that something more sinister would befall them.

Dad learned from his father, and gave me insight into the way his father taught him, which was the only way he knew, by telling me stories and parables he remembered his father told him as a boy. Each story had a serious note and they all centered on the family.

Sam Bonpensiero was a sincere and no-nonsense man. He could be boisterous when angry, a madman when confronted by superior odds, and vicious to the core when someone threatened his family. He could also be a gentle man, which was normally his persona. He had many friends both in and outside the Italian community. As a liquor man and people manager, with at times seventy-five employees, he was well-liked and respected. Forced from commercial fishing, he entered a business he didn't understand at the beginning, but he learned.

Even though he and my mother weren't great church parishioners, he did assume a leadership role as president of the Sicilian Catholic Society, *S.S. Madonna De Lume*, for several years. My mother, also a member of the society, marched in the seasonal parades down to the harbor to bless the boats. I too was baptized and became a church-goer and then altar boy in what is now historic Little Italy's Our Lady of the Rosary Church.

Dad was also around when the church priests were in need of sacramental wine or a bottle of scotch or Irish whiskey when parochial priests visited the parish. He maintained contact with his Italian friends and neighbors and later passed his presidential gavel to a Porticello boyhood friend and fisherman, Giuseppi Carini.

Once my father was asked to work for a nationally recognized liquor firm. I was so proud of my father as I listened to a McKesson & Robbins executive make him an offer to come aboard their company as a regional marketing rep. They wanted him to travel the Western states as their ambassador and show bar owners how to improve their operations. I listened when they made him the offer: $75K per year, car, expense account, three weeks vacation, and retirement plan. When the VP was done, Dad looked him right in the eye and said, "Bill, I'd sure like to tell you I'll think about it and talk to my wife. However, I can't accept your offer. But, thank you anyway."

After they left, I said, "Wow, Dad, why did you turn it down?" I couldn't believe it. "Christ, Dad, it's 1968 and that was one hell of an offer."

"I know, son. The money, company car, and retirement were great and maybe I should have jumped on it. But son, have you forgotten that I can't read or write? This company respects my ability as a bar operator. Why would I want to destroy that and our relationship by surprising them with my ignorance?"

Not very smart, heh? Think about it. My father was correct and showed me that he could see where I couldn't.

Regarding Dad's lack of education brings up an interesting side story. Sometimes in the heat of the moment, we forget about the other guy who had to emigrate from another country. We can't even begin to understand what it means to be an immigrant. I'm not referring to the dictionary term for immigrant, but more about how it feels and how you think and how you survive.

We were born and stayed here through our life and most of us never traveled to see the world. Forget knowing the world through a TV. Those images pass like gas after a good bowl of chili. Do you lose sleep over the 400,000 Sudanese who died to genocide in 2003, or the 800,000 Rwandans slaughtered in 1994? What about the one million Ethiopian urchins who starved in 1985? Or the one million children of Biafra in 1968 who starved as civil war raged, or was it genocide? We don't know, and believe me, Americans do not give a fig about how the rest of the people live. Yeah, we empathize, give donations, and send Red Cross ships. But, for all we know, we can't solve the world's problems and don't want to. That is a job for politicians who theorize.

This true-life illustration may help in understanding the plight of those who were Sicilian immigrants. My cousin Salvatore Franco Lococo, known to me as "Cuzin Frank," arrived on American shores when he was fourteen. I recently mentioned to him that I was writing about my Dad and how difficult it must have been for him as an immigrant, not being able to read, write, or communicate.

"Tell me about it," said Frank. "I lived it. Unlike your dad, who was born in Milwaukee, I was born in Porticello with a midwife in attendance. Doctors were few, far between and expensive. They were not on call for those of the *cafoni* (hick or peasant class). I've come to learn that most of my family came from that group."

As a boy of fourteen, proud, tough, and cocky from the streets of Sicily, Frank was anxious and somewhat nervous coming to a new country. In our modern perspective, it would be like arriving on Mars, where most people had food but no one spoke your language.

"That was the way it was for me," Frank said.

In San Diego, Frank learned quickly that they didn't speak Sicilian nor did the 1956 school system do right by him or countless other immigrants. We also must remember that at the time, we were a country of immigrants. They were not illegal aliens.

To educate the fourteen-year-old, the system put Frank into Roosevelt Junior High School. Of course, Frank didn't do well. He couldn't do the work, didn't understand anything expected of him and, to make matters worse, had people laughing at him. They kept him there for six months stumbling around classrooms, where he observed wall pictures of strange people (presidents) and flag symbols he didn't recognize. His plight was one of survival, daring anyone, whites, Mesicani or *Miringiani—Eggplant—Blacks*, to give him trouble.

At the time, Frank preferred to gawk at the pretty Americani girls, hoping to get lucky. Frank was feeling big time when he got to the States. Besides, his hormones were driving him crazy being around *Americani* girls. Christ, they were washed, clean and smelled good. In Sicily, few if any had inside plumbing.

"Over here, they had good teeth, wore pretty clothes, and didn't smell like garlic. Who heard of a dentist over there? The girls in Porticello were different. Hell, their fathers were trying to get them engaged or laid by the time they reached puberty."

Frustrated with the non-adapting newcomers who didn't speak the language, San Diego educators decided to do something drastic. They sent the Sicilian foursome of Frank Lococo, Dominico (Mimo) Carini, Phil Tarantino and Tony Marino across town to the poorest, most backward neighborhood in San Diego, Logan Heights. There, they attended Logan Heights High School, the bastion of the poor, the deprived, and most uneducated black Americans.

Luckily, the four were placed in a class where a young Italian-speaking teacher specialized in those who couldn't read or write. In short, he became their savior and taught them English language skills. It took about six months or so. From there, all were eventually sent back to their district school, San Diego High (SDHS), where Frank's adjustment saga continued.

While there only a short time, he got into a fight with another *Miringiani*, as he calls them, and Frank pulled a knife. He was then sent to Schneider's, a trade school for incorrigibles who didn't have social skills or could not get along with others.

After almost a year at Schneider, Frank was able to return to SDHS and graduated in 1961, the year before I graduated from college. Anyone reading this would get the impression that beneath Frank's current Mr. Nice Guy image lurks "Frank the Hammer" and they'd probably be right.

Frank was a bigoted tough guy when he arrived. Then he met Gina, whom he chased until he won her over and convinced her family that they should marry. Of course, with Gina being a nester and the class in his life, he agreed. I assure you that the years have matured and mellowed Frank. He is not the spring-loaded, ready to fight Dago. Now he is viewed as "Pussycat," purr's his one and only Gina, his queen of fifty years.

Not only are Frank and I cousins by marriage, but we have become very good friends. Reflecting on those times, Frank says, "They were tough. At times, confusion and helpless despair were my soul mates, and it was tough not understanding anyone except your family or other Sicilians."

Frank still speaks with a slightly broken accent, but he smiles as his three daughters say it is cute or darling . . . Ah, Sicilian daughters love their papas.

"Before I could speak English, I felt trapped and controlled," said Frank.

More than anything else, Frank's words helped me immensely to think back and understand my immigrant father. Too bad it was so long in coming.

※ ※ ※

Finally, before I left for my Air Force assignment, my Dad and I had an open discussion about Frank Bompensiero and his associations with the Society and why Dad didn't respect my wishes about the invitation to my graduation party. He had a difficult time putting it into words, but he tried. "You are young and will put it behind you. I have a lifetime of respect and honor for my brother and can't go against my beliefs. Your graduation from college and combined commissioning in the Air Force was one of the proudest days of my life. Your mother and I did it. You were then only one of several Sicilian families whose children went to college and graduated. To me, you were the best. No one in the family ever accomplished that, not anyone. It was just you, with Mom and my support. We shared in your accomplishment and I was so proud, I wanted Frank to see that. We did it without his help."

That day, my father finally communicated to me and I understood his depth of pride. That got me on a roll and I asked another question that had been eating at me for years. "Why did you allow your brother to come into our house, entertain his friends, insult Mom and keep on blabbing to anyone, including his daughter, that he owned the Manhattan Room, The Spot, Kelly's and the Corsair, let alone the Algiers. Does that sound like brotherly love to you? It sure didn't to me. He was a real schmuck! If you think I enjoyed playing his seeing-eye dog for almost two months after he left Quentin while watching him act like Mr. Big, you are crazy. I did that for you, not him. Christ, what were you doing, kissing his ass?"

"I know, son. But believe me, I owed Frank."

"What did you owe and why?"

"Son, we paid a bunch to get him released from prison. We paid more politicians and administrators than you can imagine. It went right up to the top in the state and everyone had his hand out. The game is played that way, all with cash.

"Hell, Joe, you know I'm no big-time knowledgeable investor. I do cash. It's what I know. I just put anything extra from the night's receipts in my pocket and some of it would find its way to a black bag in a safe deposit box. That's what I've done over the years. Good thing I did, or my brother would still be singing the blues in Quentin. No one will ever know how much it really cost. I didn't care about money. I earned it with my bars and saved and saved because I knew eventually I would need it. I never cared about money anyway. It was just a means to an end. You and your mother never went without, did you?

"No, Dad. You've always been a great provider."

Then he said, "Let me tell you something. When I arrived here in 1927, I was fourteen years old and I couldn't speak English. My father died three years before we got to San Diego. We waited and waited for Frank to send us some money for the passage. My mother finally decided to sell off an upstairs floor in our house to get the money.

"In those days, it was a lousy thirty dollars per person for passage and it took us three years to save it. When we finally got here, all my sisters quickly found jobs working at the fish cannery. Frank was into all kinds of shit. He rented a small place on Columbia, not in the old house that you knew, but another one. He was my big brother, he knew his way around the town, and we could speak the same language, Sicilian.

"Frank took care of us when I was kicked out of third grade after being there only a few days, just because I pulled a knife on a teacher. Can you imagine all the other kids in Washington Elementary third grade were babies at eight and nine years old. I was fourteen and the bastard teacher shoved me into class with them. Then, soon after I was put into a class, the teacher tried to force me to sit in one of those little student desks and it was so small, it stuck to my ass. I got pissed off. She called the principal and I pulled a knife on him. Frank found me a job sewing nets because my school days were over.

"Joe, by this time Frank was committed to Jack Dragna's family. Do you honestly think after arriving from Sicily that I gave a shit where he worked or what his belief's were. Get real, son. He was making money and helping the family survive and that's all it was about. Do you know what I mean?"

I listened, but I looked at him and didn't say anything. He paused, and then continued. "Things were tough in the twenties and Frank was into all kinds of crap, theft, robbery, etc. He didn't care and told me as much when we came back to America.

"He'd break your face if you had a wallet with money in it, and he was getting heat from Jack to start hustling and extorting money from anyone he knew that had it. That was how he operated. I won't lie. I helped him locally several times, but we never got caught until I helped him dig a hole in a backyard in Kensington so he could bury something. He wouldn't tell me what, though, and the next thing I know we were arrested. I told the cops the truth. My brother told me dig a hole and I did. Then he told me to go home and I did. Later, I guess he put a box in it and covered it.

"Some kids must have seen him because the cops came the next day and arrested Frank. Then, they came to Mom's and arrested me. But they let me go because I was underage and the boys didn't see me at Frank's."

As the story turned out, the cops kept the stuff and let Frank go as well. Frank figured the cops kept it for themselves.

"What else could you believe? Forty-eight balls of opium were in the back seat of the police car and the door opened and the bag fell on the street? No, it was in the police evidence room and found legs and ended up in the trash and they threw it out.

"Are you shitting me? Frank stared at me with his eyes bulging like I was questioning his veracity. He said, 'I sure as hell would believe that Christ walked on water before I'd believe the cops lost or misplaced the fucking opium balls. Turi, just like in Sicily, everyone is on the take.'

"Another time I helped him plumb the pipes in this house where he lived before he married Aunt Thelma. It was where he hid the vino during Prohibition. Then we got busted in a neighborhood raid and he went to prison while Nana, my sisters, and I stayed home."

"Yeah, I know, Dad. But that was his fault, not yours. You were a minor."

"So what? If he were your brother, would you turn him away if he were helping you? I doubt it!

"Besides, Joe, I never joined any of his Mafia society. I didn't believe in that crap and neither did my father. I met and knew all the players in Frank's circle of associates: Jack Dragna, Joe Bonanno, Sal Marino, Johnny Roselli, Jimmy Fratianno and the Matrangas. They knew I wanted no part of that lifestyle. It wasn't my way. I was happy being a fisherman and then cocktail lounge owner. Besides, the organization that Frank belonged to never did right by him, moneywise. But maybe that was his fault. His big mouth always got him into trouble."

"Okay, Dad, that's good enough for me." Finally, I understood.

Over the years, Sammy and Mandy provided a conservative value system for me to grow up on. It concentrated on character development, hard work, self-worth, and formal education. Unknowingly, however, these teachings clashed with Frank's modus operandi: quick money and absolute power to ensure his place in an underworld society.

One might ask, "How did an eight-year-old know about these things? Information was the key. I read the newspapers as a boy and the stories were the key. Mom taught me to read before I went to the first grade."

Besides, once the crime reporters found that their local boy Frank was an Al Capone West Coast wannabe, he was press-worthy, so they made sure he was always in the news.

Frank held to the Old country conventions. To family, he showed the face of generosity and familial devotion. Frank's "Jekyll and Hyde" facade displayed only the good son, brother, or father to his mother, sisters, wife, and daughter. Typical of those operating in the underworld of crime, Frank kept his visits to his mother's residence at 2033 Columbia to a minimum: holidays, birthdays and special occasions. This was generally accepted because all the family knew the *Spiru* (spies) in Little Italy would report on the happenings, especially of a prestigious businessman who drove a Cadillac and was involved in big business dealings that took him away on frequent business trips.

To a family struggling to make a life in a new world and accustomed to their men and women laboring in the blue-collar industries, Frank's flashy style–big talk, expensive clothes and fancy cars–was proof that he had "arrived." The family accepted his frequent absences as part of his work. They did not question him. They bought his story. They would never believe he was doing the gofer bidding of Los Angeles Capo Jack Dragna. Frank owed Jack. When you were indebted to a powerful West Coast Mafia boss you did what you were told. That was the way it was when staring into the face of evil.

CHAPTER 29
ENGLAND GETAWAY

For the world, 1965 was a year like most others. In the U.S., Lyndon Johnson proclaimed his Great Society program, while off in New York City "The Sound of Music" made its debut on Broadway. And in Germany, Nazi war crimes searches were extended. The U.S. Marines attacked a major Viet Cong stronghold in Vietnam, while China and India were in a land dispute. The English, of course, banned cigarette ads on the telly, while I had to make the worst of transatlantic phone calls home. I then sat down and wrote Mom that her newborn granddaughter was dead and that Julie had been paralyzed in an auto accident. For me and mine, it was not a good year, but the world continued to go round the sun.

✳ ✳ ✳

Upon receiving my initial transatlantic call, Mom and Dad were heartbroken. They were both concerned about Julie's paralyzed condition. The couldn't offer any more help than their love and support. Of course, we needed time to heal and nothing more. In a letter I received ten days later, Mom expressed concern over Dad. He became troubled and despondent over the loss of the baby, Julie's recovery, and my surgery.

Although a few years had passed since the bar raid, he kept busy trying to regain a liquor license but with no luck. He also seemed pissed that his brother Frank rarely called or came around after he heard about the bar raid.

Mom closed with, "Your recent tragedy really got to him, Joe. He misses you."

About a week later, I called Dad and spent a few minutes letting him know we were good and missed them a lot. Then he interrupted and responded like an old Western gunfighter leaving his troubles behind. "I think we are getting the hell out of Dodge and would like to come to England. Would you and Julie be okay with that? Can you get some time off of work?"

"We'd love the company and don't worry about me getting time off work. I have plenty of medical leave from my own surgery, but I'll tell you about it later. Your trip sounds perfect."

Julie and I thought they'd fly over and spend at least two weeks, maybe three.

❊ ❊ ❊

Mom and Dad arrived on a day in June that was unusually gorgeous for England. As I headed south on the A-12 to London, nary a wisp of cloud showed in the sky. It was blue, just like I remembered. Just one of those six or eight wonderful English days that the British dream about, then speak of in almost sacred terms.

Speaking as a native Californian, I thought the sky came in one color —blue. But after a couple of years living on the southeastern coast of England, I knew better. It was always gray. Christ, I thought, I'm becoming a bloody Limey. My neighbors were Brits, and the whole lot would hold onto every ray of sunshine and warmth like the last morsel of a Christmas pudding.

The temperature had been in the mid -70s for the past two days and the orgasmic weather was cause for wild merriment aboard the pirate radio broadcasters on their converted freighter bobbing in the North Sea.

While blasting out the great new Beatles hit, "She Love's Me, Yeah Yeah Yeah! "the D.J.'s cautioned listeners about overdoing one's time in the sun. Actually, they were alarmed because the weather was predicted to reach the 80s. In England, that could be deadly . . . and it was.

The Brits continued to dress warmly as if it was winter, and many died from heat exhaustion. We Americans joked about jumping on a crowded subway or double-deck English bus on a shopping binge during those untypical warm days in London. We never figured that we could die from the British body odor. Living in England for years was quite a learning experience.

Julie and I had great support from my military brethren at RAF Bentwaters and from our little township in Little Bealings. Our wing commander and co-workers honored my wishes when it came time for a simple ceremony in the base chapel for our baby, Samantha. I attended the ceremony, but left almost immediately after the service. I left to say goodbye and bury Samantha at Woodbridge Town cemetery without any onlookers. Just three people were present, two from the cemetery staff and me. Years later, when I could deal with the tragedy, I released pent-up feelings and wrote her a sonnet, which follows this chapter: "One Flower Gone."

✸ ✸ ✸

The B.O.A.C. jet had just landed and began taxiing toward the tower when I verified that I still had plenty of time. They would have to depart the aircraft, then go through customs, and walk the ramp.

I stood by the exit door and waited. My face broadened into a smile at the sound of my father's familiar voice, wondering aloud to anyone who would listen as he and Mom walked through the arriving crowd.

"Mandy, we have to get a Red Cap." Dad said. Dad didn't see me approach and I laughingly said, "They don't know what you want, Dad. Ain't got Red Caps in England."

Dad recognized my voice and almost knocked me over as he turned and we hugged. Mom cried as we embraced. We had not seen each other in two years, and with only an occasional phone call, we missed each other terribly.

"Joe, my God, Joe! It's you!" he shouted. "Where did you come from?"

"Suffolk, Dad. Suffolk England.

"I'll take care of the luggage." We left arm in arm for the lower level where we could claim their baggage.

Four matching rawhide suitcases, two large and two small, came off the ramp. "There they are, Joe!" Dad shouted.

Mom and Dad watched as I casually walked over to a very-well dressed man in a black suit with red carnation and wearing a black bowler. I spoke to him and the next thing they knew, the man followed me and walked up to Dad. "Excuse me, sir. I am Walter and I will handle your luggage for you, if you don't mind."

"Thank you, sir," said Dad as the luggage man placed the cases on a small wheeled rack.

"No need to call me sir. Walter is sufficient." Would you like me to present the luggage to the car, sir?"

"Yes, please, I guess," said Dad.

"Walter, if you please, here is my valet parking ticket. Can you?"

"Of course, sir. Please stay by the curb and I'll make all the arrangements."

Walter strode off like a man doing a routine mission while Dad said, "You know, I think I'm going to like it here. I like the way they talk."

Moments later, my tan VW bug pulled up, and the tires squealed as the brakes were applied.

"Careful how you mount them, Walter. We're traveling to Suffolk. The A-12 can be tricky."

"Right you are, sir. We could place the larger pieces on the hood, sir, since you do have a dilly of a tidy-tie, and I recommend that we place a smaller one under the bonnet and possibly attach one to the boot." Dad, hearing our discussion, looked befuddled.

"What did he say? I don't understand where he was going to place the luggage. Joe, you're not going to let him tie the big suitcases on the hood, are you? You won't be able to see when you drive."

"Yeah, most likely. I don't think we can secure it anywhere else." I knew Dad didn't understand the subtle differences in British car-part terms.

Dad carefully watched as Walter lifted the two large cases to the roof of the car and tied them down. He then placed one of the two smaller cases under the hood and tied the last to the trunk. I tipped Walter and said, "Please get in, we're heading for Ipswich. Enjoy the ride and sites."

At that point, I turned to my father.

"Pop, you're in England and the language is a little different. In English car lingo, the boot is what we call the trunk, and what we call the hood is the bonnet. It's a bit confusing but you'll get used to it." And so he did.

"Dad, learning English all over again can be tricky so, if you don't understand a word used, please ask. The British love to give directions. By the way, they love Yanks! They haven't forgot our assistance during World War Two. And, do not worry about the language. You'll get used to it."

I sat in my seat and pulled my belt on. In England at the time, it was mandatory. "Please wear safety belts while in England, folks. It's the law and they enforce it." I cranked up my Bug and headed down the road, on the wrong side of course, toward the A-12 and home to Suffolk County and a bungalow in Little Bealings.

After we carried in the luggage and showed them around our rented two-bedroom cottage, they were both pleased. Dad no doubt had visions of his former lifestyle in Sicily and was probably worried over what he would find. We relaxed and had a welcome-to-England cocktail, with ice water for Dad, in Little Bealings.

Then I asked Dad if he'd like to take a walk down to our local pub. That became his hideout for the next couple of weeks. He found that he liked the Brits and their camaraderie. He and I spoke like old friends who hadn't seen each other in many years. Dad mentioned that he and Mom wanted to visit Samantha's gravesite in Woodbridge Town.

The next day, bright and early with the morning dew on the heath, we drove to Woodbridge Town. Mom wanted to stop at a florist and I did. It was a bit cold and we had left Julie home. Her feelings were still raw. One day she and I would go there together and hold each other while we took a moment to share our grief, our loss and spend time with our little Samantha.

At Samantha's gravesite, Mom replaced the withered flowers with the fresh ones. There were tears all around as we grieved for our child.

About two weeks later, we decided that a tour of Europe was in order, and with Julie feeling much better; her doctor thought the trip would do her good. She wore a neck brace and I would limit the driving time. I brought home a map and plotted a sightseeing route since I was to drive. (I held the only international driver's license).

I developed a circuitous route and since we were doing it my way, we went to Belgium, Netherlands, Germany, Austria, Italy, and France, then back to England.

Dad wanted to go to Sicily. I had been there once, and it was still backward and poor in 1963 when I stopped in while on a mission. I told Dad that it would be better for him and Mom to fly down, especially since Julie would be tired after a month on the road.

We left England on a bright morn and headed to our North Sea ferry departure point. We crossed over to Calais in France and headed to Belgium and Holland for a few days, then got into Germany. It was Mom's old stomping grounds, Kaiserslautern, a city on the other side of Luxembourg. We were all hungry, so we stopped and had Mom order the food. She still spoke German and could flit between Sicilian, English, and German without a breath.

On this occasion, upon completing the order, the German waiter turned to Mom and said in English, "Your German is a little rough, *fraulein*. It sounds more like Russian." Dad teased her, saying that after all these years claiming her mother and father were Germans, he found out the truth.

"I know I'm German or I think I am," Mom said.

However, mysteries unfolded while I was researching family data on Niputi, and I found a printout from a fellow military friend, Les Snodgrass. I asked him for anything he could find under Mom's maiden name and voila, I got obsessed with the first document I read and never looked beyond. There it was right in front of me. Both John Buechler, my grandfather, and Katherine Marie Baker, my grandmother, were born in Russia. Married year, 1871. Years married, 29. It was fascinating that, at 75 years old, I found out I was half-Russian, not German as believed.

We thoroughly enjoyed our trip. We had wonderful family time together, as always. After thirty-plus days, we agreed we missed home, so we scurried back across the pond to mother England.

A month later, after I returned to work, Mom and Dad flew off to Sicily, his childhood home. Upon his return, we commiserated and it was sad.

"Son," he said, "we had a wonderful time. The people were great and the land is beautiful."

"I'm glad you enjoyed yourself, "I said, knowing full well that he was straying from the truth. "How were your cousins, the Zarconis?"

"They were fine."

"Where did you stay in Porticello?"

"We didn't. We went up the road not far to Palermo and stayed in a hotel."

"No one had an indoor toilet and shower, did they?" That I thought was a nasty retort. I knew that most people there were poverty-stricken and that is why they left Sicily. Dad looked at me, his eyes started to water up and I knew that I had touched a chord.

"Joe, I saw how those people lived and I hurt for them. The truth is that was the way I lived. I had forgotten. We were poor, proud and stupid."

"I'm sorry, Dad. My remark was out of line." His facial expression told me he understood.

"My cousins were truly very wonderful to see, but they are not well. They were poor and very humble and... I couldn't help them. Zarconi and I were kids together. Now, he's an old man and his family . . . *Ah Dio?* What can you say?" His eyes watered and he changed the subject. I savored that honest moment of empathy shared with my dad.

The Niputi ...the Nephew

"Son, I want to ask you a question. Are you happy in the Air Force?"

"Yeah, Dad. I chose this path." Knowing my father and having a feeling that he had something on his mind, I laid some bait. "Nevertheless, you know, the military can be a rough life. I am gone quite a bit. I've heard from the old-timers that you almost never get to see your kids growing up.

"So, why do it?" he asked. *Now I'll see what he has cooking in the back of his mind, I thought.*

"Well, it's all about options and what one is interested in doing for a working life."

"Joe, you know I always had a feeling about the joints and the fact that I was always the one exposed. You know, my brother was never dependent on the liquor business. He never owned the Gold Rail. That was Jack's joint and he gave Frank a piece to run it. It was never that way with our places. I built them and worked them.

"Joe, my brother hustled everything he ever obtained. He earned nothing. Leo Dia's Maestro Music and Frank's association with "his" wire business were all hustled. He always played for a piece of someone else's action around town. I don't know how he got a piece of it, but you can bet he didn't buy into it. Frank lived by looking for the next hustle. That was my brother Frank. With him, nothing ever changed. He still lives the same way.

"Hell, if I hadn't made a move with the Corsair, I'd be totally broke and screwed.

"You never knew, but some years after we sold the big house, I always had the stinking feeling that if the *Spiru* ever decided that my brother and I were partners, they might come directly after me and my businesses. That started to worry me as Frank just went about doing his business as usual thing. Knowing Mom and I would still have to eat, I decided to cover my bet. My plan worked worked or I wouldn't be here now.

"What do you mean Dad?"

"The corsair, son. The Corsair."

Dad, they took that out when The Spot and Kelly's went south. Right?"

"Well, yes and no. Yes, it was hit. But you remember Larry Taormina?"

"Sure, Dad, you mean Larry who worked at Lubach's on Pacific Highway. I recall he left there and came to work for you at the Corsair after cousin Larry departed."

"Yeah, he bartended with Larry initially, but remember Tina's Larry wanted to go on his own. He then got into the lunch truck business and eventually went back to his first interest, the bar business and bought Patrick's.

"However, Larry Taormina's bartending for me was a sham. I didn't like having my name on all the joint's licenses. So about six months before they hit us, Larry and I reached an agreement for him to buy the Corsair *sutta tavula*—under the table."

"What? Are you kidding?"

"No, son. No joke!"

"I trusted him enough to sign the liquor license and business over to him way before they ever busted the joint. I had a twenty-year lease with about ten to go at the time. I talked to the landlord and he let Larry sign the lease as a co-leasee to protect him.

"Larry and I cut a deal, with a 70/30 split for five years. My end came off the gross monthly receipts. Then Larry would own the joint outright.

He loved it because he didn't have to come up with any cash. He was clean and had a solid reputation. He'd work the

The Niputi ...the Nephew

joint, set up new bank accounts. I contacted the distributors and told them Larry would be running the joint from then on. And that Larry had excellent credit and I wanted my name off as soon as the old accounts were settled. It turned out to be a sweet deal for him and wise protection for me."

"Dad, why didn't they avoid the Corsair the night they hit the other joints?"

"That was all about timing and failure to review ownership on the ABC license. No one checked the licensing to find who owned what. Hell, they, the cops and the ABC always saw me hanging around the Corsair anyway. So they assumed that nothing had changed.

"Larry Taormina raised hell after the bust and when the cops and ABC realized what happened, they did an 'oops' over Larry being the owner. So they worked out a deal with Larry and dropped all administrative charges, and he accepted the hit with a three-day suspension. He was happy and so was I."

"Well that word never got around town or on the streets. Everyone involved was silent," I said.

"After they took my joints, I didn't know what to do and laid back for a while. At least I had enough to cover my monthly nut from Taormina. Since it was all cash, it wasn't bad." He paused for a sip from his snifter and spoke some more.

"During that time, I got tied up with Archie Avakian. You remember him, don't you?"

"Sure, you mean Archie and Jeanie from Long Beach?"

"Yeah, we used to play cards at the Del Cerro house and they went to your wedding. Remember, they would come down for a weekend visit and we'd hit the track at Tijuana. Then Mom I would go with them and play the ponies with them at Santa Anita."

"Yeah, Dad, I remember them. Why?"

"We became pretty good friends and with him owning a liquor store in Long Beach, we always had business to talk about. Then he inherited or pulled a note from some guy who owed him and he picked up the Carousel, a bar here in El Cajon. He said it was a dog and didn't make any money, and he wanted to dump it. I asked if he wanted me to take a look at it and he said, "Go right ahead."

"I took one look and within a couple of days knew his crew was stealing him blind. He didn't have a clue. He thought on-sale joints were the same as operating off-sale liquor stores, which only make about 20 percent against the gross. On-sale is a different racket. *Capish?*"

"I know, Dad, you taught me that."

"Well, long story short, I told Archie that he had a good joint but he had to fire his crew." His employees were stealing but he couldn't believe it and wanted to argue about it.

"Sammy, I've been to the place dozens of times over the past six months and didn't notice anything. They were nice people."

"Okay Archie, I'll make you a deal. Let me have the joint right now and you can keep your name on the liquor license, or make me the manager for thirty days and I'll open your eyes to making money. Then maybe we'll cut a deal where you make me a silent partner for 30 percent of the gross and I'll manage the joint while you sit back and collect your monthly cash. He took me down, introduced me to the crew and I started to manage the joint like my own. I cleaned house and brought in a new crew. The first month ended and I called him down for a count. He about shit when I handed him ten thousand in cash.

"I laughed at Archie's excitement as he said, 'Sammy, you mean I can't laugh all the way to the bank?'"

"No, Archie. Go laugh in your garage."

"Well, what happened with your deal? You working with Archie?"

"The deal went nowhere. It didn't? Archie had never seen that kind of money and got greedy. He asked me to show him what I did and how to do it. What the hell, he was my friend, right?

"A month passed and he gave me three grand for my split. Then he reneged on the deal. I guess he felt, why pay Sammy. We hadn't signed any legal documents. I took his word and handshake . . . I learned what an asshole he really was. By the way, the Carousel went under several months later and we haven't seen the Avakians since.

"Later, I found Morty Zlotoff, a contractor who had a couple of joints on property he owned. But they weren't making it. Again, it was owners who didn't understand the liquor business. Morty knew my reputation and so we put together a sweet deal. I'm going back to run his five joints and he's building a Caribbean-themed nightclub in Mission Gorge and he's calling it Calypso Joe's.

"Good for you, Dad. That sounds great." I hastened to say more, thinking that he had something else on his mind. He just wasn't ready.

"Well, what about you, son. I know you'll do well and Mom tells me you'll be up for captain soon. And knowing you, you'll make it. How do you like the Air Force?"

"I'll make captain, Dad. But, I'm not sure I'll stay for a career. I travel an awful lot. Besides, you're never around when your children are growing up. It can be tough on a marriage. With Vietnam in the wind, I'll most likely get assigned overseas after this job, and that would be two overseas assignments in five years. So, I'm not sure what I'm going to do." That opened the door and I sat back and waited for his response. It didn't take long.

"Joe, what the hell, you don't need that. You can come home and I'll put you in charge of Calypso Joe's. You can buy a new house and settle down. You'll make it in San Diego. Then, we can look for a joint of our own. We can make you the owner since those bastards came after me because of my brother."

That's all I needed to hear. I knew I was right about the raid. My father needed me to return and get him back into business. There was no way I could refuse, so I said, "That's a helluva idea. Dad. Let me talk to Julie about it." And I did. Later I sat down and wrote a short poem to my baby daughter who lay in Woodbridge Town cemetery. We would leave her in a safe harbor because I had no idea where I would be in the future.

The Niputi ...the Nephew

ONE FLOWER GONE

Time has flown leaving so few memories of you,
Samantha my flower, thoughts of you keep me blue.
Time rushed by; decades withered me at last,
But my mind, ever sharp, will not forget the past.

English Stout and sweet tart to celebrate your birth
we savored the thought—happy hearts—silly mirth.
For nine months, we sang and laughed out loud
A new babe is coming, from God in the clouds.

The bassinet so bright, your mother so happy,
excited at last to make me a pappy.
Dear infant, sweet baby, how pretty in pink,
your room is ready, new clothes, toys and sink.

Things here are joyful, they're light and so gay,
soon, maybe tomorrow will be your birthday.
Dear sweetness, little child, oh love of my life,
how could we know then a future with strife?

A car from the village going oh, much too fast,
a swerve, an impact—all destroyed—too good to last.
The doctor in blue gown, passed you to me
all swaddled in blankets, I could not help see.

The black of your hair and your pug little nose,
tender sweet lips and luscious pink toes.
Oh, such a beauty but I'm never to see,
my sweet daughter, this child, growing up with me.
Tiny white casket, she so alone and so cold,

Joseph Bonpensiero

this babe and I—my child—with no God to scold.
Misty the morn, dew blankets English yew and fir,
no birds today singing, just me alone here with her.

No peace, no, not ever, she laid to rest there,
a plot in damp ground—Woodbridge Town Square.
A wife and a daughter, a family no more
Only sorrowful memories—does this even the score?

Bitter gifts that you gave, oh God—and for naught,
You left me alone, heartbroken, distraught.
Who gathered this Flower, I cry to the sky.
Deity above—silent—there was no reply.

PART V
COMING OF AGE

CHAPTER 30

BARS, BANKING & BUSINESS

1966 was a good year as the Beach Boys released "Pet Sounds." And Bob Dylan's "Blonde on Blonde" album came out as well. President Johnson said the United States would stay in Vietnam, and Dr. Martin Luther King Jr. spoke on the Vietnam War. His speech was just about the time Julie, our newly born son, Sammy, and I made our way from Europe to New York. We traveled by sea and had a beautiful voyage aboard the SS United States, courtesy of the USAF. We settled in San Diego and purchased our first new home. And as Dad indicated, I had a job running Morty Zlotoff's "Calypso Joe's." It was a challenge until I pressed my crew into a cohesive unit and they performed as expected. However, in time, running Calypso Joe's didn't do it for me. I needed a challenge and I needed my options open.

✳ ✳ ✳

When I made the decision to leave the Air Force and return to San Diego, I discussed it with my wife, Julie, and my mother. Both of them were affected by my decision and it was important that they knew why I was doing it. I felt as if I owed Dad for all the time and effort he put into raising me. I never forgot how he gently pushed, shoved, and cajoled me and Patrick to stay on track and become college graduates.

Suffice to say, it paid off as I bought our first home, a 1,450-square-foot new San Diego ranch style on Conestoga

Avenue—and all for $19,000. With a VA loan and nothing down. Today the house goes for $500,000. Talk about inflation and false values. Man, how time makes money and perceptions fly. Too bad we sold.

I picked up the reins at Calypso Joe's, a place that held over two hundred customers, with a stage, bandstand and all. It was newly completed in Mission Gorge and we had a huge grand opening with standing room only. It turned out well. We had hula dancers and islander knife thrower/dancers for entertainment, and a specialty limbo dancer named "Boomba." He kept the crowds alive as he showed them how low he could go under the limbo bar.

Dad and Morty were pleased with the public's response to Calypso Joe's. However, in the back of my mind, I wondered how long before the newness of the entertainment wore off and then what? In six months and bored stiff, I couldn't increase my interest in the liquor business which I knew so well. It just was not my chosen field. I had learned that flying was not my game and left it; the liquor business was my father's game, not mine. So, I made the move.

As my first year out of the military came and went, I found myself missing my comrades and reading constantly about Vietnam and what our units were doing. I missed the military lifestyle and challenges. I finally had a talk with Dad and told him that I appreciated the Calypso Joe's position, but it didn't do it for me. I had left the Air Force to get him back in business but I needed to do something more in line with my education. Dad said, "I understand."

In a relatively short time, I found a position with the First National Bank. It was a two-year bank management-training program. I felt like a second lieutenant again, green and looking forward to the future. Within six months,

The Niputi ...the Nephew

I jumped at the chance when a young bank professional by the name of Jan Budding offered me an opportunity in the real estate division.

Jan was a good mentor and I spent over a year with him learning and growing until three things happened. One, Jan pressed me to take some banking courses. Dad called and asked if I could arrange to meet him for lunch. And, I met my short-term future in a businessman by the name of Mr. Nate Rosenberg.

"Sure, I'd love to have lunch. When?"

We made plans for the following Tuesday. He and I didn't get to be together often, so when we did it was special. Like a lot of others, I always enjoyed his company.

We had just finished our steak sandwiches at the U.S. Grant Grill when I noticed two beautiful women dining with a distinguished-looking gentleman across the restaurant from us. Within minutes, the man excused himself, rose, and approached our table. My eyes studied him as he strolled toward us. Although only standing about five foot six, he appeared taller. He stood proud and carried himself like a six-footer.

From his outward attire, there was no doubt he had impeccable taste. He wore a beautiful gray tailored sharkskin suit, accompanied by a deep-ruby-colored silk tie, matching pocket sash and highly polished ebony alligator loafers. He must have just left the barber and manicurist, since his hair appeared as if each hair on his silver head was individually razored, one hair at a time. His nails were short with a hint of white at the tips and were finished with a manly clear gloss.

Within seconds of his arrival arrival at our table, he unbuttoned his suit button, and then pulled out his car keys. I caught the NR monogram on his tailored white-on-white shirt and noticed this was only outdone by his NR on a gold plate affixed just above his Mezuzah. It was attached to a gold rope key chain he pulled from his pocket. His manner was gentlemanly as he came up with a smile on his tanned face. I knew the man to be Nate Rosenberg.

"Sammy, you son of a gun, good to see you. Where have you been?" said Nate.

"Nate, it's taken me two weeks just to have lunch with my son. Please meet Joe. He's at the First National Bank. He's one of two real estate loan officers."

"Real estate lending, heh? That's a great field, Joseph. How long have you been with the bank?" I stood and reached out my palm and noticed his three-carat pinky ring and matching watch, both in platinum, no doubt.

"Nice to meet you as well. I've been there going on two years. Banking pays the bills, but it's a long slow climb."

"Well, Joseph, as your Dad and I can attest, all things take time. Sorry to interrupt. I just wanted to say hello to your father. I'd love to stay and chat, but I've got an appointment with Congressman Wilson and don't want to be late."

"Sammy, I'll be calling you. We've got to talk."

Nate then turned to me. "Joseph, it was a pleasure meeting you, especially after all your father said about you. I'll be in touch." *I thought about Nate's exit remarks and knew Dad had set me up.*

We left the grill feeling refreshed, and I couldn't wait to head up the valley and hear the rest of the story. Since my father and I never played games with each other, he started. "Well, son, that was Nate Rosenberg. It wasn't an accidental meeting, as you know." His hazel-green eyes gave off that glint of awareness as he smiled and said, "The Air Force didn't take out your second sense, did it? I still can't put anything over on you."

"I learned from the best, Pop," I replied.

We both laughed and then he got quiet and serious. He proceeded to lay out a proposition by starting with, "*Figlio tutti informazioni Segreto Silenzio, Capesh?*" This meant none of his comments were to go beyond my ears.

"Joe, I've a dear friend who is a helluva nice guy whom I've known for years. He's also smart and made millions in legitimate businesses and he has fallen on some hard times. He recently called on me because he's got a huge problem and needs my help."

"So what's his problem, Dad? You've never been known to let a friend down. What's up?"

"Well, it involves several people and I'm not at liberty to speak for either of them, now. That's why I'm talking to you. You're one of the people."

The wheels in my mind started to turn and stopped at today's lunch. I interrupted with, "Was Nate Rosenberg, the man I met today, your friend in need?" Dad glanced over with a slight grin and nodded yes. I paused, knowing my father would continue at his own pace. Questions revolved around in my head as I began to think. *What was the angle? There always was one. What did Dad want from me? Could we make some money?* I was about to find out.

He continued; "Nate needs someone to help run his businesses. They are getting too big and he's unable to maintain his management style and do the things he wants to." That all sounded good to me. However, Nate didn't present the image of a man facing any difficulties.

"Joe, one day Nate came to me and we talked. During the conversation, your name came up and I told him about your upbringing on the *Giuseppina* and in the bar business, about college and your background as an Air Force officer, and how you were now with the bank. He was impressed.

He said, "Sam, your son sounds like the kind of man I was looking for to head my organization." So one thing led to another and he said he'd like to meet you. So, that was the reason we had lunch today."

"I understand that, Dad, But why did Nate contact you in the first place. He's a smart man, got the world by the balls in terms of money, business knowledge, and action. Hell, he's forgotten more about real estate than I ever learned."

I paused, waiting. Dad was taking his time. Something difficult was bothering him. "So, what's going on, Dad?"

Dad finally said, "Nate has a problem. Someone is breaking his balls and he is very, very concerned. . . ."

I didn't even pause and said in dialect. *"Pa, tu Frati si rumpi coglione pi Nate?* (Your brother is breaking Nate's balls. Isn't he?)"

Dad just smiled. "You don't miss a trick!"

"Dad, it's not hard when you've been raised to listen and learn. You did a good job. The only pain in the ass we've both shared since I've been around, I'm sorry to say, is your brother. He's bad news."

"You know you make me proud."

I now knew the score, and it was going to be my decision whether to take a leap into another business world or stay with the bank. My choice would be made knowing that the bank was not going to be forever. The answer became easy a month later when Jan Budding left the bank to take a new opportunity. And I became the First National Bank's main office real estate loan officer and was given a raise.

Taking Jan Budding's earlier advice, I enrolled in a class, Real Estate Law, and learned it was quite beneficial in resolving a long-term problem. The class instructor was a San Diego attorney named George Delafield.

During the course, George found occasion to discuss some of his interesting cases with the class. One in particular grabbed my attention. It also shows how some strands of information when placed into the hands of certain people become very important and lead to great things.

Delafield had been hired by a Midwest company to represent them in their efforts to acquire a piece of property in San Diego. George formed a third-party corporation named Ironton Inc. His charter was to buy the business, fictitious name, lock, stock, and real property from an individual at the lowest possible price. However, as we learned in class, price was never a major issue. The corporate client was not interested in the land, business, or property. They only wanted the name. Yet, they could not approach the owner and introduce themselves because the cat would be out of the bag and the price would be out of the question. The only thing they wanted was the fictitious name filing in California.

In a subsequent class, and questioning, he let it be known that the business was a cocktail lounge. My ears perked up. No other information was provided. I finally raised my hand and asked the instructor, "In this kind of a transaction, what will your client do with the bar and business?"

"Oh, we turn around, strip the name, and sell it. We don't want it." That was all I needed to know. When class was over, I called Dad and said, "We've got to talk. I'll meet you at the house tonight."

When I arrived, Dad was already there playing with his grandson.

"Dad, let me explain why I called you," I said excitedly. I filled him in on what I heard. "Dad, they don't want the bar and are willing to get rid of it at their costs. Now the only thing is, what joint it is. Dad, with your knowledge of the bar business, what joint in San Diego could this be? They do not want the place or the liquor license. They just want the fictitious name, so maybe this could be the place we've been looking for."

He thought about it for a few minutes and said, "I know the joint. It's Bob Cheron's Playboy Club on 36th and University. There has been a bar there since before World War II. It could be a helluva joint. I know Bob. He is a good guy in the wrong business, but he is one great tailor. Son, you say the land is included?"

"Yeah, that's what the attorney mentioned."

"Great. There are only a few brokers around who can handle this escrow and I'll know more tomorrow. Let's stay in touch."

I cashed in my whole life insurance policies and sold some stock and took every dime I had accumulated. Dad and I pooled our money and made a low-ball offer. Ironton Corp. accepted and we opened an escrow. It wasn't a week later that my father walked into the Playboy Club and took over the joint. He was, however, less crude than the "sheriff" who basically did the same years before at "The Spot."

Okay, a bartender and cocktail waitress and two beer drinkers were at the bar, but in his calendar of events to open this new place, Dad didn't have time for them to finish their drinks. "I am the new owner of this bar, and we'll be starting soon to clean it up and make it a great place to come and enjoy yourself.

"Are you going to serve lunch today?" a customer asked.

"No more lunches. We are not in the food business," said Dad. With that, he called some Navy friends from downtown. About ten men and a Dumpster showed up.

The Niputi ...the Nephew

When all had arrived, we opened the doors, let the light in, and started to take the chairs out of the joint. It was one filthy hole, as I recall.

Within 45 minutes, the place looked like a bombed-out shelter. Tables and chairs were gone and the carpet was being ripped out, while the bartender stood in awe. Dad finally said, "We don't need you anymore. Go home. Just leave the cash register. I'll call Bob Cheron and let him know I'm starting the makeover." Within a couple of hours, by early afternoon, the crusty bar had been removed and the guys were tearing out the false ceiling. By four o'clock, Bob Cheron and his trusty broker arrived. "My God, Sammy. We had an operating business this morning. I'm out of business and we haven't even closed escrow. You can't do this!

"Don't worry, Bob. You know I'm a man of my word and I'll get this taken care of soon. Besides, you weren't making any money. You know the sooner I get done remodeling, the sooner we can close everything, right?"

"Yeah, but you can't do it until we've closed escrow."

"Bullshit. I didn't read that anywhere in the contract for sale." I arrived just in time to see what he had done and heard Dad's comment to Bob. I laughed to myself, knowing Dad never read anything except numbers on the racing form.

"Bob, does it say I can't do this really? If it does, I apologize, because you know I can't read that well." The broker interrupted and Dad turned to him and said, "Scuse me, I'm speaking with my friend Bob." Then Dad turned back to Bob and said, "We have to talk in private. When they returned, Bob told the broker that all is okay. I have Sammy's assurances."

"It's highly irregular, Mr. Cheron, but if that's your call, we'll make it happen."

CHAPTER 31

THE STAR & GARTER

I look back now and say to myself that putting the Garter together wasn't so tough. But that wouldn't be true if you considered all the physical and emotional stress Dad and I lived through putting the place together. In retrospect, what we accomplished in 45 days was no easy feat. We both had a lot on the line and, considering our limited funding, we used it all and borrowed to the hilt. Dad had many friends who lent a hand and Dad's rep provided him the pick of the litter of San Diego's top dancers. They loved their Papa Sam. Then, just two days before we were to close the escrow and have our Grand Opening a few days after that, we had a notification from the ABC—Alcohol Beverage Control. A neighbor filed a license complaint against our business enterprise. He was quite unreasonable and could ruin everything. This was a big-time problem!

✳ ✳ ✳

I recall it was June of 1968 and San Diego's newest Go-Go hot spot and cocktail lounge, the Star & Garter, would open its doors. Not surprisingly, with Dad's gutsy operations savvy and my business drive, we completed the basic de-construction, then added new fixtures, equipment, bathrooms and a new beautiful neon sign all within 45 days from the day we opened escrow. We built it on the remnants of a World War II bar called Tony's Bomb Shelter and most recently the Playboy Club. The bright, beautiful

The Niputi ...the Nephew

Garter would be a classy cocktail lounge and a Go-Go joint using Dad's vernacular.

However, a man whose name I can't recall filed a last-minute complaint about the neighborhood bar being too noisy. The ABC was reviewing his request at their leisure, even though they were reminded that a bar had existed in the same location since before WWII. Then I thought: *What bureaucratic crock! They were trying to do it to me and Dad all over again.*

Unfortunately, the neighbor had us by the short hairs. We had our opening night entertainment, twelve Go-Go dancers, three cocktail waitresses, and two bartenders ready, except for the license. We were up against a financial time wall and needed our license to have our liquor delivered. I told Dad that I would visit the neighbor and try to smooth-talk him into being reasonable.

Dad replied, "That's fine. I've got to call Bob Cheron anyway."

Later that day, I walked around the corner and tapped at the man's door. The guy, with a brew in his paw and his beer belly hanging below a torn T-shirt, opened the door and smiled. He seemed affable. He listened as I explained our situation and then, with a Go-Fuck-Yourself air, showed me to the door.

Dad was in the office. As I entered he looked up as I said, "I tried to reason with him. Even though the SOB had a drink in his hand and liked to walk to the bar, he also didn't like the noise. I asked if he was open to any reasonable deal. "I might be open to some form of negotiation, but not here and not now."

"Don't worry. I'll take care of it," said Dad.

For years, I had heard: Don't worry! Which was Dad's secretive way of relieving or delaying a problem he didn't want to deal with. Dad knew I had a lot on my plate with the Star & Garter and a huge decision to make regarding going with Nate's business venture or staying with First National Bank.

"Joe, I'll take care of it. Okay. You go home."

"By the way, what did Bob Cheron say?"

"Nothing, he wasn't at home. Look Joe, you go home and come back tomorrow morning. I'll take a walk over and see this guy. Maybe I can convince him to pull the complaint."

I left and returned around 10:30 the next day. Dad was in the office. "Good morning, son. Glad you came in. Take this money to the bank for the cash register banks. And drop this off to Pete Case of the Alcohol Beverage Control. The booze will be delivered this afternoon and we'll open tomorrow."

"You mean the neighbor signed it?"

"Yeah, he said he was sorry the way he spoke to you. He had a bad day. This morning, he was very reasonable. Not to worry, we'll talk later." We never spoke about it again. I didn't want to know but I had a hunch what Dad used as his negotiating equalizer.

I left, took care of business. As I returned, our brash neighbor showed up in our parking lot. He noticed me exit my car. "Sorry about the other night, sir. I had a bad night."

"No problem. Please come in after we open and I'd like to show you around and introduce you to our day bartender." He replied that he would, and we shook hands. "Thank you again," I said as he departed.

From the moment we opened the doors I knew our new place would be a success. It had a special feel, an ambiance that drew people in. Dad and I both put a lot of sweat equity into the Garter to make it a showplace. I was proud that I made the commitment and felt as if I repaid my father for the years he provided me love, security, guidance, and the means to accomplish my educational objective. Yeah, so it cost me time and grade and put my Air Force career on hold for almost three years, BFD. But it was worth it to see the smile on Dad's face.

One day about a week later, Dad called me at the bank and said, "Joe, remember I introduced you to Nate Rosenberg at the Grant Grill?"

"Yeah, Dad. Nice man."

"Are you interested in seeing his business operations? I saw him downtown yesterday and he gave me his business card and wanted me to ask you if you had time to take a look at his stores."

"Sure, Dad. I'm always interested in learning and growing. I'll stop by the Garter on my way home and pick it up."

"Fine, see you then."

Nate's card was elegant with its simplicity. A plain ivory-colored linen card embossed with "Nathan Rosenberg" in gold lettering. The reverse had a note: "My office at 3 p.m., Suite 300. Confirm with secretary—619-676-2837."

I called and confirmed the time. Nate's office was across from Horton Plaza, the most prime location for real estate in San Diego. Horton Plaza sat in the center of the city center, honoring Alonzo Horton, an early city father.

As I walked toward the building that housed Nate's office, I gazed at the splashing fountain where, as a boy, I fed popcorn to the pigeons just to see if could catch one without anyone catching me. The Plaza was a nice resting place for shoppers and bus transfer passengers. Just across the street and adjacent to the Plaza at the southeast corner of Broadway and Fourth Avenue stood a nondescript building. Although my family had been in the liquor business for years and had owned the now-departed Spot Café and Kelly's Tavern, I was taught to concentrate on our business and not worry about the competition. Therefore, other than knowing that the Kings Club was on the corner of Fourth and Broadway, I had never been to the place.

I walked into the portico of the building and noticed an office locator. I was looking for one that said Nate Rosenberg. With my initial glance, I started to laugh. *This guy was something.* It started with N. Rosenberg Enterprises Ltd. and went on with over a dozen corporations embossed with permanence on a brass plate:

N. ROSENBERG ENTERPRISES Ltd.

Rosenberg Administration	Ste. 199
Nathanial Rosenberg Ltd.	Ste. 200
Nathanial Rosenberg Esquire	Ste. 201
N. R. Realty Inc.	Ste. 202
Nathanial A & B Operations, Inc.	Ste. 203
Rosenberg Construction, Inc.	Ste. 204
Rosenberg Diamond Importers, Inc.	Ste. 205
Nathan Rosenberg Photography	Ste. 206
Dick Tyrell Jewelers	Ste. 207
Nathan Rosenberg Administration	Ste. 300

Nate had the entire second floor of a four-story building. On the first floor sat the Kings Club, Nate's Go-Go bar and several business kiosks on either end of his bar. He must have had two thousand square feet on his ground floor. Talk about prime property. I was impressed. Maybe he did need someone to help. However, I was going to prove that assumptions were like assholes, we all need them, but you can't plan your day around them.

I walked into the elevator and found it only went to the second floor. I was confused over the numbered 300 suite and the elevators not going beyond the second floor. I entered a professionally decorated foyer and approached a very attractive dark-haired receptionist. She smiled and asked if I were Joseph. I was somewhat impressed that Nate had told her my name and said yes, but I couldn't find the third floor elevator.

She smiled knowingly and said, "I'll inform Mr. R that you're here."

A moment later, out from a corridor came Nate, as dapper as I recalled. This time he was in a lightweight medium brown suit with appropriate trim. He smiled and said, "Joseph, right on time, good to see you again. Follow me."

I followed him into an office resplendent with similar deco to match our bank's CEO's offices. He asked me to sit and relax for a moment while he cleared up a few pressing matters. When I sat down, the chair really relaxed me. It was made to put the occupant at ease, or should I say, put the occupant into a pleasingly comfortable position. The chair was, as I learned, classic Nate Rosenberg. Dad warned me that Nate was shrewd and always looked for an edge. He always sought a come-off-the-wall way of gaining an advantage over any adversary. It was Nate's way. In business, in poker or with women, the man had an edge. It was his specialty and he was excellent at it.

Nate's office was quite large, approximately 20 by 20 with a very intriguing split level and a hidden doorway. He had an interior designer work with his architect early on, in his planning and they created a very special office where everything was built in, hidden or built to a specific size. His desk, a grand hand-carved mahogany monster, was raised about four inches above the eyes of anyone sitting in the lush lounge chair or sofa. The office was designed with one thing in mind: luring all who entered to conduct business into a false sense of security. And, I was there on business.

God bless Dad, I thought. I recalled his warning; "Nate is a longtime friend, but don't forget, he needs you, we don't need him. He is not family so watch, listen and learn. Nate's a *pesce gane*—a shark. Then he added in dialect, "*Ma, figghiu Su Pesce cane nessuno havere dente.*" (Son, this shark has no teeth.)

Nate shuffled a couple of papers, then called on the intercom to his secretary to hold all calls. He excused himself as he pushed back from his chair, pressed a book behind his desk and a wall moved, revealing a black marble bathroom. He went in and I noticed it had a shower, a vanity with overhead faux skylights, and a waterfall with a virtual garden of plants. To say the least, I was impressed.

While Nate was gone, I got up and stretched and looked at his floor-to-ceiling library. One bright-lettered book's title caught my eye. It was higher than most and just beyond one's normal reach. I couldn't resist and stretched, pulling it down. Its title drew me in: "How I Made A Million In Las Vegas," by Nate Rosenberg. Curiously, I opened it and realized that it was written in Chinese. Nate did it again.

That was Nate Rosenberg; always looking for the edge, even if it took a little deceit to reach one's objectives. It dawned on me: *Everything was orchestrated and planned just for me. Nate was going through a lot to impress me and I appreciated that. He was a master of deception.*

I liked that in a man because at least I knew where I stood. Then I thought of what Dad said about Nate and the shark and I thought of his connections and wondered, was Nate tied to the old Meyer Lansky? If anyone was a Judah

The Niputi ...the Nephew

Mafiosi, from what I read, it was Lansky. But then what in the hell did I care. It was none of my business and to my knowledge, it didn't matter a fig to my employment.

In the white-collar world I worked in, the straight bullshit was bred into the collegiate crowd and was the mantra in the business world. Never take advantage of a situation or customer. Don't screw anyone; business is not conducted that way. But, as I learned from my father, they left out the key word, intentionally. You always heard that a businessman had to be smart to be successful. It was a tough world out there which meant someone, possibly you, could get screwed. Nate believed that most transactions had someone getting the shaft–based on his street knowledge. Accordingly, he made it his business to ensure that given the odds, he would rather not be on the receiving end.

"Joseph, let me tell you that your father is like a brother to me. In fact, you probably don't know it, but he saved my ass with your presence in my organization and saves my ass today."

Nate and I spoke on and off for about a half hour, then he received an emergency phone call. He had to leave in a hurry. "Look, Joe, something came up I can't ignore. Can I take you around my businesses tomorrow at say nine o'clock, and we can leave from here? Just pull your car into the Grant garage, just mention my name and they'll have a perk parking space for you."

"Thanks, Nate. I'll be here at nine."

I called in sick at the bank and then headed for Nate's. He sat behind his desk shuffling papers, but ready to go.

"Let's go have some breakfast," he said.

During breakfast, Nate proceeded to replay his in-depth business operations: "We have Dick Tyrell Jewelers and the Photography Studio's here and in Oceanside and the Kings Club and my business rentals in the Rosenberg building. Oh, additionally, I also have my personal accountant and one of my attorneys working out of my building as well. It makes me feel a little more secure. I'll use your real property expertise to assess the financial feasibility of doing a redevelopment project.

"Finally, I have Chez Cary in Orange County. She's my special baby, a wonderful high-end restaurant operation. We'll visit her one day. If you think that Dick Tyrell's is my Grand Prix of business, then my Chez Cary is the pearl in my oyster of fine dining."

"Assuming you come aboard," said Nate, "everything except the Chez is on the table and within the purview of your area of responsibility. I also have several business real properties in Hollywood, Los Angeles and San Diego, and we can have fun discussing the R.E. game ad nauseam.

"By the way, did I show you the big apartment across from the El Cortez?

"No, you didn't."

"We'll have to do that too. It's hot on my list. Because I trust you, I expect your honest and good name to bear one additional and specific task. Once you agree, you will release me from the task and allow me to get involved with other business ventures. *Sure, I thought to myself, and why not?*"

"Of course, Nate."

We strolled over to the Grant garage and Nate looked dapper as usual behind the wheel of his white Caddy convertible as we drove down Fourth and back around the Kings Club building.

Nate then said, "Joseph, I love this building and what it stands for. This was my Sugar Daddy of real estate

The Niputi ...the Nephew

knowledge and decision making. I turned a trick on this place which set the stage for my future."

"Joe, do you know what a subordinated ground lease is?" I turned and said, "Yes. How is that relevant?" He continued.

"Well, back in the day I was renting a stall from the owner of this building for a couple of hundred per month. I used it to perfect the Dick Tyrell jewelry operation. The war was on and money was not spent on improving the building. It was a real dump. The owner wouldn't improve it and wouldn't help his tenants as he just eked out a few bucks from his renters.

"I checked on neighboring rents and found they were several times higher. Well, as I said, I had been reading about subordinated ground leases and realized that maybe I could turn a buck. I approached the owner through a subsidiary representative—a shill, and offered him double what he was making on the rents to lease the whole building to XYZ Corporation, which in effect was me. The owner loved the idea and the lease tied him up for one hundred years.

The rest is history. I talked to my banker and got a loan to improve the building and spent over a hundred grand rehabbing it. I talked to all of the tenants, increased their rents to what the traffic would bear, and built another six stores inside. The previous owner almost shit when the wrecking crews came in. I paid him his lousy two grand a month and I was pulling down ten, and it was mine for one hundred years. You can bet I was one happy fella after I turned that trick, Joseph."

"I'll bet you were, Nate. I'll bet you were."

"You really don't need to own, Joseph. Just having control can be enough."

Nate continued down Broadway to the Dick Tyrell jewelers and he walked in like a defiant victor, or like someone who owned the joint. He introduced me to the manager and several of his sales staff. Interestingly, I noticed that Nate was almost naturally dictatorial with his people about his operations. He knew what he wanted and knew his business. He created his empire from its humble beginnings and he knew how it was to be arranged and managed. That was it! Ipso facto. I mentally reserved this piece of information for the future.

Note, he had the manager line up everyone as in a military morning standby inspection and checked their dress, appearance and cleanliness, even fingernails. They were either off-duty sailors or ex-military. He then took me and the manager back to the office and showed me the safe and his stash of jewelry, commenting aloud on the quality and beauty of several pieces.

As we prepared to leave, Nate turned and said, "Gentlemen, you ought to remember Joseph. He may be your new boss."

"That was interesting," I said.

"Most of it was fluff for their benefit." *And mine too,* I thought. Then we got in the white Caddy and drove to Oceanside, where we did the same thing to his Dick Tyrell store as well as his photography studio, a new venture he was creating.

"Joseph, there's a lot of money to be made in photography and we are just starting out." Then he said, laughing, "It's almost better than booze."

We headed north on Highway 101 and cut over to the freeway to get into Orange County. "We're taking our time, Joseph, because I want to get to the Chez Cary around noon to see how the lunch crowd is faring. In fact, I'll take you to lunch."

"Thank you, Nate. I'll look forward to it."

We pulled up in front of the Chez Cary and a valet dressed to the nines took Nate's keys, with a "Good afternoon, Mr. Rosenberg" greeting. Nate was welcomed by the staff and garnered quite a few smiling nods from guests. In short order we met Geril Mueller, who Nate said was Danish and the key manager. He and his brother Gus were the brains behind the culinary operation.

Nate rewarded their performance and loyalty after he purchased the former restaurant operation, tossed everything out, and started from scratch. Again, Nathan knew what he wanted and hired a guy named Cary Sinclair to run it. But Sinclair had long fingers, so Nate fired him and elevated the Muellers to management.

Nate showed me around with a prideful air. From the fresh flowers to the immaculate silverware, and to the red velvet lounge chairs precisely placed around the tables, it was wonderful just to walk through it. He even took me to his precious wine cellar, enclosed with prison-like bars to replicate a European castle's dungeon. We had a scrumptious fine dining experience, and that was lunch. Looking back over time past and the economy, my mind recalls the savory menu items, and the embossed menu cover comment, "One of the Great Restaurants of the Western World." And it was.

There were fourteen hors d' oeuvres on the menu with Escargots Bourguignon at $3.25 and Beluga Caviar at $8.75. Boula-Boula Turtle soup was one of six at $2.00, with six salads, Cesar Romaine at $2.00. Lettuce and bay shrimp were $2.75.

The idea of "less is more" was apparent as only two salad dressings were offered: Oil and vinegar—with Roquefort—and Thousand Island. There were four house specialties and thirty entrée dishes. The most expensive was Chateaubriand Gastronome for $21.00 and Rack of Lamb for two at $19.50. *Oh, if it were only open today. But I probably couldn't afford to eat there.*

I thanked Nate for lunch and congratulated him on his wonderful one-of-a-kind restaurant. We returned to the Kings Club and he made a walk-through to see what the action looked like. Cousin Larry, Tina's husband, was behind the bar and had a helluva crowd. He just looked up, smiled at Nate and me, and kept working his station.

Off to the side of the entry we ended up in front of a blank door that I hadn't noticed before. It had no knob, just a keyhole. Nate pulled a key out of his pocket, inserted, and twisted it and an elevator door opened. We entered and he used the key again to activate the elevator. When the elevator stopped, he said, "Please remove your shoes, we don't wear them here." The door opened into a visually black hole. He then pushed a button in the elevator and, like magic, the room came alive. Soft music played in the background while spotlights pointed at the bar and allowed soft neon colors to move along the back bar. The bar of course was filled with crystal and prima liquor. Everything was as it should be. I was in awe, having never seen an opulent view of the good life.

It was his penthouse and toy, decorated as only Nate Rosenberg could. It was absolutely decorator custom, gorgeous, professional and right out of a playboy's dream. The room had what appeared to be a two-inch lush, ivory-colored carpet throughout. It had a horseshoe-shaped bar with mirrored back bar and, wow, the bar stools and furnishings were all etched with the NR symbol. He had a Vegas-type card table, crap table and roulette wheel. All top quality, of course, and surrounded by a custom-made off-white wrap-around sofa. It must have seated fifteen people. He even had a fireplace.

"We can be more comfortable here while we talk. I use this room for important people. Everyone now and then needs a little R & R. I've had some celebrities here from Hollywood. Even Congressman Wilson and a few other political hacks have visited. Even had the governor visit, and got him bred, blowed and he walked away with ten grand from the crap table over there."

"He must have been one lucky hummer, Nate."

"Yeah, lucky my dice were on the table, Joseph. There is no luck when you're entertaining those who you'd like to thank. It's all business. Get my drift?"

"I understand, Nate. Money and the penis theory are basic." Nate chuckled at my quip.

He made me a malt liquor scotch on the rocks and said, "Please sit," as he began his "once upon a time story" of extortion, mugging and almost murder. "Crimes that only your big-mouthed, mother-fucking hood, your Uncle Frank Bompensiero, could conceive." *Now it started to make sense. Nate was afraid.*

Hesitatingly, he said, "You know him, right? You're not offended by my reference to him or his character?"

Nate was still unsure of my loyalties and I tried to ease his mind. "What character, Nate? He has none. I've had his cloud of bullshit hanging over my head all my life." It was getting close to seven, and I said, "Nate, how about calling it a night? I'd like to see my son before he goes to sleep.

How about we finish tomorrow if that's okay with you. I've had a great day."

"That's a good suggestion. Drop by around eleven." I rose, shook his hand, and bid him a good night.

CHAPTER 32
THE ROSENBERG CONNECTION

Extortion is a criminal act where someone illegally gains money, property, or favors by either using force or the threat of force. In the past, elected officials used their position to gain favors or money, and it was extortion. Now it is accepted that people in general and not only the elected can commit this crime as well. It may sound similar to blackmail, but there is one difference. In blackmail, the perpetrator threatens to do a perfectly legal act, for example, releasing incriminating pictures. Whereas with extortion, they threaten to commit a totally illegal ac like, killing and maiming. "The Mafia," says the law, "is one organization that extensively uses extortion to gain information and deal with the criminal element."

✳ ✳ ✳

I walked into the office and Nate's personal secretary gave me a "go on in" nod. As I proceeded towards Nate's office, my mind wandered and landed on the subject of influencing others. I remembered Dad telling me as a kid while fishing something about leverage and explained it this way, "Having them by the balls made them follow." Experience proved that Dad was right.

I thought about how Nate swayed people, especially since I observed him influencing others in the pursuit of a personal aim or political objective. It would be interesting watching Nate in action and seeing him toy with someone.

They all didn't have to be "in his pocket." Nate had charisma and polish and I wondered whether his actions were different than, say, an Air Force general officer or as devilish as a Frank Bompensiero. I had opportunities to view both and wondered. Frank was basically in your face crude. While in the Air Force as a young officer, I learned of an Inspector General who was often spoken about due to a supposed comment to his staff about, "*wanting that SOB off our base by sundown.*" Wells had his own style.

In essence, it was no different than watching Frank Bompensiero go from Mr. Nice Guy with a big smile on his face one moment to a snarling mad dog the next saying, "Do you know who you're fucking with and what the consequences could be?" I realized that all men have their own ways of getting to that nut-crunching point, when the individual on the receiving end knows he has been bested and finally relents.

Nate was ready to resume our previous night's discussion. "Don't worry about our conversations in here, Joseph. The place is sealed. It's like a fortress. I have it electronically swept weekly. I also have it rigged to automatically record anything said in the room. You know," and he winked.

"Well, what I'm going to tell you now, only one other person has ever heard that, and it was none other than your father. Once I tell you this story, I think things will become clear to you. Then he began:

"A while back, before I saw you and your Dad in the Grant Grill, I had an appointment with this very attractive lady at my room at the Grant, if you know what I mean." I smiled my recognition and he continued.

"Well, after a while your fucking uncle and that henchman cocksucker friend of his, Jimmy the fucking weasel

Fratianno, show up." I started to laugh and that interrupted his tirade. "What gives?" he said.

"I'm sorry, Nate, but your vernacular cracks me up. I thought I was the only one that hated Frank, but I guess I'm not alone. Please continue."

"Guess what those pricks decided? Yours truly, Nate Rosenberg, is going to be their next mark for extortion. I've worked my ass off my whole life and these two pricks think they're going to do me in and carry off the candy."

"You've got to be shitting me, Nate. I already see where this is going."

"I'll bet you do, if you know that sonofabitch.

"I've always run straight joints, within the law, and not hustled too much from our customer base. I've always been fair and, yeah, generous to a fault with the help and our customers, especially to the ladies." He and I both laughed.

"Do you know what the deal was?"

"I can only imagine."

"Well, it was all about how to keep the Jew alive and take all his fucking money. The dirty bastards!"

"There I was hanging out of a US Grant Hotel window upside down and experiencing vice-like pain crushing my ankles. As the blood pooled in my brain, I knew it wouldn't be long before I blacked out. In a momentary flashback, I recalled my high school coach yelling, "Swing around the high bar, Nate. Don't act like a monkey and hang upside down. You'll pass out."

"At least if I blacked out, I wouldn't be conscious, and then nothing would hurt. I wouldn't have to listen to myself screaming as I fell the four stories and feel my brains splatter on the pavement below. God was I scared. Fear continued to cloud my mind and I didn't know where I was.

I saw the word Kings on a neon sign and thought I might be at the U.S. Grant Hotel, but I didn't know how I got there.

"Sweat formed on my brow and allowed the semi-tight bandana covering my eyes to lift slightly. I peeked from my left eye. Oh my God, I cried to myself, as I saw the tips of my alligator shoes and the hair on my calves as my trousers slipped toward my thighs. I couldn't see what was wrenching my ankles, but then my knees were bent. 'Oh, shit,' I muttered to myself as I saw the maniacal eyes and ferocious scowl of The Bomp and the Weasel.

"I was roused into consciousness by the ugly sounds, "Come on, you fuckin' kike bastard, play nice or we'll cut your prick off and show you a real Sicilian circumcision before we toss you off the building. That means balls and all to you, Jew bastard. Your blond wife won't appreciate that, you fucker!" The Weasel laughed as The Bomp spewed out his hatred.

"Pull 'em in, Jimmy. We need a break."

❋ ❋ ❋

Jimmy "the Weasel" Fratianno was one of the worst fuckers to come out of the Midwest. He was simply a lap dog that had a, "Yeah, let me at 'em" fixation. Though Frank was a made Mafiosa, Jimmy had not earned the recommendation from his ties in the Midwest, but was trying like a whiny suck-up, begging to be "one of the boys." Both he and Frank were no doubt proud of their achievements, be they thefts, extortions, killings, whatever. It was their badge of honor, especially around those within that sicko brotherhood.

Both were apparently losers in their young lives, Frank for sure.

Neither would ever try hard to follow the straight and narrow. Accordingly, they spent time incarcerated.

Ironically, the police, FBI and other police organizations could never prove major felony murder against Frank, and I don't believe they did for Jimmy. However, both men left many a body in a variety of graves around the countryside. That's if you believe any one of a dozen writers, pundits, newspaper reporters, or government department officials who created a pseudo-official stamp of criminality on them.

After Jimmy came out to California, he contacted Dragna's family and was taken in with open arms. He started hanging with Frank, who was already connected with the L.A. family. One day, even the Weasel would be a made man, whatever that was. The local, state and federal police felt the two had Mafia connections, but that wasn't a crime. It was like saying, "He has communist connections." So what? Is that a new crime in the country? You may not like it, but what in the hell are you going to do about it? We do know that both individuals were the dregs of society and reached out to dirty everything they touched.

✱ ✱ ✱

An awakening occurred in Nate's brain. He knew where he was, why he was there. For now, he was still alive. However, being consumed by fear of the unknown, he lapsed into unconsciousness, with thoughts of his father, New York and anywhere other than where he was.

He continued to drift in and out of consciousness, or was it survival-induced unconsciousness, he didn't know. He recalled, however, why they were trying to roust him and what they wanted. Nate had been a successful businessman. He worked hard learning a business and building it up from scratch. In today's idiom, he paid his dues. He created things where nothing existed before, and his skills rewarded him with green, lots of it. No one knew how much or what his scam was. But, in Nate's case, his business was legitimate and the golden prize for pure entrepreneurship.

The two thugs couldn't care less, and only knew they wanted a piece of it.

Nate knew both of these idiots and had seen them in action over the years. Jimmy had even stayed at Nate's apartment for a period. He knew Frank's reputation. Frank would not hesitate to kill if he thought that was necessary to accomplish his objective. But, if he did that Frank would realize that if he killed the goose that laid the golden egg, he wouldn't get anything.

Everyone wanted to know how Nate's business functioned. They knew he had a slew of businesses including the Kings Club, which was an easy Go-Go operation on the best location corner in San Diego. However, they didn't know how Nate made money, big money. No one yet knew his secret. Nate could not divulge his methods to that bastard Frank Bompensiero or his rat weasel friend. They wouldn't get a dime. He'd die first, but then his lovely wife would be comfortable.

Nate had no friggin' choice. The bastards were killers and Nate began a fearful gallows laughter rush and told them to rethink what they were doing or they would end up dying broke.

Frank had been drinking and said huffily that he wouldn't tolerate any more of that lying bullshit and he wanted me to know it. I didn't know what to do, "Those cocksuckers really had me by the balls."

I finally acquiesced and said, "Okay, okay, that's enough. Let me down and come see me in a few days and we can talk at that time. I'm not used to making decisions under duress. With that, they let me go and, to add to my misery, Frank said they were keeping the broad for awhile

The Niputi ...the Nephew

so they could get a blow job,. "Of course Nate, ole buddy, this one's on you." They didn't want to feel as if they left empty-handed. The bastards!

"That was it. You've heard it all," said Nate as he stared at the ceiling from his chair. He was quiet for a moment and I empathized with the man for going over the terror that he must have felt. Nate's recollection of his encounter sent me quickly back in time.

❋ ❋ ❋

Frank's maliciously evil side was not apparent to all as he played the big, smiling, friendly businessman, father or uncle. But one day his real self came out at Kelly's bar, a joint owned by Dad and Al Garcia, a fisherman family friend back in 1954. I dropped into Kelly's to see Dad and it must have been close to six o'clock since he was sitting at his desk changing banks for the night shift. Al and I were sitting on the couch and Frank Marino, the bartender and an ex-fisherman, hovered over the desk while Dad counted the day's take.

All was quiet and routine until Frank stormed into the office. At the time, he was embroiled in his court bribery case and, when on the street, was cockily mouthing off to anyone who would listen, "They won't put a glove on me," or, "Fuck him and all those crooked cocksuckers." He was of course referring to Judge Hewicker, his trial judge, whom he hated.

He then declared, "I need to use the goddamn phone. *Tuti spiru ascutari.* (All spies are listening to my phones.)" He strode over to Dad's desk, shoving Frank Marino aside while saying to Dad, "We've gotta talk."

Frank Marino reacted by saying, "Cheese, Frank, give me a break. I'm just checking out." That was enough to send Frank into a rage. What happened next wasn't fun to watch. As Marino turned, Frank grabbed up a closed pair of scissors lying on the desk and plunged them into Marino's palm. Marino screamed and fell to the ground.

Frank stood over Marino and shouted, "Listen, you cocksucker, when I want you to speak, I'll tell you what to say and when I want you to say it! Capish?"

With that, Marino, a more physically fit and stronger man, sheepishly got up and said, "Don't ever touch me again, Frank!"

"Touch you! Are you crazy? You fucking lowlife, I'll bury your wife and kids if you fuck with me." No one in the room, including Dad, said a word. I wondered at the time, *why hasn't anyone said anything to this asshole, was it fear?*

I didn't known then, but in time, I learned.

That was Frank Bompensiero's use of intimidation and bravado. He had many people hoodwinked and lived on a reputation that I believed then and know now was undeserved.

He was reputed, by his daughter in "A Bad, Bad Boy," to sit on his couch while tears flowed over his daily dose of Lassie on TV. I guess, without someone's idyllic view of him contemplating the trials and tribulations of a dog's life, Frank's literal bad, bad boy persona never rose to the surface. Bet me!

I was thinking about Nate's ordeal, and he had an awful lot to lose. Frank and Jimmy would press for the max. Nate knew they wouldn't let up and it was only a matter of time before they'd come to collect their pound of flesh. Nate paused for a long time and seemed worn out by reliving the ordeal.

Finally, he turned to me and said, "Well, Joseph, that is the operation and the reason why you are here. I need help in running my busy operations."

Yeah Nate, I thought. You need more than that and I know it. You need a gunsel-bodyguard and I'm not one of those.

"I understand, Nate, and I empathize with you. Especially since I've been on the inside my whole life, and I've been unable to do anything about it. I have never been able to get my father to cut Frank loose. It's a Sicilian family blood thing."

"I understand that, Joseph. Yet your father showed me his colors for what is right and his feelings for me when he sent you to me. No one messes with his son."

Nate had completed his story and had opened up his storefront to me. Soon, I knew he would make me an offer and I knew that I was in the proverbial "driver's seat." I had the power and waited.

I mentally reviewed what Nate had said over the past forty-five minutes as he laid out my responsibilities and was thinking how I was going to the next step, tell him I was interested and what could I expect in salary, when again he eased into business as the pro he was.

"Joseph, I want to ask you a personal question to ensure that I am fair in what I am going to say next. Do you understand? Additionally, if you have any objections, I'll understand."

"Nate, we'll never know unless you ask. I'm no virgin, so ask away."

"Good. How much is FNB paying you to play banker?" It was 1968, I had been at the bank almost a year and a half, and I proudly said, "Six hundred per month, Nate." He then blew my socks off with a direct response while looking in my eyes. "For your services and loyalty, I'll give you $3,000 per month to start."

"That's fair and I accept. I want to give the bank notice, so I'll start in a week if that's okay with you, boss!" The power shifted. Nate was again in control. The man with the power and money really never relinquished it. He was always in charge.

We shook hands and Nate said, "Great. That's a relief to me."

"Nate, let me ease your mind a little. I'm going to tell you a quick story about the last time I saw Frank. We were at my aunt's home and he got mouthy with me and he called me outside. When he touched me, I knocked him on his ass. My pent-up rage for all the years of his B.S. let go. I gave him a real beating that he had never experienced before, including a black eye, broken ribs and a lot of kicked-in-the-gut bruising. Dad had to pull me off. I told Dad that he'd have to choose between me or his brother.

"Nate, if it's all the same to you, if Frank shows his face around here, I'll make him bleed before we call the cops." Nate's grin surpassed his inner pleasure. "I need to hear all the painful details."

I started a week later and, after he took me around introducing me to his managers, we went back to his office, and he told me he'd appreciate it if I didn't leave him alone in the building. He wanted me on a short leash. "Nate, have you had a call or a visit from your two friends from the Grant as yet?"

"No, but . . ."

I interrupted and said, "I understand and agree that I should stick close to home." Accordingly, I was either in the Kings Club checking the operation or visiting the U.S.

Post Office. Nate had invented a money machine and it was working, and I was literally his "bag man." I made myself busy picking up the bags of dollars and doing the counts and giving my numbers to Nate and to his three queens.

Nate's moola tree was amazing in its simplicity and ability to generate cash.

One day I pulled a huge mail sack off the elevator and Nate saw me pass his office.

"Joseph, put that in your office. We need to talk." When I returned, he said, "You've been here several weeks and haven't said a word about the bags and the scheme and the operation."

"Nate, I figured if it was any business that you wanted to share, you'd bring it up. The how's and why's you do things is your business. If I see something that I can do better, faster, or cheaper, I'm going to tell you how to improve it. If not, I don't fix what ain't broken."

"I appreciate your honesty and it's time for you to know how I came upon my little moola machine. Joseph there's an old World War II Navy song the recruits used to sing as they walked up Broadway, looking in the windows at all the things they couldn't afford. It went like this: 'Twenty-one dollars a day, once a month, Twenty-one dollars a day, blah-blah-blah.' "

"Well, back in the forties I was a hustling salesman working for Seven Seas and doing a few other things. I was a good salesman. I beat everyone by a mile, and my customers came back repeatedly. Because money was tight, I was looking for an angle to help the sailors buy jewelry. They would love to buy their girls or Mum a gift, but didn't have any scratch. Remember, we didn't have any credit then. Well, I figured out a way to allow them to buy, and I'd get my money as well. The one thing I had to give up in the equation was time. Then what I just said made the light go on. 'One. '

"That's all I really needed was 'one' dollar per month—nothing more, nothing less. With one dollar a month, twelve dollars a year on a hundred-dollar piece of jewelry, the machine would only have to repeat once every six years. I'd have a money machine. Since the item only cost me ten dollars, my investment would be paid off in less than a year and I would benefit for years to come. If I built a broad and big enough base, I'd make a fortune. Once I validated the numbers, I put the system into operation. You're the only one who knows how I came upon it.

"I'll bet you wondered why I have the three ladies down the hall in separate offices, when it would be more practical and economical to have them together. This way, I can individually treat each of them special and they know it. They compete with each other for little perks, which I bestow on them, a plant here, a box of chocolates there, time off here. You know an extra smile works wonders for the female of our species."

And I thought to myself, *Nate knew his women.*

"I keep them independent and baby each one. None of them know what the others do and it keeps them hopping. I have a less than three percent deadbeat rate and you can take that to your conservative First National Bank and compare. Ha ha!"

He leered, knowing he bested all, and I knew it.

"Joseph, they write to the guys in the U.S. Navy, plead, and cajole to maintain their accounts and get me my money."

Nate's idea was beautiful, and I personally thought about it with pride for his accomplishment and tenacity.

Every time I went to the Post Office, I felt good and blessed Nate's creative mind. I was now a part of it.

When I joined Nate's team, there were six thousand accounts on the books. The average bag of mail I collected each day, six days a week, had from three hundred to five hundred envelopes enclosed. Within each envelope was a one-dollar bill from some thankful sailor whom Nate had helped. There were a few payoffs and a few checks, but normally it was strictly cash, all green cash from Nate's Moola Tree. According to Nate, it only took him a few months to sell his first hundred thousand. He quit counting after his New York jewelry source told him that he had, in fact, paid for over two hundred thousand dollars in merchandise. Faithful to a fault, the Navy boys were paying Nate back a buck a month, and to Nate that meant there were millions out there.

I visited his three independent queens who cared for the Moola Tree. I knew that he wanted me to stick close to the office if someone unexpectedly paid him a visit. I made sure I was available, and, in my mind, thought about what I would say when the time came. I was ready and looked forward to it with eager anticipation.

I had been in San Diego a little over two years, working first at Calypso Joe's, then at First National Bank. I also attended most extended family gatherings. *Ziu Chich* was never around. So it was almost six years since my encounter with Frank at Aunt Thelma's and my college graduation party.

CHAPTER 33
DREADED ENCOUNTER

Fate has a way of sneaking up on you, even when you anticipate its unwelcome visit. I knew in my gut that Frank would come. He was never one to waste time when the smell of money took to the air. Besides, Nate had tossed it to him and Jimmy because he was afraid. Frank liked it when his prey oozed fear. He could smell it. "This," he told Jimmy the Weasel, "will be a long and easy payday." Frank needed, wanted and would get it. So, fuck it. He'd take the bastard for what he could. Frank never worried himself over the details or the number of things that could affect the outcome of an issue. But in this case, even though Turi mentioned that Joe might leave the bank and go to work for Nate, it didn't matter. Frank would take care of that too. Knowing Frank's reaction to unplanned events and based on Nate's retelling me of his encounter with Frank and Jimmy months earlier, they would no doubt come calling. I planned my comments and knew which buttons to press. While taking advantage of his peccadilloes, I also knew what the outcome would be.

✳ ✳ ✳

It wasn't long, maybe a week or two, before I received an interoffice phone buzz from Nate's secretary. She sounded concerned. She wanted to speak to me quickly. I went to her desk and she had a long face, as if something were wrong.

Now, I wondered, *what in the hell I was walking into.*

"Mr. Joe, I passed two men as I walked to the restroom a few minutes ago," said Nate's secretary. "When I returned, they were nowhere to be found. They have to be in Nate's office because, just before I called you, Nate called on the intercom saying he didn't want to be disturbed. Joseph, his door is always open unless . . . there's trouble."

"Not to worry," I said. "I know who came to visit. I'll take care of it."

I walked to Nate's office and stood near the door. I carried a notebook and a small tape recorder. I turned it on and placed it inside the notebook. I couldn't hear a damn thing through the massive entrance door. I rapped on the door twice and went in. Nate was in his master's chair with a forlorn look on his face. This wasn't in character for him. I instinctively knew who was off to my side and out of view.

Nate was a schemer and always looked for an edge in any business transaction. And since all of his final negotiations were held in his office, he paid special attention to its construction. Nate's under-office flooring was unusually elevated. He intentionally had his carpenters raise the floor. This surreptitious design feature allowed all office furniture, save Nate's massive desk, to be lower than his. Though most didn't recognize the declination, it forced everyone to view Nate as if on high. Guest's unknowingly felt psychologically inferior. They all had to look up at Nate's magnificence. He always had to gain an edge. In this case, I wondered what gears he had in his mind mechanism to solve his current problem with the undertakers. I spoke as I entered, saying, "My apologies for busting in, Nate, but this is a-life-or-death matter."

I placed my notebook and recorder on his desk and turned toward the couch. Over my left shoulder, I noticed Frank and Jimmy.

"Well, I'll be damned. *Ziu Chich* and Jimmy the Weasel Fratianno. Surprised to see you two here. Sorry, Nate, but I didn't know you had unexpected visitors. I'll be gone in a minute. Jimmy, I didn't mean to call you by your nickname, I know you don't like being called 'Weasel.' I apologize."

My recognition of the two men was verbal, no handshakes, or gestures. I couldn't allow them to think they were in charge. Though surely, knowing them, that's what they thought. I wanted to set the tone as being there on another matter and not to be deterred.

I studied both men's faces, looking for something out of character. The look on Jimmy's face was quizzical. He wondered what in the hell I was doing there. Frank no doubt assured him that he had everything under control. Most likely because I had intentionally tipped Dad that I didn't go directly to the office between ten and noon, as I picked up the bags of mail. But I changed that to first thing in the morning after I saw the tedious job requirement of counting money. No doubt, my presence cramped Jimmy's style. I immediately reinforced my upper hand with some figuratively gentle intimidation.

"Well, *Ziu Chich*, I haven't seen you since my graduation, which was about six years ago. Remember, it was just a couple of months after you didn't play nice at your sister's, Aunt Thelma. And you, Jimmy, you were heading off to prison the last time I saw you. How long ago was that? I forget. I'm getting old. Hell, I'm almost thirty and you geezers must be . . . well, way up there.

"I didn't know you had any business with our company. Nate has never mentioned any relationship with you."

I emphasized Nate as well as the "our" word, knowing it would confuse Frank and leave Nate in the clear.

"I guess your brother never mentioned that I went to work for Nate after I left the bank. He probably thought what I was doing was none of your business. You know, Dad introduced me to Nate one day several months ago while we were having lunch at the Grant Grill."

"That's strange," said Frank. He paused. No doubt trying to figure out what was going on. He must have been thinking, *Niputi wasn't supposed to be here during the hours of ten to twelve, but that was a couple of months ago. Sammy mentioned it in passing.*

"Well, Niputi, we have some business to discuss with Nate and we'd like to talk about it in private." *I'll bet you would, Ziu. I'll bet you would!*

"That's fine, *Ziu*. However, my issue is more important. And besides Uncle, you must know there's no privacy in Nate's office. Hopefully, you haven't said anything you should have kept close."

"What in the hell are you talking about, Niputi? The only goddamn thing mentioned in this office before you marched in was our business." With his ego-driven statement, I decided to pimp him a little.

"Well, I know that, silly," I replied. "However, I beg to differ, since you don't know your ass about your surroundings. Did you know you were being recorded and photographed from the moment you walked into the foyer of this office? Neither Jimmy or you threatened Mr. Rosenberg, did you? You didn't say anything incriminating, right?

"You've always been paranoid about the *Spiru*, and knowing Nate as I do, he's got this place rigged with more state-of-the-art electronics devices than I saw in the Air Force. Hell, he's had congressmen and governors in these offices, so you know what I'm talking about. But, it makes no matter. You see, *Ziu Chich*, within these walls, I'm privy to everything because I'm Nate's majordomo. That is, I speak on Nate's behalf and take charge of major events, like now. Especially since I have the keys to Nate's kingdom and access to his cash flow. Right, Nate?"

"He's right," said Nate. "He handles all the company cash."

"You see, *Ziu*, I am the cash bagman and you two are not going to get your mitts on any of it.

"*Ziu*, let me lay this out for you and Jimmy once and for all. I knew you were going to visit Nate to lay claim on him as your free ride. You've been dragging on him for years, but not big time, like now. You guys used to sponge off of his apartments back in the thirties and probably still would if you could get away with it. You know, over the years things change and some of us grow. And those with the family name Bompensiero have felt the heat and the stares every time you opened your pie hole and spewed out hatred. It was always the same for us, whether you committed a crime, were arrested or indicted. The family took it in the shorts because of your notoriety. You always left a bad smell wherever you went.

"Well, not any more, and not with Nate Rosenberg. You may be interested in his money, but I recommend you go learn to work for a change. Nate told me about you and your friend here, and the night at the Grant Hotel when you hung him out the window and threatened him with death. I wrote it all down, nice and proper. It's in a deposition written and notarized for the district attorney. You and Jimmy know what a deposition is, Frank, and you also know who the DA is. What you did to Nate was a no-no, *Ziu*. It's definitely extortion and is also called attempted murder."

"Oh, I even mentioned the gal's name and after getting her statement recently, I think we could add a few more charges, like forced oral copulation. That's "blow jobs" to you two, just in case the big words confused you. The deposition covers it all, and names you and your friend Weasel. I think with that and some additional documentation, you could be living the rest of your life back in Quentin."

Frank's jowls were flushed with blood, and if a look could kill, I'd be dead.

"I'm here for the duration, *Ziu!*"

Jimmy and Frank glanced at each other. Frank turned back toward me abruptly, and tried to get up from the couch, but became unsteady as he tried to rise balancing himself. So I asked, "Do you need help? Too bad your brother's not here to help you up, like he did from your sister Thelma's lawn." That did nothing but piss him off more.

"Nephew, I think you should mind your own business and . . ."

I interrupted rudely. "Look, Frank. Your tough guy bullshit won't sell here. You know better." I turned, speaking directly to Fratianno. "Jimmy, has he told you that when he tried to play tough guy with me six years ago, I almost broke his jaw, gave him a big shiner and kicked him in the ribs a few times.

"You remember, Frank?" I looked at him. "That's probably a bad memory you'd like to forget. You couldn't brag about having a twenty-one-year old kick your ass. Just think, *Ziu*, I'm almost thirty now and a solid scrapper. Combat does that for you. If you and your friend Jimmy want to become prison roommates again, just fuck with me.

"Frank, you're sixty-four years old now and I am just a punk kid of thirty who would just love to work out on both of you. Especially since you won't have surprise on your side. You are hungrier now and won't have your brother Sam saving your ass." I turned to Jimmy, allowing Frank to stew in his own juice.

"You know, Jimmy, this is family business and you and your kind don't get involved in family matters." I looked directly into his beady eyes. "Unfortunately, you were there on the third floor of the Grant, according to that little lady who provided me her disposition, so your goose is cooked as well."

By this time, both of them were nervous, twitchy and shuffling on the couch. They wanted out!

"That's enough bullshit," I said. "We can do this one of two ways. You can get up and leave peacefully, or I'll call the police and file a complaint against you. They will believe me, Frank. Remember, I'm the clean Bonpensiero, the college graduate, and Air Force officer you like to demean.

"I can assure each of you that you, Frank, will draw more heat than you can deal with. You'll be on the five o'clock news and arrested for extortion within an hour. Whatever you do, don't come back."

I opened the door. "Gentlemen, this is the easy way out."

They both rose. Frank turned and faced Nate and said, "Nate, we'll be . . .

I interrupted. "No, Frank, you won't be back and that includes you, Jimmy. I guess you didn't understand! Don't call! Don't visit and don't come back! I've already sent a signed deposition of the Grant Hotel event to my attorney with instruction that if anything happens to Nate or me, the D.A. gets the report. *Capish?*"(Understand?)

"We understand," said Frank.

"Frank, I know you'll call your brother and tell him what happened here. Don't embellish the truth. It's

The Niputi ...the Nephew

recorded and I have witnesses. You'll find Dad at the Star & Garter, that's my new joint on 36th and University. P.S., Frank, you and Jimmy are not invited to our place of business. We reserve the right to refuse service to anyone. And Frank, I don't like you."

Frank glared at me and, for the first time, he was lost for words.

With that, they left. I followed them to the elevator and watched them go down, down, down. When I returned, Nate beckoned me into the office.

"Thank you, Joseph. I never knew you had such chutzpah!" I just nodded.

"The Sicilians call it *Coglione*—balls." We both laughed.

"Nate, I've never been afraid of assholes like him. Besides, I'm just doing my job."

"After I knocked the shit out of Frank at my aunt's, I told him I'd finish him off any time he screwed with me. That's why I reminded him and played all my cards." Again, Nate smiled warmly, knowing he had made a sound decision hiring me.

"You know, Joseph, your father has never mentioned that you had an altercation with Frank."

"He wouldn't, Nate. They are blood and it was family-related. It would embarrass him. Besides, I think it embarrassed him watching me kick his big brother's butt in front of God and everyone.

"Excuse me, Nate. I need a minute to call my Dad. Frank was just taken down a notch. He won't forget and will be fuming. I don't want Dad being caught short. I'll have to explain to my Dad how it went down, which will be the truth. You'll validate my story if my Dad ever asks, right, Nate?"

"You got it, Joseph. I owe you anyway."

I left for my office and called the Garter to speak with Dad. As I picked up the phone, I wondered if I read Frank correctly during the confrontation. Frank's blood pressure and temper must have been all over the place. He and Jimmy no doubt would be in some hole, licking their wounds and scheming. I knew Frank had never before been threatened by anyone he respected, especially a family member.

Frank always counted on an edge and this time he had none. He now knew he couldn't trust me. He now had to be careful around family as well. He could end up back behind bars and didn't want that. He was getting too old for this shit. He must have fumed and thought: *That little smart-assed prick had too much fucking education. My brother Sam really fucked up giving him too much schooling. The little bastard didn't care, the cocksucker!*

I found out later that Frank decided that he would have to find another rich one to hustle. A friend in Vegas needed help with a real estate broker and investor on a loan repayment. Frank agreed to look into matter undoubtedly thinking it was "a good score." The businesswoman investor just happened to live in San Diego. Her name was Tamara Rand.

"Star & Garter," echoed in the receiver as my Dad picked up the phone.

"Dad, I've got to tell you something you won't like. Can you talk?"

"Yeah, what's up?"

"Well, the day you set me up with Nate came and went. I told you that I accepted his offer. In any event, we can sit down later and talk about the details. However, I just tossed your brother, Frank, and Jimmy out of Nate's. They were starting to put the heat on him and I barged in and

The Niputi ...the Nephew

warned Frank that he'd go to jail. I don't think he likes me anymore. The bottom line is that he will probably call you and I didn't want you to get caught unprepared."

"Well, thanks for the heads-up. You know my brother will never learn. *Testa Grudu*." (Hard head.)

"Yeah, Dad, I know. By the way, Nate is gushing over his decision to hire me. He said, "Your Pop was right, Joe."

"If Frank calls, you'll know why he's fuming. He didn't say a fucking word when I told him the college boy wrote a deposition for the D.A. about the night he and Jimmy hustled Nate at the Grant. I told him if he ever fucked with Nate or me, it was going to the District Attorney. He about shit!

"Don't worry, however. Everything is fine. I'd like to talk more and will drop by later, but I've got to run." I hung up and knew my father would stew over the latest confrontation. I thought to myself, *Dad could make amends and make nice with his brother. It was no longer my job.*

Then a couple of weeks later, Dad called and asked if I could meet him for coffee. He got a call and wanted to introduce me to someone. I drove to the Garter, picked up Dad, and headed to his favorite Denny's. We entered and he walked up to a booth where a tall, suited man sat. We entered the booth and Dad introduced me to Jack Armstrong, local FBI.

"Well, this is a pleasure" I said to Armstrong. "I finally get to meet someone in the shadows who represents the government. That didn't take long for Frank to call you after my last encounter with him. Did I scare him?"

"What do you mean, Joe?"

"Well, Jack, that's personal. He still has his pride. If Frank wants to tell you, that's his business."

"Look, Joe, I wanted to talk with your Dad, and as I figured correctly, he called you in."

"Bullshit, Jack. You're aware of what I've done for my Dad, the Star & Garter and my relations with Frank. You know where I live and where to reach me. If you wanted to speak with my Dad, you don't need me. You two have spoken before. I know that, so what do you want with me? Talk about Frank or the Garter."

"Well, from what I gather from Frank, you might have busted his chops."

"Yes, I did, Jack. He physically assaulted me at my aunt's several years ago and I kicked the living shit out of the old bastard. But he wouldn't reveal that. His ego took a big hit that day. It's a bad memory for him. However, that's not what you're interested in, is it, Jack?" The waitress came and we ordered coffee.

"No, not really," Jack said.

"Okay, then, I know what you're speaking about. My father is aware of what happened. But as I said, if Frank has told you, that's between you and him. From my perspective, the issue was resolved."

"Joe, I don't want to play cat and mouse. You know what I'm referring to and I want to make sure it doesn't go any further."

"I don't blame you, Jack. You have a vested interest in Frank and might lose his wagging tongue."

I continued as my Dad just looked on.

"Just do me a favor and we can stop dancing. We're on the same side of the law. So, just give Frank enough so he doesn't reach out to my friends and doesn't come around the Star & Garter with his hand out. Since I won't be around to help out, please do me a favor. I don't want to go down at the whims of the locals and ABC like my father did. Just keep the locals off of my Dad's back. You and I know all the forces came together to screw my father with the bars downtown because yaw'll figured Frank owned them all. That's why the retribution raiders went after him. That's all I ask."

"I'll do what I can."

"Well the ball is in your court, Jack. I'll be honest with you. My tit is in the wringer. I interrupted my Air Force career to help my father and since I hold all the stock in Sal Enterprises, Inc. I don't want to worry about my father and mother's income while in Vietnam."

"You shouldn't have to, Joe."

"I appreciate that, Jack. However, I want you to know that I don't have my Dad's loyalty to his brother Frank. If Frank smells anywhere around the joint, I'll call him and let him know that I'm not happy. But, if he doesn't get the message, you'll be next person I call. If it continues, I'll contact one of his friends."

Jack's eyes leered at me, realizing that I was reading between the bureaucratic gobbledygook of word play and I would not allow my father to go down as he once did.

We gabbed a little more and I mentioned that with Vietnam causing a major stir, I was probably going to be recalled to active duty.

Jack understood and indicated that he would do whatever he could. He lauded my career pursuits and shortly thereafter, Dad and I left.

Much later, while reviewing the news about crime, I noticed that FBI Special Agent Jack Armstrong appeared before a federal grand jury in Los Angeles and testified about Frank Bompensiero. Armstrong indicated that in order to solicit information crucial to ongoing FBI cases from Frank Bompensiero, the FBI had forgiven age-old and prior grievances in exchange for some financial largess for current information. This also included murders past and recent.

Dependent on what source you use (surely not the police), Frank had killed over twenty people in his life. However, none were proved. But the best and most reliable source of factual information would be the FBI. Why? They play for leverage and had Frank by the balls. (Quid pro quo.) They forgave him for his alleged dirty deeds. They wanted the truth and, like God, forgave. For a few hundred dollars a week and peace of mind, Frank spilled his guts, one hood at a time. Some say he had outed several hundred hoods. And, with that, I leave Frank's body count to you, him, and the FBI.

Things quieted down around Nate's and had a better relationship. Most likely this was due to our encounter with Frank. Nate seemed more relaxed. About two weeks went by and I was down at the lower Broadway location of Dick Tyrell's when he called and asked me to come back to the office. He had some military things he wanted to discuss with me. When I arrived, he beckoned me into his office. He was angry about something.

"We've run into a problem at the Oceanside operation. There's this Marine Corp general in charge of Camp Pendleton who thinks he can go against the American way and take away a businessmen's right to operate. That's bullshit. I won't allow that to happen. I love my country."

I thought about his remarks and tried to make sense out of his synopsis. I knew that he knew what he meant. It was my problem to sort it out. Christ, he was all over the map.

"What exactly did the general do, Nate?"

"The cocksucker declared all of my joints in Oceanside 'off-limits.' Can you believe that shit?"

The Niputi ...the Nephew

"Yeah, I can. It's legal within military regulations and within a commander's prerogative. Actually, he's responsible to prevent the troops from being subjected to something he views as bad for conduct, morale or good order and discipline."

"Well, screw him, Joseph. We'll go around him. I'll make a call." And he did.

With all the fancy aplomb he could muster, he first set the stage as he went through a checklist, just like a pilot doing a preflight check: Recorder on, speakers on and me as a witness. "Bessie, get me Congressman Wilson."

A moment later, Bess said on the intercom, "He's on the phone, Mr. Rosenberg. He'll be with you shortly."

"Hello, Bob. How the hell are you, Mr. Congressman?" He schmoozed. He went on for a couple of minutes and concluded with something like, "Oh, Bob, I wanted you to look into a small problem I'm having with one of our illustrious Marine Corps base commanders at Camp Pendleton. Apparently, the local businessmen and civic leaders have convinced him that my Dick Tyrell Jewelers and the photography shop are bad operations. The S.O.B. has had the gall to place my business operations off-limits. Can you believe that?"

"Bob, you know I run legitimate businesses, no crime, no drugs, everything up and above board. I always have and always will. My stores are the same as in San Diego and I insist that my managers conduct their affairs in accordance with recognized standards and accepted practices. Now, these jealous cocksuckers are trying to give me a bad name and ruin my businesses and reputation as well. I won't stand by and let that happen . . . "

Nate paused as he let the congressman have a moment to figure out what he could do.

"Well, Nate, I'm going to be out of town traveling to the Orient on official government business soon and may not have the kind of time necessary to resolve any differences between your businesses and the Marine Corps. However, I may be able to make a few phone calls and inquire and then ..."

Nate interrupted and dropped his hammer in a calm and unpretentious voice.

"Bob, I've got several hundred thousand dollars invested in my Oceanside operation and because of this fucking general, my business is off 95 percent. Bob, make a call or do whatever you must. I want the 'off limits' postings removed before you go off with the misses to the Orient. I'm not going to wait while you play political bullshit. That's your business. Do your thing.

"Congressman, aren't you coming up for re-election next year?" The direct confirmation of his forthcoming election was a tacit Roman dictum reminder: *Quid pro quo*. Something for something, and it always would be.

"Not a problem, Mr. Rosenberg. I'll take care of it and be back in touch soon."

"I know you will, Bob. Don't forget where I live. My penthouse is always available to you. I think I owe you some payback for beating me at poker the last time we met," Nate said, laughing.

No doubt, Nate left the politician with a thought. Another cash contribution would be forthcoming. Nate closed with a perfunctory, "Thank you, congressman."

"You lost to him at poker?" I inquired.

"Hell no!" said Nate. "He played four hands of make-believe poker and won fifty grand. Can you believe that?"

"Sure, Nate. You must be a lousy poker player." Of course, I knew it was an obvious campaign donation, remembering *Ziu Chich* saying, "They're all on the take."

Two days later, we got a call from Nate's attorney, who had been working the issue from a different angle. I got a buzzer from Nate and went to his office, where he sat cozied up to his desk with a Cheshire cat's grin on his face. He said, "Joseph, I believe that power of persuasion is working fine. Appears as if our Pendleton general is a warrior and is off to Vietnam. The 'off limits' has been lifted.

"I'm off to the Penthouse for a steam bath, massage and a female air start." He paused and buzzed his therapist, saying," I'll be up shortly. I need the works."

Nate was heading up to get some relaxation and as he gingerly crossed his thick white carpet, he turned and said, "Ain't life grand, Joseph."

"Yes sir," I replied. Especially when you have the power.

CHAPTER 34
THE LAST HURRAH

1969 was a year of firsts and lasts. Apollo 11 landed on the moon and Richard Milhous Nixon succeeded Lyndon Baines Johnson as president. The Beatles gave their last public performance, and after 147 years, the last issue of the Saturday Evening Post hit the stands. The NFL's Super Bowl III MVP, Joe Namath, led the Jets and upset the favored Indianapolis Colts. Finally, Dad and I had to listen to a man trying to come to grips with his miserable lot in life. Frank Bompensiero called the Star & Garter and asked Dad if he could come and talk with us. Frank supposedly had some revelation. Actually, he was venting about his past and predicting his future. He made some admissions to us that seemed important to him. I listened and on occasion asked questions only he could answer.

✯ ✯ ✯

San Diego's newest Go-Go hot spot and cocktail lounge, the Star & Garter, had been opened for a couple of months. Business was good and the operation was solid. However, I can say now that we were lucky to get the place opened.

I hadn't seen Frank since we had our encounter at Nate's, and he hadn't called Dad either. He was probably too embarrassed to call and tell his brother that his son got to him again. He was most likely licking his wounds.

In time, something finally got to him and so he called his brother. There were no requests or invitations that I

The Niputi ...the Nephew

was aware of on either side. I believe Dad finally decided to side with me. At least I would not bring the cops sniffing around.

From the moment we opened the doors, the Garter was successful. Dad and I both put a lot of sweat equity into the Garter and made it a showplace, and our on-stage girls were beautiful. We were both proud. Moreover, I felt as if I had repaid my father for the years he provided me love, security, guidance, and the means to accomplish my personal objectives.

Yeah, yeah, so it cost me time and grade in the Air Force but, what the hell, it was a three-year sabbatical and I learned much more than I would have elsewhere. And it was well worth it seeing the almost perpetual smile on Dad's face.

I recalled giving my father a call from Nate's the morning I told Frank to go screw himself and not to come back. Dad listened intently as I told him what transpired. He said, "I'll take care of it . . ."

I interrupted, "Dad, it's all over. There is nothing to take care of. He's your brother, Dad, not mine. I have no respect for him or what he does. However, I know he'll turn to you if he needs help, just like you did when you sent me to help your friend Nate.

"Whatever you do with him is your business. But, do it away from the Garter. I'm not going to jeopardize the liquor license because of your stupid brother."

Dad was taken aback with my candor. However, about three or four months into the Garter's operation, Dad called me at home.

"Joe, my brother called and wants to meet us at the Garter." I stared at the phone questioningly. With personal feelings aside, I was in control of my own destiny. My position in the Garter was solid, literally and legally. The business, corporation and liquor license belonged to me. I had formed and owned Sal Enterprises, Inc., the corporation that controlled the stock. I owned the land as well, under a separate deed of trust under my name. Dad could do nothing about it and I wasn't concerned.

I said, "Dad, what do you think he wants?"

"I have no idea. He just said he had something important to tell us."

"I'll see you there around ten a.m."

"Sounds good."

When I arrived the next morning, he had done all the day's ordering and restocking. As I walked in, he said "You want to play some eight ball?"

"Sure." We started our game and I broke, and as I did I recalled our previous time playing pool when Pat was in town. "Hey, Dad, do you remember how you beat Pat and me the last time he was here?"

"Yeah," he laughed. "You were easy." We small-talked around the table, always looking for an edge, and Dad beat me three out of four games as we waited for Frank.

Frank showed around one o'clock and was directed to the office. At the time, I was in the storeroom adjacent to the office and saw Frank barging in the door like he owned the joint. He never changed. I closed the stockroom and entered the office, where Dad was making a bank for the night shift. "Hello, Ziu Chich."

"Nice place you've got here," said Frank, trying to be pleasant. He didn't give a shit about the joint, but he was jealous it wasn't his.

"Thank you. We're going to keep it that way. What's on your mind?"

"How about a drink, Niputi?"

"Sure, *Ziu*. But not like old times. Those days, like my father's businesses, are long gone. The Star and Garter is mine."

"What about your father? Doesn't he count?"

"You don't have to ever worry about my father or my mother as it pertains to income, Frank. Although we all can't say that, can we? I don't believe in wasting time, *Ziu*. We have a business to run." At least I referred to him as Ziu to ease the tension.

"So, what's on your mind?"

"I came by to tell you both that I will be hit and soon." He smirked and whined that probably his own family fraternity brothers would take him out. I knew the "fraternity brothers" comment was aimed at me, his college-graduated nephew whom he only tolerated. I jumped in with both feet.

"Fraternity brothers, no less, *Ziu*. You must have done something bad for them to want to bury you."

Frank must have sensed from my comments that I had a short fuse. I wouldn't play cat and mouse with him. He had been civil up to now.

"I know I've pissed off quite a few people over the years. It's my nature, I guess," Frank said. "I've also broken it off in the ass of some insiders, and for those guys paybacks are a bitch. To get back to my point, have either of you heard about a nationwide search for a pedophile suspect?"

"That TV crap. Yeah, so what?" said Dad.

"Armstrong put the arm on me the other day."

"Who is Armstrong?" I asked.

"Jack Armstrong, a local FBI guy," replied Frank.

"He's been after me for years to blab, but I've never had anything to say to him. A couple of weeks ago, I'm minding my business having coffee and reading the paper in Denny's and here comes Armstrong, asking if he can join me. I said, 'Sure, Jack. Anything for the FBI.' Jack sits and notices I'm reading the local rag about the ongoing search for the sex nut, and he about blows me over. He says. 'You're a grandfather, aren't you?' "

"Yeah, so," I replied.

"You've been reading about this pedophile that we're after.

"So?"

"So, what if he gets here and stops off at your place while you're having coffee and grabs one of your grandkids. What then?"

"That got me thinking. The guy is asking me for help trying to find a cur-dog pedophile stooge. Can you believe it?" Then he said, "You know I don't like queers and degenerates, right, Turi?"

"Yeah, I know."

"Remember that queer Liberace back in the fifties. Ha ha." I thought back to Liberace and Frank's big mouth at the Manhattan Room, Dad's first joint in San Diego. I remembered that it cost my parents all their savings.

"Yeah, Unc. I remember that you encouraged my father to blow the only honest deal where he could own a piece of a millionaire to be. Yeah, I remember."

Frank looked down and smirked and continued. "Well, I told Jack that he never blabbed about anything, let alone business that did not concern him. Remember, Jack, I pleaded the Fifth over one hundred times in Judge Hewicker's court back in the fifties."

"Ziu Chich," I asked, "what was the question the DA asked you?"

"They wanted to know if I was the individual known as Frank Bompensiero. I wouldn't answer and pled the Fifth.

It pissed 'em all off," he said laughing. "But now, what Jack is asking bothers me. So I tell him, it's everyone's concern Jack, even yours."

"You know, Turi, I love kids and watching TV and the Westerns and dog programs like Lassie. So just being courteous, I told Jack I'd keep my ear to the ground and if I heard anything, I'd let him know. He appreciated it and I think it made him feel good."

"Brother, the more I thought about this creep pedophile, the more I got pissed thinking about those *disgratiato* sons o' bitches. Anyone abusing kids eats at me, *Manaja* (Frustration). *Those Cretinu bastia* (Friggin cretin bastards.)

"The parents of pedophiles should have to watch their seed's *Mincia and colognes* (prick and balls) ripped from their bodies. That would get their attention. But, you know what pisses me off? It's those friggin *Spiru*. They can't catch the miserable bastids, but have time to follow, harass and break my balls.

"On the way home, I thought about it more and more and made a few calls to a couple of guys, and one thing led to another. After a few days—*bada bing, bada boom*—and I called Jack Armstrong and asked him to meet me for coffee at Denny's.

"I gave him a time, date and actual address of the asshole. Of course, the guy was there. He was not going to run anymore," said Frank. "Someone put a pissed-off hungry dog on the degenerate and he ate a mouthful of the bum's shorts, if you get my drift. He won't be molesting any more kids." Frank did his gallows laughter bit.

"No shit, *Ziu*. You found the guy?"

"Who me, nephew?" he laughed. "The friggin *Spiru* will never have the connections we do. The cops are only as good as their stool pigeons, and we have them all. That's why the Feds panic when they try to hide someone. They know that ninety-nine percent of the time, if we want someone bad enough we'll get to them."

"Then, a few weeks later, some of the guys and I were tossing the bull and I mentioned feeding the pedophile to the sharks. No doubt, they blabbed. The organization doesn't appreciate any big mouth, especially mine. But none of them want to piss me off now. They've got too much to lose. It's not like the old days.

"They know I'm not going to talk about business after all these years. If they didn't believe that, I'd be dead by now. Besides, there are too many politicians and union bosses on the take. They like things just the way they are. Screw them all."

"Paro Frati" (but brother), interjected Dad. "Why would they come after you for some bum? I remember you saying *Tu Familia* had its own rules. So why would they come after you?

"In their minds, they worry that I'm going to say something. They owe me nothing. My years in Quentin were due to my own dealings with Berry and Bonelli and the California politicos. They only wanted their cut and I didn't offer them any, either. All that dried up when Bonelli and company ran across the border to Mexico and everyone but me got off."

Then, in a rare gesture to his brother, Frank turned and said, "Sammy, if it wasn't for you, *mi frati*, I'd still be talking to the walls in Quentin."

Turi smiled and said, "I know, *Chichu*, I know."

"I would have been left holding my schwaanz in prison for thirty-five years if you hadn't interceded. They never felt they were part of the Bonelli thing I set up. Besides, that fucking De Simone and his pimp Roselli wouldn't lift a finger for me.

"Their codes of honor, and we take care of our own, is all crap. That was Hollywood shit, the cops and their college punks. Do you think *la Cosa Nostra* thing had a secretary-general taking notes and writing down vows in a set of scrolls, like the Bible?" Frank said, laughing. "Dead Scrolls would be more like it. Hell, none of the mustached Pete's could read. Have you forgotten, Turi? None of us left Sicily reading. You can't read now and you've been away from Sicily since 1927.

"The last generation with all their schooling and the likes of De Simone as a boss was bullshit. Our code was simple and that cocksucker wasn't smart enough to understand it. Jack taught it to me when I first got to L.A.

"You ask, I give, you owe. Simple! Open your mouth, talk about business to anyone, and die. That's it! If that doesn't make you want to follow the rule, you'll be reminded after you die when your wife, kids, all the family go tits up. Get the picture? Simple, hah, hah hah. It worked for everybody—businesses, labor unions, everybody."

"Yeah," I said. "Voluntary membership, honor through intimidation and death the expiration date."

"You got it, Joey."

"That shouldn't be too tough, *Ziu Chich*, especially since you were able to do it," I said sarcastically. "No sane person would like those odds!"

"Maybe those that came from a different country?" said Frank.

"What bullshit," I said. "You and Dad were born here. I've got copies of your birth certificates from the same ignorant midwife who couldn't spell Bompensiero correctly when Dad was born."

Sammy, preoccupied with counting money, ignored the comment while Frank took the insult as a direct hit and leered at me.

"Nothing has changed, *Ziu Chich*, except I'm older now and have lot of scar tissue. I don't do bullshit anymore without a reason of my own choosing."

Sammy turned to his brother as Frank's puffy face reddened and his blood pressure rose. Frank swallowed hard on the remainder of his Johnny Walker Black.

"You know, Ziu, I'm going to change the subject, if you don't mind. I could never figure why you hated the Jews as much as you do. First, you try and fuck Bugsy Siegel out of Hollywood and Vegas, but that was Dragna business and you screwed that up. Then you almost nailed his henchman, Mickey Cohen, and you missed again. Then you screwed up the Algiers for us and the Khans. Then, Nate Rosenberg. I've always wondered, why? Because they made money and were smarter than you and your guys, or were they just easy marks, especially Nate, who was a fucking business genius?"

"Bugsy was business, company business." Frank said.

"Yeah, but you missed by a mile from what I've read, or was it B.S. or just another bad shot." I said, laughing. "I hear you can't shoot too straight. I can give you some lessons. I'm a marksman and don't miss." I thought he was going to blow a gasket.

"Niputi, you can bet your smart ass that I wacked Siegel, that son of a bitch. Blew his fucking eye right out. That cocksucker fucked with the wrong guy when he played around with Jack Dragna. We made sure of that."

"Let me talk about one more thing, Frank. Remember when I said I was almost thirty years old?"

"Yeah, so?"

"Well, it's been 22 years since you came to my father's house at 2018 Union Street in the old neighborhood and intimidated my father and mother to cook your fucking big dinner for De Simone and Adamo. The same two men who screwed you the night of the dinner. But, that's not what I've been pissed about all these years, and mostly why I kicked your ass at Aunt Thelma's seven years ago.

"Frank, I for one don't give a shit if one of your friends blows you away. No big fucking deal! If anyone deserves it, you do. In fact, it's overdue. And, as far as respect is concerned, I won't even go to your funeral. You've never amounted to anything except an ill-mannered *cafoni* (clod). Besides, I'll never forget that you insulted my father by telling him his scotch was shit. Then, you tinkle your scotch glass at my mother as you took over our house as if she were one of your waitresses.

"In that house, she was the only one who told you off. She was not one of your waitresses.

"Now, Frank, on behalf of my wonderful Mom, if you want another drink in my bar, you can get your old ass up and gruffly ask for a lotta ice, like you did my mother. Tell the bartender your *Niputi*, your nephew Joe, said it was okay to give you another drink. Make sure you say please, since you never did before. And Frank, if you don't want to do that, just get the hell out and don't ever come back."

There was silence as I looked at him and Dad. Then I said, "I'd better leave before I do something I'll have to bury."

I walked out the door. To my knowledge that was the last time Frank ever came into the Star & Garter. I would see him one last time in about a year. Then, unfortunately, it would be several more years before Frank Bompensiero got what he deserved.

CHAPTER 35
A FATHER'S PASSING

If you live long enough, you will lose someone you love. It could be possibly a father, mother, brother or child. If you haven't, you will. And, believe me, you haven't endured one of the most painful events you'll ever experience. I know of the pain I speak of. I have lost two fathers, a mother, and two children who were eighteen years apart. Our infant baby died as the result of a needless auto accident on her initial birthing day. And we lost our eighteen-year-old son when a drunken fool crashed into Sam and his motorcycle, one block from home, after visiting his girl. We don't see much of our youngest son, Matthew, anymore. Ever since his older brother Sammy died when Matt was fourteen years old. He's had a difficult time. However, he created two beautiful girls, Samantha and Rachael, my granddaughters. Now at 44 years old, he resides in a quiet place and hopefully finds solace. All my family losses were tragic, however, I never felt the loss as much as the death of my father.

It was March 1970. My wife Julie and I, and sons Sam and Matt, were living in a duplex just off Mather AFB, near Rancho Cordova, California. It was convenient, affordable, and adequate for our needs. However, with all the excitement of having our Matthew, our newborn, we hadn't even taken time to drive to San Diego to meet his grandparents.

Though we stayed in contact with Mom and Dad, she called one day quite upset.

"I'm concerned with your Dad's health. He's been having a few bouts with intense migraine headaches. He even banged his head against the walls until he cracked the flesh and bled." I asked the logical question.

"What did the doctor say?"

"He won't go."

"Tell him I'm taking some time off and we're coming down so he can meet his grandson Matthew." She thought that was a great idea. I made the arrangements and several days later we drove to San Diego.

As I expected, Dad was suffering from something far worse than he or I could imagine. He was sloughing off the malady as "just a bad headache. I've had 'em for years."

However, the next morning while watching TV, Dad was playing with Matthew and then yelled, "*Jesu Christu*, take Matthew!" I took Matt, called for Julie, and gave her Matt as I helped Dad rise. He wobbled and tears welled up in his eyes as he stumbled forward to grab the edge of the wall. He then banged his forehead repeatedly as blood squirted from the open wound. I grabbed a towel and pressed it on his forehead to slow the bleeding.

"Julie, give Matthew to Mom and run down and start my car."

"Mom, call Dad's doctor. We're heading to Mercy Hospital."

Dad yelled out, "I'm okay."

"Like hell you are. This is no bullshit. You have a problem and can ignore it, but I'm not going to pretend it doesn't exist. We're going to the hospital and find out what in the hell is wrong with you!"

I held Dad up, leading him to my car, and with Mom talking to him we raced to the Mercy Hospital emergency room. Fortunately for Dad, Dr. Sam Assam, a neurosurgeon, was on duty. He asked Mom about Dad's prior experiences and she recanted his recent bouts with headaches. Dr. Assam called for a spinal tap and the results told him that Dad's spinal fluid was clouded with blood. "This means his brain is bleeding," said Dr. Assam.

X-rays of Dad's head followed, and Dr. Assam sat Mom and me down and explained Dad's condition. "It's obvious from the X-rays, coupled with the spinal tap, that Sam has an aneurism in the midst of his medulla oblongata. Surgery is necessary for survival. He is critical."

With thousands of little nerve tentacles coming off the brain stem, the shocking aneurism was obvious, large, and bulging from a weak wall of a substantial vein. I wondered, *Will he clamp or bypass it and how?*

Dr. Assam then said it's a difficult procedure to get to the affected aneurism without injuring nearby nerves.

"What are the critical nerves and how do you get through those nerves, Doctor Assam?"

"I'm sorry, but we have to cut through them." With that, I knew Dad would never be the same. He was fearful of surgery and I spoke to him to make him understand that he had no choice if he wanted to live.

The operation lasted almost thirteen hours and Dad survived. However, Dr. Assam offered guarded encouragement about his recovery. Mom didn't understand. She thought surgery would correct the problem. Later I said, "Mom, hope for the best but expect the worst."

I spent precious moments with him one last time after his neurosurgery and told him to keep fighting. He had worked so hard and now it was his time to enjoy the fruits of his labors. His mouth was already twisted and part of his face was paralyzed as he listened to me. I found him aware but inconsolable.

Mom and I both knew he wouldn't want to live that way. With tears in my eyes, I thanked him for being a great father and told him I loved him. It was hard saying goodbye to my father, who was only 57 years old—a man whom I still miss and love to this day.

I left the room, saying softly to my mother, "Mom, his recovery will be difficult at best, so prepare yourself. He doesn't want to live in his present state and the truth is that neither of us want him to live as a vegetable." I left her little hope.

She understood. I left the waiting room and called Julie and advised her of his condition." Get the boys ready. We're going home. I can't do anymore now."

I called and checked in with Mom every other day for three weeks. Finally, my cousin Tina called to let me know that Dad had died. I felt relieved that his suffering was over. Mom said his devoted sisters came to the hospital night and day. No one mentioned visits from Frank, but I figured he showed up.

I knew Frank was around somewhere, but I didn't hear from him and had to contact him. A strange and secretive call came in one evening a few days after Tina notified me of Dad's death.

Julie was caring for the boys following dinner and I was studying for a management exam. The phone rang and Julie answered it.

"Is Frank Bompensiero there?" asked a man's voice.

"Just a minute, please." She scurried down the hall to our bedroom where I studied. My thoughts broke away from legal administration as I heard the door crack open.

"What's up?" I asked." Julie had a quizzical look on her face and I knew something was wrong.

"Hon, there is someone on the phone asking about your Uncle Frank."

I took a second to think. *We've been here almost two years and no one outside the military, even relatives, ever called for me, Dad or Frank. Now someone was asking about Frank. What the hell?* I motioned her to get the boys to their room. I picked up the receiver and decided to play hardball.

"Hello, whom did you ask for?"

"Frank Bompensiero. We have been friends for years."

"Really! Well, you and I are not friends, . . . and where did you get my number? Well, friend of Frank, I'm his nephew. Why don't you call him?"

"I've misplaced his number. We . . . ah—"

I interrupted. "We, my ass. *Tu Pezzu di Minchia.* (You prick.)

"Call your mother, information or the FBI. They know his phone number. Don't call my house again. My father just died. Now is not the time for me to be dealing with Frank or any of his Goomba buddy shit. *Capish?* I am Federal, *Tu Strunza* (you turd), which means someone's listening. So asshole, tomorrow when the FBI drops in on you, you'll know why."

I hung up and smiled. *That Dago asshole will start whining and end up shitting his pants for scaring my family.* I had Frank's number that Dad had given me and called him.

"Hello," said the voice. I recognized Frank.

"*Ziu Chich*, this is your *Niputi*. Just listen! My wife just received a call a few minutes ago from some Goomba cocksucker wanting to know where you were. He was not a

Spiru (spy-cop.) I told the fucker where to get off. Now I'm telling you, Frank. No one, I repeat, no one from your life is to call me about you. Don't you realize that I am a federal employee? I've given the FBI permission to tap my phones. *Capish?*"

"I'll take care of it," said Frank. "One other thing, *Niputi*. I'll be having a little gathering on Shelter Island for my brother. The guys want to pay their respects. Would you do me a favor and drop in?"

"We'll talk about it, *Ziu*," I replied. "And make sure you take care of that other matter we spoke about. *Buona Sera.*"

Although I generally kept Julie informed, I didn't expect her or the boys to be caught up in the family's Mafia bull. The Sicilian pageantry and potential religious zealotry had driven me crazy for years. That was for those who were brought up in the culture. The family women didn't mean anything by it, but they were raised that way and still had some strange beliefs.

All of the women would be in black. I knew this from watching their dress throughout the years as their husbands died. However, Dad personally rejected the ritualistic crap. Neither Mom nor I would tolerate the outward display of emotion over my father's death. I witnessed many local funerals as an altar boy. On one occasion, the wife of a deceased fisherman tried to climb into the open coffin with her husband. This would not happen at my father's funeral.

※ ※ ※

As I recalled my father's face and his suffering, I had flashes of another nightmare, Frank's coffee meetings with Jack Armstrong of the local FBI. Frank mentioned that Jack was bugging him and had met him for coffee several times. That thought sounded the alarm as hairs on the back of my neck stood on end.

The word may have leaked. Hell, who knew, maybe the FBI let the word out? They were as bad as anyone and would lie to achieve their objectives. Or what if Frank's associates wanted to distance themselves from his mouth? They didn't like him anyway and often called him "The mouth that roared." They knew he was a loose cannon who should be dumped in a ditch. Frank more or less let that be known to Dad and me when he brought the subject up at the Garter back in 1969.

What if those idiots thought that with his brother gone, Frank would be easy prey? Frank was a big mouth; of that, there was no doubt. But he had been a church mouse in Quentin and had maintained his oath of silence. Yeah, but that session didn't involve the Mafia. But now with the *Mickey Mouse Mafia*, as De Simone 's house became known, Frank's position in the pecking order was reduced. Then Frank became irrelevant as De Simone lost his job as Capo and Johnny Roselli's protector, Sam Giancana, died. Frank, almost ten years after release from prison, was now irrelevant. Eventually, someone must have found out or saw him speaking with Jack Armstrong at Denny's.

If there was a purge, who would be caught up in the mess? No one in his Mafia cause respected him and would rather have him dead. Frank's friends believed in their solemn code, and they could be heartless as the old-school Sicilians. At times, they could conceive of eradicating an entire family. It had been done before. The possibility existed that my family, my sons and I could be in danger, even though we were not involved. Frank's friends were, of course, *pazzo* (crazy). I would have to do something, and soon.

The Niputi ...the Nephew

I was concerned for my mother and called her, giving her some support until I got there.

"Mom, look on the bright side. Dad didn't suffer. He died with dignity. But, don't expect me to do the Sicilian black mourning crap thing.

"I know," she replied.

"Mom, I don't believe in that and neither did he. You might pass that on to the family. I'll be at the funeral in uniform. He liked me in uniform. And Mom, I'll be wearing Dad's favorite lime green sports jacket, tan slacks, and his favorite loud tie at the house. I'm doing it to celebrate my father. I'll see you at Aunt Grace's. Julie will fly down with the boys the day after tomorrow."

Mom interrupted. "Joe, we got a call from your Uncle Frank and he wanted to speak with you."

"Yeah, I know, Mom. I already spoke with him."

"What did he want?" she queried.

"I'll tell you later. It wasn't important."

"Bye for now, Mom. I love you. See you tomorrow afternoon."

I thought about what Mom had said and her tone. She was easygoing and didn't want to ruffle feathers. She had done enough of that in her life and now without me by her side, she would fall prey to the intense family pressures. She no doubt had a lot on her mind. In addition to the loss of Dad, she was like most quickly widowed women, wondering how she would get on and financially survive? I knew the answer.

Dad didn't have insurance, which of course was for the *Riccu* (rich). Although he made a lot of money, he lived well and spent lavishly on Mom. They spent a bunch on the horse races every season. To relieve her angst, I stole a moment alone with her a day later. I looked her right in the eye and said, "Mom, don't worry about the future. All would be handled to your satisfaction. I promise." Then I hugged her. In these difficult times, she overlooked the one big insurance policy Dad believed in—me.

After arriving at my aunt's, dressed in the lime-green sports jacket, blazing yellow silk tie and beige trousers, I shocked all those in black, including Mom. I figured my outfit would blow the hoods' cookies. But I changed into my uniform before I left to visit Shelter Island, just to be a pain. Uniforms always made Frank uneasy. I figured that maybe Frank's friends would feel the same way.

I drove off to Shelter Island knowing that I had time to relax and enjoy the serene view of the bay. It would take me no more than fifteen minutes to get there. As I drove I thought about Dad and some of the complications of my future. Yes, I was back in the Air Force, and soon would finish my graduate degree. I had volunteered for Vietnam. I tried to get Mom to leave San Diego and live with me, Julie, and the boys in Rancho Cordova. Besides, I was selfish and didn't want to worry about her, Julie and the boys while Mom was alone in San Diego.

The smell of the salty air came through my window as I pulled up in front of the Shelter Island Inn's valet parking. Attired in my Air Force dress blues with rank and decorations shining brightly in the sun, I stepped from my car. I stood looking around to see where the FBI and plainclothes police parked. I feared that they would follow me to the island. I was also looking for uninvited hoods, press, and anyone else I didn't care for. I climbed the stairs and felt strangely alone and pulled the doors open to the hotel lobby. It was almost vacant, most likely by intention. I caught the time on the conch shell-framed clock over the Polynesian outrigger above the archway and it read 10:50.

I wondered: *What was waiting for me?* I had been there before, but those times I was there to party or to hit on some babe in the Aloha bar. Now, those were the last things on my mind as I walked up the stairs.

I was early for the get-together, but normally tourists by the number would have filled the lounge and bar area, laughing, and talking between sips of fruit-laden rum drinks. However, on this seemingly bright day it was unusually quiet. I thought they must be outside enjoying the cool breezes and soaking up the Mediterranean-like San Diego sun. I was wrong. The place was silent and barren. No one was home, or so I thought, as a well-dressed man approached from behind some drapes that separated the major dining room from the lobby.

"Excuse me, sir. Can I help you?"

"Yes, sir. I'm looking for my uncle, Frank Bompensiero. Is he here?"

"Yes. You must be his nephew Joe. We couldn't miss you in your uniform. We have been expecting you. Just follow me."

We went down a corridor and he pulled back a drape and cracked open a door, which led into a large private room. I heard hushed voices as I entered and wondered this seemed more than just a few guys to pay respects. Someone must have owed Frank, feared him or just comp'd him a place to meet.

There was a small bar and tables off in a corner of a large room. Frank sat in a huge red leather booth surrounded by three men. I recognized Jimmy the Weasel but not the other fellows. I looked around and recognized a few others in the crowd including Joe Piazza and Bill Biaggo.

Joey saw me and walked over.

"Piazza, my old pal." I said. We shook hands and embraced.

"Sorry about your Dad, captain."

"Thank you, Joey." We hadn't seen each other in ten years. We last partied on New Years of 1960 when he and I spent a month in Mexico City and Acapulco. Then, he was enthralled with Frank and his supposed station in La Familia. Joey wanted in real bad. He wanted to be one of them. Now he was. I thought, *what a waste of a smart bright talent.*

I realized that Frank had assembled about thirty of his Mafia brotherhood. Many, I hadn't met. It was a show. Frank was holding court of his Mafia *Goombas*. I thought, *what fucking gall*.

I walked over to Frank and did the obligatory embrace and said, "Hello, *Ziu Chich,*" and nodded to Jimmy.

Frank said, "All my friends wanted to pay their respects to my brother. Some flew into town. In fact, I'd like you to meet an old friend of mine. He gestured to the nattily dressed man sitting next to him who rose, and put out his hand. I reached out in kind as Frank said, "This is Anthony Spilotro. We go way back. He's from the Midwest and works out of Vegas now. We have done some business together. "He looked younger than the crew, more like my age. Anthony spoke saying, "Hello Joe, glad to meet you. Sorry about your father."

"Hello, Anthony. Good to meet you too. I appreciate you coming.

Spilotro replied, "Anything for your uncle Frank. We've been friends for years." Bingo! My mind recalled his voice signature. Spilotro was the voice on the phone several days before. I couldn't let him think I didn't know.

"Well, Tony, it's great to see you in person after hearing your voice on the phone the other night. If you ever call again, use your name, I deal better when I know whom I'm speaking with." Spilotro's facial expression and quizzical eye confirmed my suspicion.

Frank interrupted with, "Joe, would you mind meeting the guys?"

"I don't mind, *Ziu*, as long as I can get through the line and get back to Mom and my family."

We walked around the room, pressing the flesh and listening to their condolences. He introduced me to quite a few Boyz from out of town who must have owed Frank.

Frank introduced each man. Then he confirmed my thoughts.

"Though your Dad was not affiliated, those that knew him respected him. The others came because they have heard me telling how he stuck by me when I went to prison."

Most, I thought, *didn't know Sammy Bonpensiero from a fig leaf.* Frank, no doubt, called them in to see who still respected him.

"It would have been nice having them come to the funeral," I said. "But the church will be full of *Spiru* with the press and their cameras."

"Don't I know! That's why we met here. It's more validation of my business thing *(Mi Cosa Nostra)*. I wanted to see who would show."

"That reminds me, *Ziu*. Was your friend who called my home, Spilotro? His voice sounded similar. Frank, of course hedged.

"*Niputi*, that was a misunderstanding. No problem."

"*Thank you, Frank!*" I knew the prick was lying as usual.

"No, that was a misunderstanding. No problem."

Thank you, Frank! I knew the prick was lying as usual.

"How about a drink, *Niputi*?"

"Fine. Courvoisier, *Ziu*, and I'd like to say a few words."

"Sure thing," replied Frank. "Gentlemen, my nephew Joe."

I stood up and thanked all the attendees for coming and made some small talk about my father appreciating the gesture, etc. Then I closed, "If I haven't personally met you today, please understand I'm on a time line and accept my apology, no disrespect intended, but I have to leave."

Joey Piazza walked up and tipped his glass in my direction and spoke so all could hear.

"Here's to Sammy Bompensiero, a man of our times. A good father and my friend."

Ziu Chich chimed in, "Here, here."

Then something unexpected happened. Frank turned to me and said, "*Niputi*, we've got to talk." I walked with him off in a quiet place in the room. He leaned close and in a low voice said, "Is there anything you or your Mom need?"

"Are you serious, *Ziu Chich*?" I was blown away.

"Yeah," he said.

I then asked, "What do you mean when you say need? Are you talking about money?"

Frank looked questioningly at me and replied, "Anything."

I continued devilishly turning the knife and said, "Mom is stuck with about fifty thousand in medical bills, which should cover the hospital, and another ten grand for the funeral. Other than that, we are fine. I'm taking care of her long-term needs. As you know, Dad, like most Sicilians, didn't believe in insurance. But he believed in me and knew I'd take care of my mother."

Frank's beady eyes sort of glazed over. He knew I was mocking his question to help. Actually, I was stabbing him

The Niputi ...the Nephew

in the heart for a final time. I knew he was thinking that I was just a disrespectful little prick. But, I wouldn't play his game.

Over the years, I had asked Dad if his brother ever offered him a dime. Dad laughed.

"Who was going to give it to him?" Now, Frank tried to feed his ego and play the Big Time Boss charade as he had done for some many years. He never achieved stardom except as a "do-fer" and killer. He also never accumulated any money. He only spent.

Frank knew I watched the cash flow and was aware that Frank accepted cash from my Dad for years, almost like homage. He expected it. However, now he could no longer use familial pressure or guilt to squeeze dollars from his brother, and he knew I wasn't going to move an inch. The tide of familial passion and respect had come and gone. There was no reason to see Frank again. We had nothing to say. It all had been said before. I offered my hand and Frank said, "See you around, *Niputi.*"

As I walked away, I felt like it was finally over and the cloud had lifted. I made a beeline towards my car. I had a funeral and family to tend to and an Air Force career in front of me. However, I had the eerie feeling that Frank would show up again. And, he did . . . seven years later. Though dead, he was still flaunting the Bompensiero name in *Time* magazine.

CHAPTER 36

OFF WE GO
...INTO THE WILD BLUE YONDER

As a boy I looked forward to flying and to join the Air Force and have a flying career. I had the support of my family and knew that one day, disregarding the occasional change in course, I would accomplish my objective. I did, but in my case I took a circuitous route. As some of the promos say, you can do anything you set your mind to. I have found now in my seventy-fifth year, 2014, that the cliché' appears true, at least for me. The following encapsulates the rest of my military career and hopefully provides closure to some of my readers' questions about my zany career travels as I have moved about forty times.

✸ ✸ ✸

Many have asked me how I did an about-face when my father died, leaving San Diego and the Star & Garter to re-enter the Air Force. For me, it was easy because I never lost sight of my career objective. I had to deal with moving priorities, as do most people. I was flexible. It wasn't easy. However, when the Garter opened and my father seemed happy again, I started to plan. I went to the Air Force and they had no need for me, but I realized that Vietnam was still ongoing. So, I went to the U.S. Army. They had aircraft, more than the Air Force. I knew they could use an experienced officer. I applied and they said yes. Both the Army

The Niputi ...the Nephew

recruiter and I waited patiently for the Air Force to send them my records. They didn't.

When I told the Air Force I was going to resign my USAF commission, they called me. "Mr. Bonpensiero, do you really want to go in the Army?"

"No," I said. "But you don't want me back and the U.S. Army will give me a direct commission as a captain. So, I'll serve them."

"Please wait until Monday. We'll send you a formal response by courier." And I did.

Early Monday morning, a courier banged on our door. In the packet were military orders directing me to active duty as a captain, USAF, effective September 1969. Somehow, I stretched enough to get back into the Air Force.

Within weeks of Dad's dying, Mom decided to come live with us, especially since she knew I'd be heading for Vietnam. Julie and I looked for a house big enough for all of us. We gave notice to our landlord and departed the duplex. Then we purchased our home in Rancho Cordova with the G.I. Bill. This was our second home using my VA loan. It was a beauty of a two-story home and Mom could have her privacy and own space.

After a year of good times, I received departure orders for Vietnam and my plans fell apart. Mom decided she wanted to be back with friends in San Diego while I was gone. Then, Julie joined her and said, "Well, I don't want to live alone in Sacramento." Talk about mice leaving a sinking ship. We sent Mom to San Diego and she looked for a condominium.

I also was able to find an officer who wanted our house, but couldn't buy it for a year. But he and his family would live in it, pay my mortgage and we'd open an escrow while I was in Vietnam. With few options and the days rushing by, it sounded good to me. Mom called and found a condominium in San Diego that she loved. I put a down payment on it and found Julie a rental house. We bid adieu as I boarded a plane heading north to Alaska on my way to 'Nam.

Things were well stateside, but I forgot to keep my mouth shut when I arrived in 'Nam and volunteered to recover a downed C-123 Provider aircraft several days after arriving at Phan Rang.

My team of five found it with a damaged landing gear and doors in a rice paddy on a firebase known as Gia Vuc. The Viet Cong shot at us randomly every day for ten days. We took cover and returned fire. They tried to nail us several times, but thanks to the sole Rambo-like misfit, an Army Ranger at Gia Vuc, and his indigent Montagnard aborigines, they kept them off our backs while we worked on the aircraft.

My guys completed repairing the aircraft and I called "Mother" for an aircrew. For ten days, we ate nothing but G.I.-issued chili powder from a five-gallon tin, mixed with water. Our reward was massive weight loss resulting from Gia Vuc intestinal revenge. Enough said about that. I never volunteered in Vietnam again,

But upon my return to my hooch at Phan Rang, I almost killed my first pilot. A hooch neighbor and wiseass prick who decided to welcome me back by placing a stuffed "cobra" coiled to attack in my bunk.

I was happy to complete my tour as aircraft maintenance officer working a twelve-hour night shift from midnight to noon, seven days a week. During my off hours I played "Chef D'Hooch" for my twenty-one cohorts. One home-cooked meal a day gives the provider big time power.

My unit was the 315th Tactical Airlift Wing, and had multiple missions which included moving cargo, spraying

Agent Orange and spraying skeeters. We were known as the "Ranch Hands." One day in October 1971 I got the word that my new boss--Major Dick Minot and I were going to take the birds back to the USA. The war had started to wind down.

In December, the multi-month mission ended and, as promised, the Air Force decided to billet me at Air Training Command Headquarters, Universal City, Texas. However, I was sent to a short term logisitics officer's course in Colorado.

Four months later, I enjoyed a broadening experience, that of working in the engineering section for all T-37 jet training aircraft for the Air Force. That assignment lasted for three years. Then, within five years of my father's death, we were on our way to Holland, where the seed for my *Niputi* memoir began.

All the while, I maintained operational control of the Star & Garter from afar to protect my mother's financial holdings. That took some doing. Then I was proffered another European assignment to Germany on the USAFE Inspector General's staff. My almost two years of constant travel were rewarded by being selected to the Air Force's premier electronics surveillance system, the Airborne Warning and Control System (AWACS) wing, at Tinker AFB, Oklahoma. That became an awesome opportunity and resulted in my selection as Component Repair Squadron Commander. This turned out to be the best year-plus job I've ever had. And I can say with pride that working with over 750 USAF electron wizards was the high point of my career.

My reward for hard work was meeting new professional men and women in the Air Force. I made new friends on multiple missions and activities that few people ever do.

With classified assignments, Vietnam combat and participation in the cadre attempting to free Americans hostages in 1980 in Iran, it was all worth it. I wrote a short story about the event entitled, "Fractured Plan, Failed Mission."

A severe heart attack at 45 years of age, when I was in the best shape of my life, and a week later suffering the tragic loss of my eighteen-year-old son, pushed me to the limit. I was still a USAF/IG Inspector, logistician, aircraft maintenance officer, and accident investigator, and was once again cleared for worldwide assignments. However, I opted for retirement as a lieutenant colonel. Yeah, there may have been a promotion in the future, but at the time, I knew I was physically and emotionally spent. I needed to spend more time with my remaining family. I enjoyed my career opportunity in the Air Force, ending it after twenty years in May 1985 at Norton AF Base.

CHAPTER 37
MY MAFIA PERSPECTIVE

Over the years, a number of people have asked me about the Mafia. I respond with a playful, "How the hell do I know. I wasn't a member." But, if you contact the federal government, possibly the FBI has something to say about it. I understand the intrigue of being so close to an enigma for so long and not being able to put it into a simply understood comment. But possibly that's what made the cult sustainable for so long. Besides, after Jack Armstrong FBI boy wonder figured out how to break Frank's spirit, Bompensiero started to sing and I commented on that.

✳ ✳ ✳

Some folks have asked what the word *Mafia* means, and who started it. The simple answer is, I don't know. It appears clouded like the mysterious Sicily where it began. In Sicilian, the word *Grazia* means thank you, and the word *Bona* means good. But, *Mafia* means what? — Sicilian secret society! A quick review of The American Heritage Dictionary defines *Mafia* as a "Secret Terrorist Organization beginning in Sicily in the nineteenth century and/or an alleged international criminal organization."

The Britannica World Language Dictionary ties its definition to the Sicilians as: "A Sicilian secret society characterized by hostility and frequent violations of law."

This definition is clean and neat. However, with the use of "alleged" in the former definition, one might consider whether the crimes committed in the USA were attributed to those Italians with crooked intent or the Mafia, in fact.

When the FBI finally woke up to the existence of the criminal organization and started to treat it as such, they couldn't identify it. I believe my dictionary source and the FBI's interpretation were far off the mark, because they fail to identify the word along the lines of its cultural origins, thus it retained a somewhat mystical orientation.

Much speculation surrounds it, but the as-good-as-it-gets answer comes from a renowned scholar and professor, Diego Gambetta, Ph.D., and his thesis, *The Sicilian Mafia— The Business of Private Protection*. His work is one of the most thoroughly researched and well-written books on the enigmatic Mafia I've read. His effort is an amazing piece of academic social study, providing a rational explanation and concept of operations for the Mafia in the Sicilian society, with offshoots of its societal impact in America.

According to Gambetta, the very word *Mafia* was most likely generated externally and from an unknown source. Suffice it to say, the term *Mafia* may have its roots in the idea of a "family unit" and akin to Sicilian business expansions, which invariably started and flourished within a family-named unit, as in a fictitious business name (e.g., "Bompensiero Olive Oil Company").

This familial naming process created a means of distancing themselves and their criminality from common street thugs and everyday criminals. These early founders wanted respect and honor. Rather, they demanded it and would have it. Thus, they wanted to be known as "men of honor"—the term applied to sworn members of the family organization. "Man of honor" indicated pride and added a cultural family dimension to the term. Possibly, this was the underlying reason the Mafia never expanded beyond its Sicilian borders into Italy. However, through its émigrés who departed Sicily and went to America for the opportunity offered, the term found root and prospered.

(As an aside, Joseph Bonanno, boss of one of the original five New York families, frequently used the term "my tradition" or "my family" when referring to the Mafia. However, he never used the word *Mafia*. As I explained earlier, the word was forbidden in our house. This may explain why Bonanno titled his biography, *Man of Honor*.)

Once published, governments, scholars, and students alike hailed Gambetta's work. He provided a sound understanding of the foundation theory, motivation, creation, and nature of the nineteenth-century Mafia association. He highlights interesting aspects of the society's credo and commandments. Those who accepted membership swore: "Not to touch women of other men of honor, nor deal in prostitution, or steal from or kill other men of honor." Additionally, they had to refrain from introducing themselves as members of the *Phi Beta Mafia*—as any other fraternity member would. To commit any of the above meant improper behavior, and this was not tolerated.

Use of ritualistically lit candles, ashes, vow cards and chants that had religious and pagan overtones were borrowed from their Catholic and pagan beliefs. Each of these ceremonial doo-dads provided more mystery and led to secretive drama for the induction into the dark world of the Mafia secret society.

Gambetta's research further provides ample support for tolerant interchange between the Mafia and the Italian government at large, as it was noted that the Mafia does, in fact, respect the law. However, the Mafia's rudimentary proviso contributes protection to those in the government who fail to satisfy. Finally, he explains how the eccentric rituals, behaviors and communication, via the complex sneers, gestures, or looks of its members, make sense in an organization of this nature.

Another world traveler and scholar, Will S. Monroe, Ph.D., predates Gambetta's study of *Lo Mafia* by almost ninety years, and I was able to procure it through the efforts of Google's Save the Books program. It approaches the Mafia from a different perspective, as Monroe visited Sicily in 1909 and studied its people, culture and, as an adjunct to the society, the Mafia.

He formulated a base interpretation/definition of the word *Mafia*. In his work, *Sicily, Garden of the Mediterranean*, Monroe states: "The Mafiusu in nineteenth century Sicily was an ambiguous term and signified a bully, arrogant but also fearless, enterprising and proud." His work also details more items discovered about the Mafia rituals.

Sicilians in general, including my uncle, couldn't define the word *Mafia*. And he didn't want to talk about it. However, the traits identifying the Mafia type put forth by Monroe fit Frank Bompensiero's persona and demeanor. He had all those traits and I've tried to depict those errant qualities in *Niputi*. Arrogance and bully come to mind, short-sighted and bigoted. Nonetheless, Frank was also fearless, enterprising, and proud while identifying with the movie genre gangster of the times.

As time progressed, new stories and more adaptation became the rage. Adding more color to the heaviest criminal elements facing the FBI and thus, the Mafia, came into vogue with Mario Puzo's 1961 novel, *The Godfather*, and its phenomenal success. People didn't identify the Mafia with the actual criminals, but with the great acting and story told in Francis Ford Coppola's follow-on film trilogy. This rode a wave of financial success, and Hollywood capitalized on perceived bad Sicilian/Mafia behaviors, exploiting the genre in films like "Goodfellas" and "Gotti" and the like.

We relished the performances of Marlon Brando as the aging Parino *Capo di tutti Capi* (Head of All Heads and a Godfather), along with Al Pacino and the rest of the "Goomba" cast performances. However, those were performances created out of the mind of the author and creative scriptwriters. In reality, unlike a few who were dapper dressers and strutted around looking bad or cool, their real deal involved extortion, vengeance and murder. It was real blood that flowed—not the stuff of stage props and makeup.

My perspective on the criminal history of the Mafia borders on my arms-length experience with my uncle and his associates, when coupled with the historic realities of the Mafia's climb between 1900 and the 1970s—its American beginnings and subsequent demise. All bad-guy Italian/Sicilian men are not Mafia. However, if you are in Italy and meet a Sicilian, your first thought is Mafia. All Sicilians are painted with the same brush.

Though Al Capone was the king of *Goombas* and America's most notable celebrity criminal, he would not have qualified for induction into the Mafia. He was an American-made Italian, Brooklyn-born to Italian immigrant parents who were not Sicilian. So, he became his own criminal brand, the "Capone Gang," where he was able to cash in on smuggling booze, prostitution, turf wars and bribing police and those in government office. It took the Internal Revenue Service to finally get him into prison. The police couldn't.

From Al Capone to Meyer Lansky and all the players in between, to those on the other side of the street, from J. Edgar Hoover to Eliot Ness, et al, they all recognized that "Organized Crime" was not, in reality, an "organization."

The term was an invention with thoughts of a unique entity headed up by a powerful symbolic and influential boss—the "Don."

Most assuredly, Frank Bompensiero enjoyed the 1972 and 1974 *Godfather* film portrayals and took glee as he saw himself as one of the successful bandits in the film. But, it never happened as portrayed on the screen, and he knew it as well. I have no doubt that he was saddened by his inability to climb the mountain of criminal success in *Privitera Lo Familia.*

In their private sanctuaries, storytellers are supreme in their imaginary views while creating adventuresome heroes and knaves in their writings of the Mafia. They didn't think of it as a social institution or political/economic unit trying to survive in a world filled with strife. They couldn't even depict an organization like the Mafia destroying itself from within as society and technology progressed.

With younger minds entering the population, when technology allows for major theft with the click of a mouse and millions of dollar transfers, it would seem ridiculous to attempt brain-washing the (post-Mafia era) youth, using a crime relic based on an archaic economy and time. The former paganistic, ritualized and mystified concept of men who used extortion or strict brute force alone to achieve objectives was no longer viable. Thus, the dismantling of the Mafiosa family loomed on the horizon as a younger, more educated population found other ways to make a quick buck.

The Sicilian Mafia that I speak of participated in protection, extortion, smuggling, prostitution, union control, gambling, and government employee bribery. Oh yeah, and murder, mostly internal or for business reasons. Their enterprises included all things detrimental to the progress of society and were monitored and witnessed by the police and FBI. I believe that through time and its dysfunctional structure, the Mafia concept in the USA fell apart.

One could ask why we do not read about the Mafia in the press? Honestly, I don't think anyone cares. The Mafia is not important. It doesn't impact people's lives as it once did. The world has other, more terrifying bogeymen to fear: Muslim terrorists for one, Wall Street manipulators and government bureaucrats for another, and cyber scammers.

What of the people of Sicily, the island dwellers, a simple and warm people, trying to survive and, yes, the resident Mafia? They may be gone from America's shores, but what of their Sicilian survival? They all didn't leave the island.

In mid-June 2014, during the final writing stages of *Niputi*, television newscasters announced that Pope Francis, the current Catholic pontiff, visited Calabria, a Sicilian town. There he comforted the jailed father of a three-year-old boy killed in a mob ambush, and he condemned mob violence against children. Supposedly, this was caused by *'Ndrangheta*, one of Italy's most dangerous crime groups.

Pope Francis had harsh words for the Italian Mafia and the *'Ndrangheta*, describing the crime syndicate as "the adoration of evil" and saying that all Mafiosi "are excommunicated" from the church.

You might think this condemnation from the Pope strikes fear into the craven hearts of the Mafia. However, and there is always a however, Chad Pecknold, assistant professor of theology at Catholic University of America, said that the Pope's comment was "just something he said in a homily, which is not a vehicle for disciplinary excommunication pronouncements."

I, for one, do not believe that the criminal nature of the *Mafia* with its swagger, bravado, bullying and intimidation, is gone from the earth. As long as the mysterious gene for evil lies in one's DNA/heart it will be used against man ... and you may be the next one targeted for extorted protection.

I now offer my final comments on *Ziu Chiich*, Frank Bompensiero, the law and the FBI's enterprising special agent Jack Armstrong. Frank continually bragged: "I did my time and always kept my mouth shut." This was part of his contrived pride and loyalty to his thing, "*Cosa Nostre--*"My Cause.

This he did as long as he was clear of the law. That is until FBI agent Jack Armstrong found Frank and Jimmy the Weasel Fratianno with their hands in a crooked Arizona highway construction scam and manipulated Frank into joining his team. Fear made Frank a stooge for the FBI. Something, he'd never admit to in daily life. But, in the end Frank proved that he was no everyday mediocre stooge. He negotiated for a smaller version of his mental data base of Mafia organization knowledge. As long as he didn't have to cough up his pal Joseph Bonanno in Arizona, others in Chicago, New York, etc., he was okay with the deal.

Thus he retained his supposed loyalty to *La Familia* out of fear of dying, proving Frank was human. Moreover, we learned that the police and government's ability to control the streets and keep the population safe is quite dependent on informers—whistle blowers.

Frank knew he was on his way out, as he admitted to me and my Dad, his brother, one day in the Star &

Garter in 1969. However, he was lying to us both, as he had been on Jack's FBI payroll since 1966. I finally feel vindicated as I read of Jack Armstrong's FBI successes in several articles released in national newspapers. On February 10, 1977, the Washington Star Syndicate journalist Nicholas Gage tossed some interesting information into the mix and I selectively paraphrase the substantiated commentary and input from federal court records. It was interesting to note that Bompensiero was the FBI's most highly ranked Mafia underworld informant. He had been reporting to the bureau about their activities for almost 12 years. And, Frank's murder was the most damaging of a series of 23 murders, which wiped out a nationwide group of FBI informants. As Jack Armstrong admitted while in witness before a Los Angeles Federal Court "Bompensiero was the highest-ranking informant to help the government in their fight against organized crime." Later, he added when asked of Bompensiero's contribution in terms of criminal numbers, Armstrong admitted that Frank's outing of Mafia members was in the hundreds of criminals.

Almost eight months after the execution of Frank Bompensiero, San Diego's notable Mafia *Consigliere* (counselor), the *Des Moines Register* revealed on October 2, 1977, "The killing of Bompensiero, like a pebble tossed in a pond, began to send off ripples that have grown until they now threaten to shake the structure within the Federal Bureau of Investigation itself."

For the sixty-five years I knew Frank, I gave him a modicum of undeserved respect out of familial tradition and mainly respect for my father. However, his demented schemes and infamous deeds had an undeserved impact on those of us who also carried the family surname. He drew police, FBI and media attention like flies to a dung heap which in turn affected our lives. At least through Niputi, I was able to wipe away the vitriol and Goomba mouth of how Frank was. He was the "Big Mouth" I always knew him to be *and this platform allowed me to clean the slate. Bastante!* Enough said.

EPILOGUE

Some have asked me if I think crime pays? That's for you to decide. For me, it depends. I think not in terms of the Mafia. Most that I knew, with the exception of Salvatore Marino and Joe Bonanno, never acquired real riches. The majority had nothing to build on. They couldn't get the money churning like old Nate Rosenberg's moola machine.

However, there were those in the white-collar world, from what I've read, that made a ton. Joe Kennedy stands out. John F. Kennedy's father not only made his fortune on the nefarious side, but it also helped pay the way for John to win the election for president. Besides being a billionaire, Bernie Madoff was thief among thieves and no one to call friend. However, before his errant ways were discovered, all respected him.

I have considered that there could possibly be a bad gene within a baby that ekes along happily growing undisturbed. Then as it matures, it awakens and presses men into criminal attacks on each other. Maybe one day, modern medicine researchers will find it.

In the dysfunctional "Mafia, La Familia, or My Tradition," being bad really stands out. Some of them are pure mean. However, I was surprised to learn that many who chose the criminal way live as long as anyone else, in some cases, longer. The final death of key characters in *Niputi . . . the Nephew* are listed in a chart that follows.

The chart reflects when and how they met their maker. Of the seventeen characters mentioned, only five were murdered. My Uncle Frank was one of those. Of the remaining twelve, eight died of a heart attack. Of the remaining four, two criminals blew the statistics all to hell. Momo Adamo killed himself. And Jimmy "the Weasel" Fratianno spent his windfall from *The Last Mafioso*, then hid under much-needed FBI protection, also squandering his "tell us all" inducement checks. He supposedly met nature's Alzheimer's along the way and died in Oklahoma.

Of the two remaining players, the only decent man not affiliated with the West Coast Mafia, but who knew them all, was *Turi*—Sammy Bonpensiero, my father. He passed away following surgery at fifty-seven years. Me, I'm slow and still kicking in Vegas at seventy-five.

We all know that nothing lasts forever. Like all living things, thoughts, spoken or written, changes do occur in time. As I've noted in my life, if man and man's institutions don't change with the time, they will perish.

NIPUTI CHARACTER MORTALITY CHART

Name	Cause/Death	Birth	Died	Age at Death
Adamo, Girolomo "Momo"	Suicide	1898	1956	58
Ardizzone, Joseph	Murdered	1884	1931	47
Bompensiero, Frank "Cigar"	Murdered	1905	1977	72
Bonanno, Joseph	Heart Attack	1905	2002	97
Bonpensiero, Joseph "The Niputi	Alive in Vegas	1939	----	---
Bonpensiero, Sam "Turi"	Aneurism	1913	1970	57
Bonelli, William E.	Heart Attack	1895	1970	75
Desimone, Frank	Heart Attack	1909	1967	58
Dragna, Ignacio "Jack"	Heart Attack	1891	1956	65
Fratianno, Aladena-Jimmy "Weasel"	Alzheimer's	1920	1999	79
Marino, Salvatore Sr.	Heart Attack	1898	1974	76
Marino, Angelo	Heart Attack	1925	1983	58
Matranga, Gaspare	Heart Attack	1926	1999	73
Matranga, Joseph	Heart Attack	1910	1999	89
Mirabile, Tony	Murdered	1894	1958	64
Piazza, Joe	Heart Attack	1936	2005	69
Roselli, John	Murdered	1905	1976	71
Rosenberg, Nathan	Heart Attack	1913	1970	57
Spilotro, Anthony the Ant	Murdered	1938	1986	48

SPECIAL REMEMBRANCE TO NATHAN "NATE" ROSENBERG

I apologize to my readers for not being able to display a photo of Nate Rosenberg in Niputi's photo album. A handsome, distinguished and intelligent man, he was a mentor. I appreciated his advice and in kind, he was happy for my presence during a fearful time in his life.

Somewhere after almost sixteen geographic moves following my Air Force retirement, I lost my photographs of the Star & Garter. Dad successfully operated the Garter albeit for one short year. I continued its operation until I sold it circa 1978-1980.... Today, it still operates as a bar under a different name at 3596 University Ave in San Diego, Ca. Mom followed Dad thirteen years later, succumbing to a stroke while reading a novel. A sweet loving mother and friend to many. She will always be missed.

BIBLIOGRAPHY

Bonanno, Joseph, "A Man of Honor." Simon & Schuster, NY, NY, 1983

Bonpensiero, Joseph., "Chocolate Moon." Amazon's CreateSpace, 2011

Brasselle, Keefe, "The Cannibals" Avon Books, NY, NY, 1968

Benjamin, Sandra., "Sicily- 3,000 years of Human History." Steerforth Press, 2006

Cary, David, Ph.D., "A Bit of Burlesque." Tecolote Publications 1997

Corona, Peter, Ph.D. "Little Italy—The Way It Was." Trafford Publishing, 2009

Demaris, Ovid, "The Last Mafioso." Bantam Books, 1981

Gambetta, Diego. Ph.D. "Sicilian Mafia-business of private protection ." Harvard Press 1996

Herhod, Scott, Mob related murders-San Jose, San Jose Mercury 2011

La Sorte, Michael. Ph.D. "La Merica" Temple University Press, 1985

Lait, Jack & Lee Mortimer., "USA Confidential." Crown Publishers 1952

Monroe, Will S. Ph.D. "Sicily, Garden of the Mediterranean." Google, Public Domain, 1909

Moore, Judith, "A Bad, Bad Boy." San Diego Reader, 2009

San Diego Union/Tribune. News stories/Obituaries, San Diego U/ET, 1939–2005

Des Moines Register, News Stories /news articles/editorials Oct 1977

Privitera, Joseph F. "Sicilian Dictionary & Phrase Book", Hippocrene Books, 2003

Rappleye, C. & Becker, E "All American Mafioso," Johnny Roselli story; Barricade Books, NY, 1991

Reid, Edward. "Mafia." Random House, NY, NY, 1952

Reid, Edward. "The Grim Reapers." Regney Co., Chicago, 1969

Sifakis, Carl "The Mafia Encyclopedia." Checkmark Books, 2005

Taylese, Gay", Honor thy Father." World Publishing, 1971

U.S. Treasury Dept. "MAFIA." Harper Collins, 2007, Bur of Narc

ACKNOWLEDGEMENTS

Niputi took several years to write and I had a lot of help in its development. Thank you Lynne Smith, my early mentor and writing instructor at LongRidge Writers Group who showed me the road. Kathy Kirkpatrick of Gentracer Inc., also deserves a thanks for her tracking our Sicilian roots. Also thanks to Simone Arias—poet and educator, for her deft precision in editing my poems.

A special thanks to my cousin Tina Bompensiero-Corrao Matranga. Her vivid recall of events filled in the gaps and lent validation of my dimming memories. Thanks to Pete and Joey Buompensiero, brothers who provided a different perspective of the teenager Frank Bompensiero. Also thanks to "Frank" Lococo, who contributed his own gut-wrenching Sicilian immigrant experiences. He expanded my view of my father as an immigrant teen.

To my muse, editor, writing assistant and dear friend, Marcia Buompensiero, a.k.a. Loren Zahn. She cracked me upside the head as writer's rot fried my brain and she was always there, a call away. I truly appreciated her collaboration on *Niputi*. A gifted writer, her San Diego-based murder mysteries, *Dirty Little Murders* and *Deadly Little Secrets*," will hook you. Buy em. Dave "Ole Geezer" Feldman, my final editor, thank you. Dave, a master journalist, author, and educator was kind enough to share his sage craftsmanship polishing up Niputi's rough edges—and there were many. A ride in his fiftyish Citroen "Gangsta car was a treat." Most of all, thank you my roomie, partner, and wife Caryl. She captured the fly-droppings in *Niputi* in spite of my heckling.

Truly steadfast, she gave needed support throughout the years of *Niputi's* development. Thank you all.

Joe

ABOUT THE AUTHOR

Joseph S. Bonpensiero

Joseph "Joe" Bonpensiero was born in San Diego's Sicilian ghetto of "Little Italy," aka "Wop Town." At seven years old, he worked aboard the family fishing boat. Though a seasoned fisherman by his late teens, his parents Sam and mother Amanda, had other plans for him. They encouraged him to pursue an education. Joe earned a B.A. from San Diego State University and a USAF commission-- later adding a Masters degree. He chose an Air Force career with multiple world wide tours to Vietnam, Europe, Libya and Saudi Arabia, et al. While serving as a USAF Inspector General's staff investigator, an incident occurred which forced Joe to expose years of troublesome and pocketed Mafia related family matters. Moreover, he details personal experiences and vignettes of Liberace, Lena Horne, J. Edgar Hoover, crooked government bureaucrats and Mafia members.Joe began writing "Chocolate Moon," a *Tom Sawyerish* account of his family life with youthful adventures at sea." In his second book, NIPUTI...the Nephew, Joe details the family's guilt through association endured because of Frank's notoriety. He then divulges intimate facts, events and machinations of Frank's psychopathic nature. KIRKUS national review and others have said of NIPUTI: "Bonpensiero seeks to bury the hatchet about his mobster uncle. He delivers...tightly knit narrative ...entertaining... the unfolding of an American life colored by the Sicilian immigrant experience." Joe and his wife Caryl are retired and reside in Henderson, Nevada. He continues to write to tell his stories and improve his craft. He is a member of the San Diego Writers/Editors Guild and the Henderson Writers Group.

www.ingramcontent.com/pod-product-compliance
Lightning Source LLC
Chambersburg PA
CBHW071644090426
42738CB00009B/1417